Alternative World

Alternative World

Nares Craig

Housmans Bookshop Publications

Alternative World–Nares Craig
First published March, 1997
Housmans Bookshop Limited, 5 Caledonian Road, London N1
Copyright © Nares Craig

ISBN 0 852832 51 6

Typeset by East End Offset Ltd
Printed by BPC Wheatons Ltd
Cover design by Nares Craig and Sherborne Design
Cover photograph of children at Jose Echeverria School, Pinar del Rio, Cuba
Cover photograph © Nicky Bolster

Dedicated to everyone open-minded enough to question traditions, and consider totally new ways of ordering our lives and the world as a whole.

Foreword

It has been suggested to me by critics, both sympathetic and less sympathetic, that throughout this book I have apparently assumed that the 'open-minded' are equivalent to 'like-minded'. In all but one vital respect I would answer that I have made no such assumption, appealing though it may be.

My wish and intention has been two-fold. Firstly to provide the reader with a realistic, though necessarily depressing, description of the current state of the world—together with some historical background and some widely accepted predictions as to the future. Secondly to outline alternative modes of economic and political organisation such as I believe essential for the survival of humanity in any viable form.

I fully appreciate that much of what I propose is controversial. It is for this reason that I dedicate it to the open-minded in the hope that it may act as a catalyst in the evolution of a new and truly positive approach that can be embraced by a whole range of people who currently hold widely disparate views.

The one respect in which the 'like-minded' criticism may well be justified is because I believe that every human being is essentially as important as every other. In 1623 John Donne more beautifully expressed this basic moral tenet which I trust is shared by you the reader:

No man is an Iland, intire of it selfe;
every man is a peece of the Continent,
a part of the maine;
if a Clod bee washed away by the Sea,
Europe is the lesse,
as well as if a Promontorie were,
as well as if a Mannor of thy friends
or of thine owne were;
any mans death diminishes me,
because I am involved in Mankinde;
And therefore never send to know
for whom the bell tolls;
It tolls for thee.

Contents

Acknowledgements

My wife Thora's wide-ranging experience (including as a state-registered nurse member of the first UK medical aid unit during the Spanish Civil War, and founding the first trade union for nurses in 1937) made her an invaluable critic and adviser during the researching, drafting and editing of this book. My grateful thanks are also due to her for many months of dedicated work on the word-processor; likewise to our son, Jonathan, for his patient guidance in its use and for expert assistance in the production of interim and final versions.

Nares Craig was born in 1917 in the week of the Russian Revolution. He was educated at Charterhouse and Trinity College, Cambridge, and served as a captain in the Armoured Engineers in the 1939-45 war. While commanding tanks adapted to carrying special assault equipment, he re-designed the Baily Mobile Bridge to increase span capacity and reduce operating casualties. After qualifying as an architect, he worked at the UK Building Research Station on investigations into housing design, production and erection processes, which were recorded in over fifty technical publications. This work resulted in invitations to lecture in various Third World centres, and later to the development of the low-cost *Brecast* system which was used widely in earthquake- and hurricane-prone areas. He thus gained first hand experience of the harsh realities of lives both in the villages and shanty towns, particularly in Latin America and the Far East. In 1984 he wrote *Preventing the Holocaust*.

Christopher Hill is former Master of Balliol College, Oxford and Chancellor of the Open University. He is the foremost historian of the English Revolution and his many books include *God's Englishmen, The World Turned Upside Down, The Experience of Defeat, A Nation of Change and Novelty, Liberty Against the Law, England's Turning Point* and *The English Revolution 1640*.

INTRODUCTION
by Christopher Hill

When I first read Nares Craig's Alternative World I was very impressed by its all-embracing scope, its wide humanity and its implicit call for action to deal with the crisis which he showed to be approaching for humanity. His analysis of the threats to the human race and the world seem to me not overstated.

His book deserves the serious attention of all of us. Its thesis is that for five centuries the powerful nations of the First World have used their military might to exploit the Third World, reducing its populations to poverty and degradation by looting and enslavement. The establishment of independent states in what used to be colonies, by what Craig calls 'one of the greatest confidence tricks in history', has as its consequence control of the trade of the 'independent' nations of the Third World by small minorities in the First World who cream off the profits. What we think of as 'improvements' - scientific and technological advances - have in fact not improved the condition of humanity as a whole. That the condition of the majority in the Third World has deteriorated is the well-documented argument of chapters one to eight of this provocative book, backed up by much factual evidence and horrifying statistics. In terms of mere human justice, Craig insists, the imbalance created between the First and Third Worlds during these five centuries should be reduced. The First World owes a vast debt to the peoples of the Third World.

But this is more than a question of justice. This is not a starry-eyed book. Craig's conclusion is that, after centuries of exploitation of the Third World, both it and the First World are in consequence seriously sick. A real possibility exists that this illness may prove terminal unless drastic and immediate changes are made. Despite technological and scientific advances, and increases in knowledge, the condition of humanity as a whole has deteriorated over the past five centuries. When Christianity was forced upon the native peoples of America and elsewhere, it was argued that it was only right that they should pay for the inestimable benefits of being introduced to true religion. And pay they did, gratefully or not. But Christianity has not solved the Third World's problems. Over large areas of the globe, resources are misused because there is no overall planning—wanton destruction of forests, for instance, world-wide soil erosion, an uncontrolled population explosion which threatens natural resources in many areas. 'Countless millions live in absolute poverty and suffer

7

the agony of diseases from malnutrition and death by starvation.'
Money-making is the only genuinely world-wide religion of today.

Craig's figures are alarming. Average education expenditure per
child in the poorest Third World countries is 2 dollars per annum, as
compared with $6,000 per annum in the First World. Illiteracy is in-
creasing in the Third World by 25 million a year. Women and children have no rights in most Third World countries. 50% of the
fortunate few who achieve higher education migrate from the Third
to the First World, taking their expertise with them. If this process continues unchecked, Craig foresees escalating ecological disasters which,
'sooner or later will lead to explosive revolts by the have-nots, with
unpredictable consequences'. Military rule, thought control through
the media, denial of human rights, terror, are all employed by the
elites who rule the independent Third World ex-colonies.

The second half of the book (Chapters 9 to 18) outlines what Craig
considers the solutions necessary if civilisation is to survive. Some of
them may seem utopian in present circumstances. Craig wants to force
his readers to recognise the disastrous consequences for the future of
the human race if we fail to take decisive remedial action in the immediate future. We must, he insists, start thinking seriously about the
alternative possibilities facing humanity if it is to survive. And we
must not only think but act.

There have been prophets of doom in all ages, but few have argued
their case so clearly and convincingly as Craig in his Conclusion. He
puts the case for 'an alternative world, consisting of cooperative societies based on true, fully democratic socialist principles...renounc-
ing individualism' and 'working together for the equitable use of
resources to provide good lives for all.' The World Council of Churches
has said that 'the amoral, wasteful and cruel system of capitalism' is 'the
root cause of the poverty and powerlessness of the majority of the
people.' We cannot afford it any longer.

Craig faces head on the facile view that the collapse of East European regimes proves the superiority of the free market to socialism. On
the contrary: the Russian Revolution came in the most backward European country, the last one would have chosen in which to try out
an experiment in socialism. Nevertheless, with all its defects, the
USSR. produced many great achievements in education and science.
The resistance of its people to the onslaught of Hitler's armies contributed decisively to the final defeat of fascism.

The proposals in this book call for serious discussion among democrats everywhere, since world-wide agreement will be needed for
their implementation. Planned development for a 'world without

money' will not be accepted without long and divisive arguments against those who benefit by the present system, or lack of it. 'Alternative energy policies', however rational, will be opposed by powerful vested interests. 'The only lesson of history', cynics have said, 'is that the lessons of history are never learnt until too late.'

The main theme of this book I find unanswerable. Capitalism has many achievements to its credit, but these very achievements now call for a decisive reorganisation of society. Competitive capitalism is now causing more harm than good to humanity; the future must lie with more democratic forms of organisation, capable of collectively planning world development to meet the impending crisis which Craig has depicted. But the democratic transformation of society will be a hazardous, long-term and difficult task. With control of all the organs of information and persuasion—press, TV etc—in the hands of rulers of the First World, how is this transformation to be achieved?

If Craig is right in supposing that the future of human life on earth as we know it is at stake, the answer is clear and it is a challenge to all of us. The programme for immediate action set out in Craig's Conclusion is very ambitious. However it comes, the transformation will meet with widespread resistance from powerful groups in both Worlds. To take only one example, the abolition of all armed forces and weapons in all nations by January 2001 AD is a very sensible idea, but it will be opposed not only on 'patriotic' grounds but also by all those who make vast profits out of arms production and sales.

On rational grounds Craigs programme seems incontrovertible, but how are we to implement it? How, in the first instance, do we get it discussed all over the world? Or do we decide that he is asking too much of us, and that the world may survive for our life-time: posterity can look to itself? Over to us.

PREFACE

The motivation for writing this book was the belief that the world is so seriously sick, in so many different respects, that its illness will soon become terminal, unless fundamental changes are made. The aim has been to help strengthen the resolve of the many dedicated men, women and young persons world-wide already involved in numerous ways with averting further decline, and promoting progress. Part One summarises the most serious threats to humanity and our world, as a reminder of the various evils which need to be consigned to history. Part Two provides a picture of the practical realities of how life could be transformed for the world's peoples, if only pressures for change were to be successful.

In spite of the impression of improvements created by technological advances, the condition of humanity overall has actually deteriorated throughout recent times. This is evidenced most critically by the plight of disadvantaged people everywhere, often 'living' in conditions of such degradation that most First World citizens cannot conceive them as being possible in which to exist. Countless millions suffer the agony of diseases from malnutrition and death by starvation.

Younger people, faced with all the uncertainties of the 21st century, are entitled to ask those who have experienced most of the 20th'What went wrong, and what kind of alternative, better world can we help to construct?'

Armed conflicts continue to plague the world, compounding its many problems. The need for universal, lasting peace has never been greater, and is fundamental to the creation of an alternative world, in which the idea of resorting to force would be inadmissible. In the words of Rousseau: 'War is the man-made institution which makes one ashamed of being a man.'

Leaving aside the threat of wars, the greatest obstacles to humanity's progress are traditions, and perhaps the most damaging of all is the deep-seated concept of 'them' and 'us'. World-wide, children are taught, and too many adults accept, that 'they' are 'well-born', better educated, and therefore bound to be right. This is in spite of the chaotic state of affairs that those in authority have either wilfully promoted or allowed the world to slip into by default.

Traditions are fundamental to perpetuating the status quo, and have thus been nurtured for centuries by the elites of this world. Of course, many traditions relating to honest, helpful human behaviour are important and must be preserved. But those traditions which are harmful include emphases on the roles of monarchies and elites generally, acceptance of armed forces and therefore wars as normal and even glorious, and respect for the wealthy with disdain for the poverty-stricken. Further negative, ingrained concepts include individualism, male superiority, 'might is right', the sovereignty of states, and national chauvinism.

The aim of this book is to make the case for an alternative world consisting of cooperative societies, based on true, fully democratic socialist principles. In this context, it is necessary to comment on the collapse of the 'Socialist Sixth of the World' as it was referred to, with optimism, in the title of the famous book, published in 1939 by Hewlett Johnson, Dean of Canterbury. First, capitalist societies, going their own 'free-for-all', individualistic and competitive ways, demand few organisational efforts by anyone; in fact, the free market protagonists deliberately eschew planning of any kind as bordering on the unethical.

By contrast, cooperative societies call for dedicated, intelligent and patient leadership efforts, to guide people towards renouncing individualism, with its lure of disproportionate rewards for the few, and instead, to lead them towards working together for the equitable use of resources and optimal lives for all. Not surprisingly, such high quality leadership was never available in sufficient numbers in what had been the vast ill-educated tsarist empire, nor later in Eastern Europe. Thus followed the inevitable gravitation towards central control, giving rise to, at best, state rather than democratic socialism.

In fact, the first attempt to create a socialist society took place in what was probably the most inauspicious environment of all. Furthermore, from the outset, the Soviet Union was hounded by the rest of the world, both militarily and economically. The final factors contributing to eventual failure were the insuperable difficulties facing the various central leaderships in coping with such a plethora of cultural, linguistic, agricultural, climatic, industrial and many other problems over such a huge area, spanning seven time zones. However, it is important not to forget that the USSR did produce many achievements in the educational, scientific, construction and other fields. The Soviet Union also withstood almost the entire weight of Hitler's armies, at the cost of 20 million dead and unprecedented destruction of productive capacity, and played a key role in the final defeat of Hitler.

The author rejects the currently fashionable view that events in Eastern Europe have proved the 'free market' to be the only viable form of economy. On the contrary, capitalism itself is proving to be an amoral, wasteful and cruel system which the world can ill afford to retain any longer. This view is very well borne out by the following excerpt from a statement in 1988 by the World Council of Churches:

We personally see and experience the reality of poverty, powerlessness and death that is imposed on the majority of the world's peoples by the economic systems that are maintained by and serve an extremely powerful minority. The capitalist system, which controls both the First and the Third Worlds, is the root cause of the poverty and powerlessness of the majority of the people.[1]

Morality has now sunk to an all-time low, with the promotion of money-making by any means to the status of the only genuinely worldwide religion. In its name, ethics give way to profits. Compounding the ongoing human tragedies, there will be continuing ecological disasters resulting mainly from First World greed and, sooner or later, some forms of explosive revolts by the have-nots, with unpredictable consequences. Those ruthless elites, dedicated only to preserving their own lifestyles, should pause to think through the horrendous results of their misdeeds and laisser-faire attitudes, which will almost inevitably rebound on their own offspring, if not on themselves.

It is frustrating enough to know that there are very many progressively minded men and women around the globe whose talents are unused, who could well, given the chance, run a vastly better alternative world; we can but hope the younger ones may still get that opportunity. That frustration is increased, for our generation, by the prospect of leaving the world in a worse state than when we entered it. Thus it seemed that writing this book represented the natural task to attempt.

1 *Campaign Group News*, February 1989

Abbreviations in text
1m   ... one million
1bn   ... one billion (1,000 million)
pa   ... per annum
GNP ... gross national product
SU   ... USSR before 1991
UK   ... United Kingdom
US   ... United States of America. Note: It is important to emphasise the correct definition of the territory between Canada and Mexico. In recent years the term 'America' has become increasingly synonymous with just the US, which is naturally resented by many other countries within the two American continents.

Endnotes are at the end of each chapter in Part One and at the end of Chapter 18 in Part Two.

Part ONE

EXISTING WORLD 'ORDER'

Compelling reasons for change

Chapter 1

RICH WORLD, POOR WORLD

Since, at present, money dominates the world, the most obvious differentiation between its constituent regions is in terms of their comparative wealth. 'Rich World' could reasonably be applied to North America, Western Europe, Japan and Australia, even though they all contain significant segments of poverty. Similarly 'Poor World' could be applied to most of Central and South America, Africa and Asia, although they contain some segments of wealth. The rich world has been defined as the 'West' or 'North', and the poor world as the 'South', or 'less-developed countries'. However, the short-hand terms 'First World' and 'Third World' will be used for convenience in this book because they are most widely understood today. The term First cannot be taken literally because several great civilizations existed in the 'Third World' millenia before much of the First World was discovered; neither can it be taken to imply inherent precedence in quality.

DOMINATION BY THE FIRST WORLD
The historical perspective

When commerce and trade are on the agenda, Third World countries are treated as if on equal terms with the rest of the world. The First World, as a whole, conveniently overlooks the huge, incalculable debt that it owes Third World countries in respect of all the human and material resources plundered from them over five centuries. This plunder did not take place in the dim and distant past, but continued until quite recent times: for example, the slave trade was only outlawed in the British Empire in 1833. This unprecedented, incalculable world-wide debt comprises two main elements: profits from the sale of captured slaves and their subsequent labour, and the value of looted precious metals and a wide range of raw materials and products.

In her book, *The Creation of World Poverty*, Teresa Hayter says, 'The British started off their accumulation with piracy, but the biggest profits were to be made in the slave trade'. As Professor H Merivale put it in a lecture at Oxford University in 1840: 'What raised Liverpool and Manchester from provincial towns to gigantic cities?...Their present opulence is as really owing to the toil and suffering of the Negro as if his hands had excavated their docks and fabricated their steam engines'. And Walter Rodney says:

> The profits were fabulous. John Hawkins made three trips to West Africa in the 1560s, and stole Africans whom he sold to the Spanish in America. On returning, his profit was so handsome that Queen Elizabeth became interested in his next venture and provided him with a ship. He returned with such dividends that the Queen made him a Knight; on his coat of arms he chose the representation of an African in chains.

Over the 400 years up to 1870 estimated totals of between 10 and 20 million human beings were 'shanghaied' from Africa and shipped across the Atlantic when approximately one sixth of them died; the survivors were sold as slaves. It is known that in the 18th century alone, France made profits of approximately £50 million and Britain £75m from selling slaves, and Britain made an overall profit around £250m from the production of sugar by slaves in the West Indies. (The sums are in the values of the time.) It must also be remembered that those 10 million men and women were picked for deportation deliberately, because they were fit and in their prime, and thus represented an unimaginable loss both to their families and to Africa. Finally, when this revolting traffic was brought to an end, the British 'merchants' who had been involved were compensated to the tune of £20m. for their 'loss of profits'.

Again from *The Creation of World Poverty* Hayter says:

> In 1757 British attention shifted from the West Indies to India. The famous Bengal plunder began to arrive in London soon after, and its arrival coincided with what is generally considered to be the beginning of the Industrial Revolution in Britain. It has been estimated that the total British plunder of India between 1757 and 1815 amounted to £1,000m. Ernest Mandel adds up the value of gold and silver taken from Latin America

up to 1660, the booty extracted from Indonesia by the Dutch from 1650 to 1780, the harvest reaped by France in the 18th century slave trade, and the profits from slave labour in the British Antilles and those from a half century of British looting in India. These, Mandel says, are the most substantial amounts for which figures, of a sort, are available; but they add up to over £1 billion or more than the capital value of all the industrial enterprises operating by steam which existed in Europe around 1800.

Apart from the straightforward looting, the First World interventionists of the time proceeded quite ruthlessly to reorganize agricultural production on a monocrop basis, so as to streamline production and profits. These interventions upset ecological cycles because, previously, 'crops were harvested and consumed in close proximity to the areas in which they were grown, so sewage and other wastes could be returned to the ground, thus maintaining the organic content and trace minerals in the soil. The new organization meant transporting agricultural products over thousands of miles, rarely returning organic wastes to the soil, but allowing them to be dumped in rivers and oceans. Thus soils are being impoverished in an irreversible manner.'[1]

The 18th and 19th century domination converted Third World countries into suppliers of raw materials for the First World, and markets for manufactured goods from it, thus undermining both their own industries and their ability to feed themselves. In the process, Europeans took much of the best land for themselves, especially in Latin America and Africa. In Kenya, for example, Lord Delamere obtained 100,000 acres of prime land for one penny per acre.

By 1914, colonies 'belonging' to certain European countries together amounted to over half the world's total land area, and contained over one third of the world's population. It would be not only impracticable, but also totally out of place to attempt to put a compensatory price tag on that long-running rape of the Third World's people and resources. Instead, First World countries should acknowledge that the least they can do now is to give without stint to raise Third World people's living standards into line with their own, and thus enable them to participate fully in the improved forms of world society proposed in Part Two. The very terms 'First World' and 'Third World' could then be consigned to the 'trash-can of history', where they belong.

First World Attitudes

Former World Bank President Eugene Black, drumming up support for aid in the 1950s said: 'Our foreign aid programmes constitute a distinct benefit to American business. The three major benefits are [a] providing a large and immediate market for US goods and services, [b] stimulating the development of new overseas markets for US companies, [c] orienting local economies towards free enterprise systems in which US firms can prosper'.[2] In 1968, President Nixon said: 'The main purpose of US aid is not to help other nations but to help ourselves.'[3] In a manner reminiscent of the proselytizing missionaries, First World countries, particularly the US and UK, have sent their representatives around the Third World to try and influence countries to privatize existing nationally owned industries such as railways, communications, airlines and the like. US authorities in the 1970s referred to food as a 'weapon...a powerful negotiating tool' and to grain shortages as giving Washington *'virtual life and death power over the needy multitudes, thus making food primarily both a source of profit and a means of economic and political control over the world at large, and particularly its poorest parts.'*[4]

The following Reagan administration statement, marked 'recently declassified', was exhibited at the 1986 UN International Year of Peace conference. It said:

> We [the US] have about 50% of the world's wealth and only 6.5% of its population. Our real task is to devise a pattern of relationships which will maintain this. We need not deceive ourselves that we can afford the luxury of altruism and world benefaction. We should cease to talk about human rights, raising living standards, and democratizations. The day is not far off when we are going to have to deal in straight power concepts. The less we are hampered by idealistic slogans the better.[5]

Professor Mullard, of Amsterdam, speaks of the European community 'now needing a firmer coherence, if it is to establish a real presence in the future. A reaffirmation of pre-war attitudes to the Third World, and a self-image of superiority may well be the glue that is needed for bonding.' However, Yasmin Alibhai argues that 'few non-whites could psychologically participate in the reconstruction of the myth of a superior whiteness and give it unconditional loyalty. Worsthorne has said their allegiance may be with the "enemies of the West", namely the Third World.'[6]

Promoting what they term 'lifeboat ethics' (meaning some have to be thrown overboard or we all sink), University of California academics Drs Hardin and Paddock have been advocating letting people starve to death in societies that fail to cut their birth rates. They were supported by a US National Security Council official, D Ellerman, saying 'to give food aid to countries just because people are starving is a pretty weak reason'.[4]

Economic Relations

Investment in most Third World countries showed a dramatic collapse in the 1980s, heralding further economic decline rather than recovery. During the period 1984-89 there was a net transfer of resources from poor to rich countries of $137bn. The World Bank was set up ostensibly to assist the Third World, but is controlled by the major First World nations with 60% of the votes, and dominates Third World governments. For example, a Costa Rican economist, Maria Trejos, says 'our whole society is being transformed...the World Bank is undercutting our country's political independence by placing conditions on everything we do, setting our policies on pricing, money, subsidies, imports, exports, banking, agriculture, and so on. We are losing our sovereignty.'[7] Due to international machinations, prices of the majority of Third World exports fell drastically, often as much as 30% during the 1980s, while prices of essential imports such as fertilizers and machinery rose. At the same time, it has become common for the First World to supply obsolete equipment, while charging heavily for up-to-the-minute technologies.

Ex-President Nyerere said in 1989:

The worst thing of all in Africa is a feeling of hopelessness—a loss of the will to fight—an intolerable feeling of dependence. We can't even scream. We are afraid that the aid we do get might stop if we do scream, or if we argue against the powerful in the UN or GATT.

First World countries erect 50% more import barriers against Third World countries than against each other according to a 1988 World Bank study, which concluded that this trade protectionism 'reduces Third World national incomes by almost twice the amounts of First World aid provided.' The *Guardian* (27/11/90) commented 'these measures are legitimate when aimed against foreign suppliers whose export prices are below cost or subsidized, but not when aimed at harassing foreign suppliers who happen to be more competitive than domestic producers.'

In 1984, the UK gave only 17 cents per capita to UNICEF, as against $3.75 to $4.75 per capita from the Scandinavian countries. But in fact the UK actually gained, because although donating £6m, UK manufacturers received orders worth over £7m for supplies from UNICEF. A report by the UK Overseas Development Institute states that the February 1991 Gulf War affected the economies of at least 40 Third World countries as seriously as natural disasters, resulting in direct costs to them of well over $12bn. 'Hundreds of thousands of imported workers from developing countries have had to flee the Gulf region, abandoning savings, possessions and livelihoods,...millions at home were dependent on receiving their financial support...now they have to be re-absorbed into their own countries, already suffering from widespread unemployment.'[8]

The multinational corporations

There are over 10,000 'multinationals' in operation, with around 100,000 subsidiaries. Between them they control approximately 90% of all commodities exported by the Third World; 12 or so of the largest together control most of the world's production of oil, petro-chemicals, tyres, glass and paper. The combined turnovers of just the 10 largest multinationals exceed the combined GNP of a large group of Third World countries. For every dollar invested, they recoup 2, 3 or 4 times over in profit. John Vidal (*Guardian* (8/5/92) tells us that:

> The top 500 companies of the world now control about 70% of world trade, 80% of foreign investment, and 30% of world GNP, or about $300bn pa. Many now control larger development budgets than half of Africa and negotiate like nations. In many cases they control or influence whole industrial processes from demand to extraction of raw materials, through to manufacturing, banking and end use. Almost by definition they control the pollution and poverty that go with these processes.

Unilever, the world's largest food company, has annual sales exceeding the combined GNP of Ethiopia, Chad, Nicaragua and Mozambique. Just six companies dominate the world grain trade, handling around 90% of US wheat, maize and oats exports. The malign capacity of the multinationals to influence international bodies in their own interests is illustrated by excerpts from an April 1991 article in the *Ecologist*, which refers to the UN's Food and Agriculture organization as 'a famine machine...benefiting the rich and powerful at the expense of the poor...in effect creating the conditions for mass starvation.' The

FAO employs 6,000 people and spends $343m pa officially to 'raise nutritional levels and living standards and eliminate hunger'. The *Ecologist* claims it is in effect a front organization for the multinationals, dambuilders and agrochemical firms to promote high-tech agriculture which boosts yields but benefits only a rich elite while it devastates the environment. The FAO is accused of 'dragging peasants into the market economy and promoting export-led development.' The 'green revolution' has replaced ecologically sound native systems with costly hi-tech methods which benefit only rich farmers and customers who can afford to buy the food. Poor farmers are made landless and driven into urban slums.

President Allende told the UN in 1972 that Anaconda, Kennecot and other companies exploiting Chilean copper had, by then, made over $4,000m profits over the previous 42 years from an initial investment of under $30m. The weakness, if they exist at all, of trades unions in the Third World is evidenced by the generally very poor wages and working conditions endured by employees of the multinationals, which are determined, as always, to maximize their profits.

Those working conditions are comprehensively and clearly explained by Teresa Hayter in *The Creation of World Poverty*:

Multinationals take people at their fittest and cheapest and discard them when they become disabled, ill, old or merely exhausted through pressure of work. They hire apprentices and fire them when their 'apprenticeship' ends; they sack workers just before they are entitled to any security or minimum wage; increasingly, they hire children and sack them before they become entitled to adult wages; some 80 to 90% of workers are women who are cheaper than men, but both they and the men are hired young and fired when worn out, say at 30; the preponderant age of employees is 14 to 24; a 50% to 100% turnover of labour pa is common. In Hong Kong, a British colony, but ignoring British labour legislation, 34,000 children work, half of them a 10 hour day. Hours of work are in general very long; in Hong Kong 60% of adults work a seven day week. In South Korea the 84 hour week is common; bus conductors work 18 hour days and garment workers 14 to 16 hour days, and at peak demand 2 or 3 days continuously without sleep. Information on wages is scattered, but, for example, in electronics, hourly rates in Hong Kong, Singapore, Korea and Jamaica average 30 cents, compared with over $3 in the US, a tenfold difference. In India, Indonesia, and Korea, wages range from $2 to $12 per week. As a result, for some large firms, wages bills account for only 7% of sales receipts, while profits account for around 30%.

The rock-bottom, indescribably terrible outcome of the multinationals' ruthless approach to maximizing their profits from the Third World was the industrial disaster, on 3rd December 1984, at Bhopal in India. Nearly 3,000 were killed immediately and 20,000 were injured seriously. Around half a million Bhopal residents continue to suffer the crippling after-effects of the methyl iso-cyanide gas; half of them will suffer permanently and resulting premature deaths still occur daily. 'The multinational concerned, the US company Union Carbide, had never warned the Bhopal City Council that the pesticide manufacturing process was dangerous. A similar plant in the US itself, had been deliberately sited in an isolated area.'9 'There is much evidence to suggest that the Bhopal disaster was the result of cutting costs and safety margins to terrifyingly low standards. Yet Carbide has never been tried; the facts of what actually happened have never been fully explored in a Court of Law; and no liability has been established.'10

In spite of evidence of poor management and shoddy maintenance, Union Carbide (one of the world's ten largest chemical companies) denied liability and produced an 'independent investigator' to support their case; but the scientist concerned turned out to have been paid by them. The company was spared paying crippling compensation of up to $15bn when they succeeded in persuading the US courts in 1986 that the case should be tried instead by the Indian courts, resulting in each claimant receiving the outrageously trivial sum of $470 'in full and final settlement' for either suffering or bereavement. For comparison, an industrial disaster in the US itself which resulted in asbestos disease, resulted in awards of $40,000 to each of the 60,000 victims involved.11

If a disaster similar to that at Bhopal had occurred in the US itself, the compensation would have reached such astronomical amounts as to put the company into immediate bankruptcy. As it turned out, when news of the $470 award become known on the New York stock exchange, Union Carbide shares immediately rose by $2.

The enormously powerful pharmaceutical companies are in the forefront of attempts to tailor world patenting laws to the benefit of the multinationals as described by *The Nation* (18/3/91):

The proposal is to extend patents to all products and processes, which are new, useful, and unobvious. This would allow the multinationals to gain control over much of the world's genetic resources, most of which are embedded in seeds and herbs in tropical Third World countries. The multinationals hope to gather information from the Third World, manipulate it with rapidly evolving biotechnology expertise and then patent the new seeds, pharmaceuticals or other products. The Third World will receive nothing in the bargain, because under the proposed regulations, naturally occurring organisms would not be patentable, though genetically altered ones would be....For example, a gene isolated from an African cowpea, when inserted into crops ranging from soya beans to maize, provide excellent resistance to insect pests...observers believe the gene will be worth hundreds of millions of dollars to its inventors. But the question is...who are the inventors?...those who isolated the gene or the West African farmers who identified the value of the plant holding the gene and then developed and perfected it? Forcing Third World countries to accept US-style patent laws would strengthen the monopoly powers of multinationals, drive up the prices of drugs and other products and devastate fledgeling Third World high-technology companies.

The dissolution of all the old ostentatiously held empires 'belonging' to the First World, and their replacement by so-called independent nations represented one of the greatest confidence tricks in history. Representatives of the multinationals have all too easily slipped into the places of the old colonial administrators, and straight political 'ownership' has simply been replaced by equally impoverishing economic domination which has been described aptly as 'recolonisation'.

Media thought control

First World leaders have spared neither effort nor expense to disseminate their idealogy world-wide, in order to promote and consolidate the capitalist system. In *The Nation* (12/6/89) B H Bagdikian states:

A handful of mammoth private organizations have begun to dominate the world's mass media. Most of them confidently announce that by the 1990s they will control the majority of the world's important newspapers, magazines, books, broadcasting stations, movies, recordings and video-cassettes. Moreover, each of these planetary corporations plans to gather under its control every step in the information process, from creation of 'the product' to all the various means by which modern technology delivers media messages to the public. 'The product' is news, information, ideas, entertainment and popular culture; the public is the whole world. Combining the thrust of all these corporate forces produces economic power that dwarfs that of many nations. Time Warner, for example, has a total value of $18 bn, more than the combined GNPs of Jordan, Bolivia, Nicaragua, Albania, Laos, Liberia and Mali. These lords of the global village have their own political agenda. All resist economic changes that do not support their own financial interests. Together, they exert a homogenizing power over ideas, culture and commerce that affects populations larger than any in history. Neither Caesar nor Hitler, Franklin Roosevelt nor any Pope, has commanded as much power to shape the information on which so many people depend to make decisions about everything from whom to vote for to what to eat.

In the *Guardian* (7/1/91) John Pilger recalled that at the height of the First World War, Lloyd George confided to C P Scott, editor of the *Manchester Guardian*: 'If people really knew, the war would be stopped tomorrow; but of course they don't know, and they can't know.' Seventy years later, the notion of the journalist as a teller of truths unpalatable to ruling elites, as a whistle-blower in the public interest, has been fatally eroded. This is in great part the result of the 'communications revolution' (as described by Rupert Murdoch) that has produced not an informed society, but a media society, in which vast amounts of repetitive information are confined to a narrow spectrum of 'thinkable thought'. The US sage Walter Lipman referred to this process as 'the manufacture of consent'.

Probably the most significant factor favouring the mind manipulators has been the wholesale spawning of television and other items of electronic audio-visual equipment—thus relieving millions of the trouble of reading or even learning to read. Over the past 25 years in the US, newspaper circulation per capita has fallen 30%, while TV viewing has increased 40%. At the same time, the US College Boards standard aptitude tests for high school reading and writing skills fell 62 points to their lowest level in 1991. Just one of the many detrimental effects of much of what is offered on TV was highlighted by a UK Broadcasting Standards Council study in 1990 which found that children cannot distinguish between reality and fantasy in TV drama, and often fail to identify the 'goodies' and the 'baddies'. The children were also found likely to take personalities, particularly those in authority, at their face value; for example becoming confused when a policeman became a 'bad person', assuming all policemen to be automatically good.

THIRD WORLD SUFFERING
An indictment of First World leaders

The world is overflowing with resources of all kinds, far too many of which are squandered on wars and other anarchic, wasteful activities. Yet, in spite of this plenty, two-thirds or more of humanity are doomed to live out their lives in conditions which most First World inhabitants could not even conceive of. In this context, statistics do not well suit the subject. We are not discussing bags of cement but human beings—all of them having the potential to lead as full and rewarding lives as those led by the more fortunate in the First World. Whether it is one or one and a half billion who live in absolute poverty, with all its attendant agonies, represents a diversion when it is clear to any fair minded person that it is insupportable for a single fellow human being to suffer such pain and misery. Let us simply record that many millions of people are born, 'live', and die, usually prematurely, in totally inadequate dwellings, and often in no shelter at all; over 600 million are estimated to be homeless. Interminably, they face hunger, lack of pure water, ignorance and illiteracy, not to mention numerous diseases unknown in the First World. In South Africa for example, the richest country on the African Continent, seven million people lack adequate shelter, and in the 'settlements' 200 people share one toilet.

The scourge of malnutrition and diseases

Humans cannot live effectively when chronically hungry; they cannot work or study properly, nor think beyond the immediate need for sustenance; *malnutrition stunts mental as well as physical abilities*. Over half of the entire populations of many Third World countries are malnourished; millions are driven to scavenging in rubbish dumps, eating animal foodstuffs or newspapers soaked in water. Twenty years ago the total of hungry Africans was 90m, now it is 140m and by the year 2000 is feared will be 200m; the greatest suffering is amongst women and children in rural areas. Taking Brazil as just one example: although it is a land of plenty, one third of all children are malnourished and 350,000 of them die annually. At least 50 million Brazilians are underfed, not for lack of food, but lack of money to buy it. The much respected priest, Dom Helder Camora, once said: 'When I give food to the poor, they call me a saint. When I ask why the poor have no food, they call me a communist.'

If malnutrition does not result in death, it often results in mental or physical deformities, for example, over 10% of the whole African population suffer from some form of disability. Globally, there are at least a quarter of a million new cases of blindness in children annually, around half of which are due to lack of vitamin A, which could be provided, if not by fresh fruit or vegetables, then by a half-yearly pill costing a few pence. Being disabled in the First World is traumatic enough, but to exist in the typically harsh environment of the Third World with one or more permanent disabilities defies description. Many of the appalling diseases virtually unique to the Third World are caused by the complete absence of safe water supplies and effective drainage systems - both of which are taken for granted throughout the First World. Around 2bn Third World citizens lack pure water and are driven to drinking contaminated supplies resulting annually in very many deaths. Even after contracting diarrhoea, the commonest killer, very high percentages of sufferers can be cured simply by 'oral rehydration therapy' which requires only sugar and salt with pure water.

On top of the age-long health struggles against the old established enemies such as cholera, malaria or bilharzia, the Third World now faces the shattering impact of Aids. Contributors to the 1991 international conference on HIV predicted that, by 2010, 90% of Aids sufferers, around 50m people, would be in the Third World. The disease is already wiping out whole communities in parts of Africa and has the potential to erode labour supply so badly that cultivation will be curtailed and mass starvation result. There are grounds for hope that Aids cases will level off in the First World in the 1990s. By contrast, in the Third World the previously predicted average life span in Africa, for example, of 62 years by 2000 is likely to be cut to 48 years. Aids will undoubtedly kill millions throughout the Third World, which is particularly vulnerable because of the universally poor infrastructure of the health services: in Africa for example, some countries total health budgets for all medical needs, not just HIV, amount to only $3 pa per person.

Endless deaths from starvation

Of all the unendurable miseries of Third World lives, the slow, agonizing death through starvation represents the ultimate rebuke to the First World for allowing humanity to sink to such depths. Only when dramatic concentrations and migrations of starving people become labelled 'famines' does the First World pay limited attention. Apart from invariably inadequate support from Governments, this usually takes the form of appeals to the public for charitable donations, often supported by various entertainments. In early 1991, declining response to such appeals was given the distasteful tag of 'donor fatigue'. Such appeals have very limited impact in the context of ad hoc attempts to pump millions of tons of food suddenly through totally inadequate supply lines. Worse, the whole scenario of leaving each crisis for charities to solve assists

First World Governments to continue shrugging off their collective responsibility to put an end forever to the terrible plight of the Third World in all its manifestations. The special attention paid from time to time to major famines, largely through media emphasis, also successfully distracts First World attention away from the fact that famines are only the 'tip of the iceberg' and that death from starvation is ever-present, on a huge scale. *Every three days, as many children alone die from starvation as the total death toll at Hiroshima.*

Few dogs or other pet animals in the First World would be allowed to endure the barbaric cruelties of starvation inflicted on millions of humans in the Third World. The *Guardian* (25 & 26/4/91) gives some idea of what starvation really means:

> When normal foods disappear, the starving eat wild grain, tubers, wild berries, corn husks, coconuts, shrivelled blades of grass...relief workers have seen men on camels eating leaves from the same trees the camels are feeding on, and migrant women boiling grass roots and leaves into a vile, frothing, repulsive green mass...the 5m now facing death in South Sudan are eating roots and bark, and some mothers unable to feed their children have been driven to suicide...many are naked and it is cold at night.

Peter Hillmore explains that:

> Death from starvation begins when metabolism is reduced and the body shuts down on unnecessary physical activity, producing familiar lethargy signs, and the heart slows down. In the Third World human bodies have little reserves of body fat to start with, so the onset of protein loss is rapid. For example, doctors estimate that *a Western child would have to starve for about three or four weeks before reaching the physical condition in which an African child starts.* Because of this protein loss, their guts atrophy, vital organs are reduced in size, vitamin deficiency increases, raising the apathy. They lose any desire to move. Unable to produce glucose for the brain, the liver desperately produces an unsuitable chemical alternative. Death follows either from a disease, or from insufficient strength to breathe.[12]

Divisions in the Third World

By comparison with the immensely rich First World, the Third World countries as a whole appear extremely poor, but none the less there is sufficient wealth within most of them to sustain significant elites. With very few exceptions, Third World countries subscribe to the same capitalist, free market economies as the First World, which means that any form of equality amongst their citizens is not only not achieved, but is not even aimed for. All of which makes the prospects for the average, very poor people of the Third World doubly bleak: they face not only the dominating greed of the whole First World but that of their own elites as well. In Latin America, for example, the poorest 20% of the population have only 3% of the total income, and exist on a daily average of 600 calories below the minimum requirement. The richest 5% of the population absorb 30% of total income, and consume 2,000 calories daily in excess of the minimum. In Brazil, the incomes of the wealthiest families are 200 times that of the poorest. In the East, Thailand has a very high growth rate; but the benefits are not shared by its poorest 10% whose share of GNP has actually dropped to 2% while that of the wealthiest 10% has risen to 40%.

In India, society is divided into no less than some 13 different levels, from the 'Untouchables' at the bottom, to the elitist Brahmins at the top. This whole caste system is enshrined in, and perpetuated by, the Hindu religion. The stranglehold which that religion has over its adherents is illustrated vividly by the following almost unbelievable dispatch from Ajoy Bose in the *Guardian* (2/4/91):

> Two lower caste youths and an upper caste girl, aged 15, were hanged publicly by their own fathers goaded by a vigilante mob, in an Indian village last week. The three were punished for defying the Hindu ban on inter-caste marriages. Roshni, the daughter of an upper caste land-lord, ran away with her lower caste boyfriend, Brijayandra. The two lovers were helped to elope by another lower caste youth, Ram Kishan. The weeping parents were kicked and beaten into putting the noose around the necks of their children as the entire village watched. Rashni and Brijayandra did not die at once but were dragged alive along with the corpse of Ram Kishan on to a funeral pyre; they tried to drag themselves out but were pushed back with sticks by the mob.

Elitism in the Third World is not just home-grown, it is fostered deliberately by the First World. Supporting such capitalist elites, President Truman said: 'All freedom is dependent on freedom of enterprise....the whole world should adopt the American system—the American system can survive in America only if it becomes a world system.' In furtherance of this aim, First World countries, particularly the US, have invited representatives of Third World elites to visit them at no expense for training and indoctrination in the many branches of the free market system. Commenting on the tie-ups between local elites and First World interests Susan George says:

> The economic choices made by these alliances bear directly on how the great majority of poor people in Third World countries live. They even decide, put crudely, whether or not they will eat. Unless we understand how and why the poor have been sold out through the joint efforts of their own privileged countrymen and their foreign cronies, we will continue to ascribe food shortages and even famines to 'natural forces', 'population pressures', and so forth.[13]

A further unhappy form of division in the Third World exists between the rural areas, still containing usually over 50% of the people, and those in the urban areas where fringe benefits are available to some, by virtue of living in proximity to the civil servants, the military, the merchants and other elites. It is, of course, through the latter's hands that any funds (whether income, loan or aid) entering a country must pass and thus risk being 'siphoned off' in various ways, leaving the rural populations as very unlikely recipients. Some economists have even questioned the whole ethic of aid giving, because of the dangers of misappropriation and the bolstering of local elites at the expense of the poor. Of $47bn aid given in 1989, 10bn came straight back as deposits in First World bank accounts.

The ugliest aspect of elitism in the Third World is crude physical repression. Throughout the Third World, the ratio of soldiers to population is 1:250, as against 1:4,000 for doctors. In the First World, resources normally permit any demanding members of the population to be 'bought off'; in the Third World, resources are comparatively limited, and the potentially restive masses far more numerous. Therefore, to protect their wealth and privileges from their fellow countrymen, Third World elites have increasingly involved their armed forces, who regrettably, have been only too ready to oblige, in some cases assuming total control. One of the many terrible examples was the Pinochet dictatorship following the coup of 1973. An official Chilean Government report, published in March 1991, chronicles the death of 2,279 people—mostly innocent civilians, 49 of them children under 16—in most cases after suffering appalling torture.[14]

Similar terror was inflicted on the people of Indonesia in 1965, following another military coup, in which a million people were massacred and President Suharto seized power. Following withdrawal by the Portuguese in 1975, the Indonesian army illegally occupied East

Timor, and over the following years killed 200,000 of the population of 600,000. An exceptional report by Hugh O'Shaughnessy (*Observer* 7/4/91) states that the East Timor people live in permanent fear for their lives but that the young ones are defiant, saying: 'If we resist they kill us; if we don't resist they kill us; so we might as well resist.' Jakarta's appetite for East Timor is undoubtedly strengthened by its off-shore mineral and oil wealth, described recently by neighbouring Australia's Foreign Minister as probably worth 'trillions'.

A special UN study by a Kenyan lawyer revealed that, during the five year period up to 1982, over 2 million people were executed worldwide without proper legal proceedings. It named Iran, South Africa, Argentina, Guatemala and Colombia as some of the worst offenders at the time. An extreme example of elite edginess is provided by the Sultan of Brunei, reputedly the world's richest man, so concerned about possible unrest in his tiny country with under 250,000 population, that he ordered fighter aircraft, patrol vessels and other military equipment worth £500m from UK arms manufactures.[15]

Severe curtailment of human rights is widespread in the Third World. Writing in *The Nation* (11/2/91) Professor Edward Said of Columbia University says: 'I do not know a single Arab who would not readily agree that the monopoly on coercion given to the state has almost completely eliminated democracy in the Arab world: it has introduced immense hostility between rulers and ruled, placed a much higher value on conformity, flattery and getting along, than on risking new ideas, criticism or dissent.' In Africa, the *Guardian* (9/5/91) reports that 'summary execution, arbitrary arrest, exile or prolonged detention without trial, are the common experience of academics in many African countries; they form vulnerable targets as Governments have felt threatened by academics developing the spirit of critical inquiry.' Such persecution of intellectuals robs countries of the very people most desperately needed for planning against disasters, and contributing to fruitful development generally.

The ultimate, terribly wounding example of divisions within Third World countries is actual civil warfare between contending sections struggling either to retain or gain control, sometimes continuing for decades. These conflagrations are often fuelled by outside support for reasons both of politics and of arms sales profits. Outcomes of such internal wars are naturally calamitous, resulting in economic ruin and dislocation, often ending in famine which in turn becomes more difficult to alleviate because potential food suppliers fear their aid will be diverted to armies rather than to the starving. In Africa, for example, at least half of the 40m people at risk from starvation, have been affected by civil wars. In Mozambique, the most acute case, 37% of children have been dying before reaching age five,compared with 1% in the UK.

In the 1970s, an International Labour Office report drew attention to the fact that, in the great majority of Third World countries, 'growth' was not resulting in a reduction of poverty, and went on: '*it is no longer acceptable in human terms, nor responsible in political terms, to wait for benefits to trickle down until they finally reach the poorest groups.*' Regrettably, divisions within the Third World countries have become, inexorably, even more entrenched since that report was written. However, it is noteworthy that in the very small number of Third World countries which have achieved more egalitarian societies, considerable advances have been made. In Cuba, for example, illiteracy has been largely eliminated; there is a ratio of one doctor per 480 population; child mortality has been cut to the best of First World levels and life expectancy increased to 76 years.

The inequities of land ownership

Worldwide, approximately 2% of all landowners, each having over 100 hectares, control 75% of all global land; just one quarter of owners control over 50% of the world's land. Immense inequities exist in the First World, but in the Third World access to land is critical to survival. In the case of the minority who own small plots, each famine forces the sale of part or all of them to buy food, and thus the discrepancies in ownership widen. Only about half the world's potential agricultural land is actually cultivated, because many large owners look upon land primarily as an investment. For example, in Paraguay only 3% out of the possible 20% of all land is farmed; and in Brazil, areas of farmland equalling the size of India remain uncultivated. In the Third World as a whole, an average of 70% of rural populations, ranging from 50% in India to 85% in Bolivia, own no land at all, not even the tiny plots their hovels stand on. They cultivate land owned by others, and pay 'rent' for doing so in the form of a proportion of the crops raised.

In Africa as a whole, 75% of rural populations own only 4% of all land. In Java, just one percent of farmers own over one-third of all land, leaving over half of all rural families with none. In the Dominican Republic, seven out of every 1,000 owners have half the arable land, while 300,000 families have none. In Bangladesh, the greatest obstacle to agricultural development is not the periodic floods, terrible though they are, but the inequitable access to land. Resources are in the hands of the few who have managed to benefit most from the various aid programmes. The 35% of Bangladeshis who were landless at the time of independence in 1971 rose to 60% by 1991.

In Latin America, only one third of the rural populations have any land at all, and even that amounts to only one percent of the total. In Brazil, half of all land is in the hands of 1% of the population, resulting in there being 20m landless peasants. A tentative Government proposal for land reform in 1985 resulted in the Brazilian big landowners spending $5m on private armies to combat the peasants, and the trades unionists and priests who supported them. The *Guardian* (2/3/91 & 12/10/91) reported that more than 1,750 people have died in Brazilian land disputes, but only 24 trials have resulted; also that slave conditions persist on some ranches to which men have been brought from far away with promises of good wages, and are then held prisoner and shot if they try to escape.

Education, illiteracy and 'brain drain'

Compared with an average education expenditure per child in the First World of $6,000 pa,in the poorest Third World countries an almost meaningless $2 pa is available; the Third World has less than one quarter the number of teachers per child than in the First World. As with other aspects of Third World conditions, the situation is worsening; for example, educational expenditure per child in recent years has declined by one-third in Africa and two-thirds in Latin America. Less than half of all Third World children have the chance to learn to read and write; 250m five to 14 year olds lack any possibility of attending school at all: if they all held hands they would encircle the earth four times. Further, children commonly drop out of primary education for various reasons including expense, sickness, distances to walk and pressures to earn during school hours; rates of dropping out, compared with 5% in the First World, are 30% in poor, and 50% in very poor countries. Barely 20% of all Third World children obtain any secondary education, compared with 90% in the First World.

Not surprisingly, the appalling outcome of this terrible neglect of the young is that, worldwide, there are now around 1bn illiterate people, approximately half the adult population of the Third World, and this total is rising by 25m annually. two-thirds of all illiterates are women. In the poorest countries under 40% of adults are literate; for example, in sub-Sahara literacy is 34% for men, 17% for women; in some countries illiteracy afflicts 90% of the people and 100% of the women. The catastrophic effects of illiteracy, both for individuals and their communities, defy adequate comment.

At the opposite end of the scale, some Third World countries have managed to establish various forms of higher education, resulting in the output of fully qualified doctors, engineers, and other professionals, some of whom remain to enrich their own communities. Many, however, are seduced away by the vastly higher salaries in the First World, and thus constitute the notorious South to North 'brain drain'. *The loss to the Third World of so many of their desperately needed skilled people has led to the process being likened to a sophisticated 20th century version of the slave trade.*

The value of the 'drained brains' to the First World, (estimated by the UN at \$50bn during the 1960s) in fact approximately cancels out the value of 'aid' given to the Third World. Whereas the First World sends technical advisers to the Third World on a temporary basis, the Third World loses double their number of qualified professionals permanently. During the 1970s, half the graduate nurses, doctors, surgeons and dentists left the Philippines. Between 1982 and 1985, some 100,000 skilled professionals are believed to have left Mexico for the US. There are more Ethiopian doctors in the US than in their own country.

The special plight of Third World women

Living conditions throughout the Third World are abominable for men, women and children alike; but for women they are especially severe. Having survived the odds against females growing up at all, women become, in most cases, burdened with the main responsibility for nurturing their families. In many places, women, often with children, spend half their waking lives fetching and carrying water and firewood, sometimes walking up to 15 miles daily in the process. Although women represent 50% of humanity, they contribute some 65% of the world's total working hours, yet receive only 10% of world income and own barely 1% of world property. A Tanzanian study in 1985 showed women working on average 3,069 hours per year compared with 1,829 for men. Women suffer appalling physiological trauma; annually, throughout the Third World half a million die during pregnancy and childbirth, and up to 80m illegal abortions are performed with a 15% death rate[16]. In South Africa, if a husband dies or walks away, the wife and children are evicted from the home with nowhere to go.

Despite Third World women contributing such heroic efforts, the scales are always tipped in favour of the males, whose greater physical strength is seen as crucial in all the varied battles for survival. That this preference for males often assumes grotesquely tragic forms is illustrated by examples from the world's two most populous countries. In China, in the early 1980s, the authorities admitted that, because of the determination to have sons, tens of thousands of mothers and midwives were murdering infant girls, with resulting imbalances as great as 5 boys to every girl in some areas, posing obviously severe problems for the future[17]. In India, the same bias towards males is aggravated by the traditional obligation of a bride's parents to contribute a significant 'dowry' to the bridegroom. One report states: 'The plain shocking fact is that India kills her girls. They die in infancy for want of medicine and food reserved for men and boys; and later in childbirth, their weakened, malnourished bodies are unable to cope with the frenzied urge for boy babies.[18]

Another report states: 'Struggles for survival in the Third World mean that male children are vastly more welcome than females. This is particularly noticeable and recorded statistically, in India, where annually, 3m girls born die before 15, and of these, half a million die due to gender discrimination. A daughter is seen as a liability involving a dowry. 300,000 more female than male children die annually. Clinics doing prenatal sex-determination tests advertise shamelessly: 'Spend 500 rupees (£15) now and save 500,000 rupees (on dowry) later'. Discrimination against females continues into adulthood; in New Delhi alone, it is estimated that approximately 600 women are burned each year in 'dowry deaths', in which the husband's family kills the bride so they may be free to keep the dowry and demand afresh from the next set of in-laws. Numbers of women in India dropped from 972 per 1,000 men in 1901 to 933 in 1981. This is in stark contrast to the position in Europe, where women outnumber men.[19]

Horrors of third world childhoods

Article 32 of the UN Convention on the Rights of Children stipulates 'the right of the child to be protected from economic exploitation and from performing work likely to be hazardous…or to interfere with the child's education'. To the deep shame of world society, as with other excellent UN exhortations, this one continues to be flouted in the most despicable and heartless ways. Globally, over 100 million child slaves and countless millions more receiving pittances only, work in often appalling conditions, and many millions lack education completely.

That the use of child labour is truly international is illustrated by this report:

About 120,000 children (as young as eight years) live and work in the garbage dump known as Smokey Mountain in Manila, picking over the rubbish for items to sell and scraps to eat. In Colombia, children work in the mines for 12 hours daily. In India, they weave carpets and sweat in dangerous glass factories. In Brazil, Portugal and Italy, they sit in cramped factories gluing shoes together. Children have no trade union rights or industrial power, so are often worked even longer hours than their adult counterparts. Investigations have found cases of *children as young as 3 chained to the work-bench*.[20]

Child labourers in Mexico are believed to number between 5 and 10m. In Bangladesh, most children have to work, sometimes 14 hours per day, every day, earning only one penny per hour. Malnourished and sick boys of 10 or 12 pull heavy handcarts collecting garbage. Girls are driven into prostitution, commonly at age 10, sometimes as young as seven years.

The following two reports relating to India present pictures of conditions which are regrettably to be found in many other countries as well:

In India, with over 80m adult unemployed, 55m children labour for pitiful wages and sometimes for none at all. 50,000 children, for example, work in hideous conditions in the match and fireworks factories of Tamil Nadu. Countless tens of thousands labour in hellish conditions at brick kilns and in stone quarries.[21]

In the late 1980s, in India, only 46.5m children were in school, out of 175m. under 14. More than 45m were working in appalling conditions. In one area, children start work at the age of three and earn 6p for a 12 hour day, on glass making, diamond cutting , brassware and hand and power looms. Thus the labour cost of a carpet, retailing in London for £5,000, can be as little as 100 rupees (£3) if woven by children. They are virtual prisoners, malnourished, in cramped conditions, with poor light and often sleeping at their looms. Beating and torture are common, and lung disease caused by wool dust is endemic. In Aligarh can be seen children of seven or eight, covered in black dust, bending over polishing machines for upwards to 20 hour shifts, inhaling emery powder and metal dust the whole time. Typically, ramshackle buses and trucks set off at 3 am to tour outlying villages, where agents are employed to ensure the children are awake and ready to leave for work. Each vehicle picks up 150 to 200 children, some only three years old, mostly little girls, for a journey of up to two hours before starting work.[22]

The *Observer* (6/7/91) reports that up to 1,000 children, aged 12 to 14 years, were being used to dig tunnels, because of their small bodies, in the Amazonian Rondonia tin mines. At an even lower level than those actually earning a wage (if under one penny per hour can be so described) are the millions of Third World children who are actually slaves, an estimated 75m of them in Asia alone. A common form of child slavery is termed 'bonded labour', in which children are forced to work to pay off their parents' debts. In Thailand there are some 2m child slaves, who can be purchased for $10 per head, working under appalling conditions. The *Guardian* (16/8/91) reports that Peruvian Government officials saw the bodies of over 50 children in a mass grave 800 miles South East of Lima. The children, estimated to be 10 to 14 years old, are believed to be victims of exploitation by gold miners, sawmill operators and ranch owners. A local official said the abuse of child labourers had become so common that bodies floating in the river were 'almost natural, no one pays any attention'.

A pitiful, poverty-driven form of abuse of Third World children is the practice of selling young girls as brides or prostitutes. This is described in the *Observer* (26/1/92) in relation to India:

> 13 year old Zahida explains… 'my father is out of a job; my family is poor; I have no choice'. She can be bought for 10,000 rupees (£250); a TV set costs more in India. Rani, 14, was bought for £15 when she was three and now works as a prostitute; her adoptive 'father' acts as her pimp and keeps her earnings. In Hyderabad there are some 100 marriage 'brokers' who can find a young bride in a few hours, arrange everything including documentation to circumvent any legal problems, and take commissions from both parties. When a sobbing little girl called Ameena was rescued by an Indian Airlines stewardess on her way to Saudi Arabia with her new 60 year old husband, her marriage certificate said she was 32; her school records showed she was 11. Her poor rickshaw driver father had sold her for £130.

The *Guardian* (12/2/92) reported that, all over the Amazon region of Brazil, 9, 10 and 11 year old girls, from poor families, sometimes sold by their fathers, were being enslaved by brothel owners, with newly arrived virgins being auctioned off to the highest bidder. The girls reported ill-treatment, torture, abuse and slavery, and beatings or killings if they attempted to escape.

Yet another category has to be added to the many forms of assault on childrens' rights in the Third World. A 1996 report from the Swedish Save the Children Fund states that there are now a quarter of a million child soldiers world-wide, some as young as seven. They fought in over 30 wars in 1995. They were used as executioners, assassins, spies and informers, and were often given drugs and alcohol before fighting. 90,000 child soldiers were killed in the Iran-Iraq War. An important factor is that modern light weapons enable children to kill with ease. An AK-47 rifle, often costing only $6, can be stripped and reassembled by a child of 10. Warlords have found children in some ways better soldiers than adults —they are obedient, easy to coerce, do not demand pay and are less likely to run away.

Against the background of millions of children dying slowly from malnutrition and industrial diseases, must be seen the increasing numbers of children dying sudden, brutal deaths by execution, notably for example, in Brazil, as described in the two following reports:

> These murders, rapidly increasing in numbers because not properly investigated, are carried out by 'para-police' groups with a self-attributed mission to 'clean up the cities' by executing 'kids who might become criminals'. There are at least 7m children living rough in Brazil, some in flimsy shelters, some in sewers.[23]

> The election slogan of a Brazilian policeman standing for Congress is 'a good bandit is a dead bandit'. But for many in Brazil the term 'bandit' applies not just to hardened criminals, but to the thousands of children who begin life on the streets, begging, pilfering, and sniffing glue to dull their hunger. In 1989 in Brazil, approximately 400 children, many under 10, were murdered by death squads made up of policemen, police informers or self-styled 'justice-makers'. Of approximately 60m children and adolescents, 40m live in poverty, and 13m in absolute misery.[24]

Reporting the killing of over 470 children in Rio de Janeiro in the first half of 1992, the *Guardian* (7/6/92) referred to the local practice of killing children to preclude the development of criminal adults, or 'killing them before they mug you'. A child was found on a beach with a sign saying: 'I killed you because you have no future.' A young Brazilian told a TV interviewer that they had only one option: turn to crime or starve. Worried businessmen are reported as paying killers, one of whom said he had killed about 150 street kids, mostly nine or 10 years old; another had killed 90 children.

Similar atrocities against children in Guatemala are reported in the *New Internationalist* (June 1991), including the violent deaths of over 40 street children in just six months of 1990 in Guatemala City alone. Many were found with their faces disfigured and their bodies dismembered; the burning out of eyes and cutting off of ears is common. Volunteer rehabilitation worker Bruce Harris believes the police were responsible for at least 13 of these deaths and the abuse and torture of a further 50. To even hold such a belief is dangerous in Guatemala, where, since 1967, over 40,000 have disappeared after abduction by 'security' agents and over 100,000 killed. But to press for prosecutions of police officers is, in the words of one journalist, 'almost suicidal'. The above report describes the case of a 13 year old boy who died of a rup-tured liver 10 days after being kicked senseless by four police officers. The inscription on the plaque above his grave reads: 'I only wanted to be a child—but they wouldn't let me.'

THE INTERNATIONAL DEBT CRISIS
Origins of the crisis

The most important factor originating the great debt crisis was the sudden quadrupling of oil prices in the early 1970s. This resulted in vast 'money mountains' which the producers invested, in the main, in the First World's banking system. The banks, in turn, almost forced it on Third World Governments at quite low interest rates, without apparently caring greatly who had control of it or how it was spent. Debts of billions were thus incurred by Governments which were often dictatorships, and rarely consulted their peoples about how the money would best be spent; on the contrary, they often spent it on arms to repress them. At the same time, large proportions of the loans were squandered, or embezzled and sent out of the recipient country into private accounts in Swiss and other banks. By November 1982 the whole process had gathered such momentum, and become such an established part of international financial dealings, that the Managing Director of the International Monetary Fund, Jacques de Larosiere, appealed to the banks to continue lending to the Third World because if they stopped it would imperil the whole world capitalist system.

Debt—facts and figures

During the heyday of the lending spree, 1973 to 1982, the profits of the 7 largest US banks from Third World loan 'servicing' rose from 22% to 60%. These profits were at times augmented by their use of monies received back by them in the form of investments by corrupt officials. Since Third World countries have often been unable to repay either interest or capital amounts, these are added to their accumulated debts so the accelerating extent of indebtedness rushes forward. This is further complicated by the Third World countries having to obtain yet more loans in order to pay interest on previous ones. 'Debt servicing' can thus well absorb half of a country's export earnings, and in several African cases—if paid in full—would take several times their entire earnings. According to UN data, Third World countries make regular 'debt servicing' payments to the First World which amount to nearly five times the amounts received by them from the First World as aid; the interest rates involved with those payments are commonly four times higher than the current rates within the First World.

In round figures, the grand total of debt owed by all Third World countries to the First World bankers is now around $1,500bn (equivalent to around $300 for every living person in the world today), on which the annual 'servicing' obligation is around $250 bn. Such astronomical figures all but defy comprehension, especially in the context of the desperate poverty of most of the debtors, and it is hardly surprising that the scenario of widespread debt repudiations is discussed increasingly. Predictably, the First World lenders do not take kindly to that prospect. With characteristic directness, a US banker commented to paul Fabra of *Le Monde*: 'If any Latin American country repudiates its debts, we have the legal machinery all ready. It would be lightning-fast; we would seize all the country's assets on land, sea and in the air. We would black all bank accounts of its citizens; not a single one of its ships could dock or a single plane land anywhere outside its borders without being immediately sequestered.'[25] On 11/9/91 US Vice-President Dan Quayle said: 'African governments must face the challenge of paying off debts and not expect them to be cancelled.' Such threats ill-become those who created the problem, by pressing countries to accept vast loans, at fluid interest rates, without considering whether conditions were ever likely to enable those countries to repay the interest, much less the capital.

All the circumstances point to repudiation being the only realistic solution. Cardinal Arns of San paulo has commented:

> When we borrowed, interest rates were 4%, now they are 8% and at one point were 21%. The people are expected to pay off these debts through low wages and hunger. But we have already repaid the debt once or twice over, considering the interest paid. We must stop giving the blood and the misery of our people to pay the First World.[26]

The combined debts of all Third World countries amount in fact to less than 5% of all Western banks' commercial lendings; thus their total write-offs would hardly be noticed. First World insistence on both capital and interest repayments can only be described as both spurious and vindictive.

The unendurable burdens of debt

In her powerful book *A Fate Worse than Debt*, Susan George has articulated the present crisis as follows:

> The Third World War has already started...it is tearing down practically all the Third World. Instead of soldiers dying, there are children, instead of millions of wounded, there are millions of unemployed, instead of destruction of bridges, there is a tearing down of factories, schools, hospitals, and entire economies — it is a war by the US against the Third World. It is war over Debt, with its main weapon, Interest, a weapon more deadly than the atom bomb, more shattering than a laser beam.

Debt burdens in the majority of Third World countries have risen from around 10% to around 30% of their GNP, resulting in steeply increasing malnutrition, and infant mortality rates of 50% in the worst urban conditions. Inflation regularly causes dramatic food price increases, and diseases previously almost eradicated are returning.

A report by the European Network on Debt and Development shows that: 'Britain is squeezing cash out of the world's poorest countries by demanding levels of debt repayment which far ouweigh new loans or aid, and has been a net recipient of cash from the Third World since 1981; only the US has a longer record of taking more money from the developing world than it gives out', (quoted in the *Guardian* 23/9/96.)

A study in Bolivia showed that those in employment had to work four times harder in the mid-1980s than in the mid-1970s, to be able to purchase the same amount of food. It is known that the effects of the debt burden in the poorest parts of Latin America have driven whole families to suicide; the parents first killing their children before destroying themselves. A dispatch from the Argentine reported that 'people are so poor here now, that they attack and rob one another; there is no community spirit left; mothers are bringing their 13 year old daughters to the brothels.'[27] During the 1980s, over 200m people have joined the 'absolute poor'—those who do not have enough to meet the most basic biological needs for food, clothing, and shelter. These now number 1.2 bn, almost a quarter of humanity, and two-thirds of them are under 15 years of age. Over 40 Third World countries ended the 1980s with average incomes 5% to 25% lower than at the start. 'Pressures on the poorest, from First World lenders, to fulfil monetary targets, cut spending, and promote privatisation, lead to massive environmental destruction which, together with the greenhouse effect, will increase the absolute poor to 5bn within 50 to 60 years, if present trends continue.'[28]

One of the most profound warnings of the lasting damage to humanity arising from the wanton selfishness of the First World, as represented by the debt crisis, was given in this excerpt from the 1972 Report to the UN, by Ward and Dubois, *Only One Earth*:

> But it is not only the pollutions and degradations of the atmosphere and the oceans that threaten the quality of life at the planetary level. There are threats, too, of disease spreading among undernourished children, of protein deficiency maiming the intelligence of millions, of spreading illiteracy combined with rising numbers of unemployed intellectuals, of landless workers streaming to the squalid cities, and worklessness growing there to engulf a quarter of the working force. An acceptable strategy for Planet Earth must, then, explicitly take account of the fact that the 'natural resource' most threatened with pollution, most exposed to degradation, most liable to irreversible damage, is not this or that species, nor this or that plant or biome or habitat, not even the free airs of the great oceans. It is Man himself.

THIRD AND FIRST WORLD COMPARISONS
Economic comparisons

At the time of the Industrial Revolution, the ratio between the average wealth of the richest and poorest countries was approximately 2:1. By 1900 the ratio had become 10:1, and by 1990, 50:1, on average. For example, World Bank figures for 1990 show that the ratio between the US and the poorest (then Rwanda) was, in 1967, 82:1; by 1988 that ratio had widened to 142:1 between the US and Mozambique. From further World Bank statistics, it is also clear that between 1970 and 1980 every man, woman and child in the 17 richest nations, enjoyed individual income increases averaging $900, while for the 1bn people in the Third World the increase was just $3 over the same decade.[29]

A breakdown of the global economic picture in 1991 shows approximately one-quarter of world population in rich or near-rich countries enjoying rising GNP; half in countries with static GNP; and a quarter in countries whose GNP is actually falling. The UNDP's Human Development Report for 1992 shows that by that time the richest 25% of the world's population were receiving around 83% of total world income, while the remaining 75% were subsisting on the balance of 7%. Sub-Saharan Africa, with a population of approximately 500m has a total GNP which is about the same as that of 10m Belgians, and less than that of the New York metropolitan area.[30] The annual incomes of some 1bn people in the Third World approximate to the cost of a couple of new tyres for a family car. More wealth is stolen in the US than the total wealth that many countries actually have. If their present 'growth' rates were to continue, it would take the poorest Third World countries three to four thousand years to catch up with present First World levels.

Other comparisons

Apart from the many economic disadvantages actually imposed on them by the First World, many Third World countries suffer tremendous natural disadvantages simply through being where they are on the globe. The majority of, and usually the worst, earthquakes, hurricanes, floods, droughts, desertifications and other disasters occur in these countries; also many pests, unknown in the First World, such as locusts, malarial mosquitoes, flies and snails causing sleeping sickness and bilharzia, continue to plague them. All these and other destabilising phenomena add terrible burdens to already frail people and their economies. The world's demographic balance is shifting fast, with the proportion of the world's people in the Third World growing from around 70% in 1960 to around 85% by 2025. In the 1930s, one of Hitler's notorious grounds for his aggressions was Germany's alleged need for more 'lebensraum' (living space), but now, in the Third World, many countries are already genuinely packed to overflowing. Not only do vast and increasing numbers of people require space to exist on, but throughout many Third World countries, living space is already diminished by vast areas of jungles, deserts, swamps, and mountainous regions. In Egypt for example, 98% of the population live on just 2% of the country. Even now, the average Third World citizen has only around one hundreth of the amount of usable land available to him as compared to a citizen of North America.

In the First World the ratio of doctors to population averages 1:500; in the rural Third World the ratio is around 1:200,000; some 1.5bn people are completely without access to any form of medical care.

Infant mortality rates in India in 1987 were 152 per 1,000, compared with 7 per 1,000 in Sweden or Japan. Average life expectancy in Third World countries ranges from 20 to 30 years less than in the First World. Third World countries have only about 7% of the world's scientists and engineers, and face overwhelming difficulties in trying to deal, by themselves, with their environmental and resource problems.

Around 100m people in the Third World, particularly in the cities, spend their entire existence like stray dogs on the pavements—without shelter of any kind. The International Labour Office reports that employees in the Third World work one-third longer hours but receive one-tenth of the wages for equivalent work in the First World. *The average US citizen eats twice as much protein as his body needs; to meet this demand, more grain is fed to US cattle than is consumed by China and India together.* While the poorest 400m people are so undernourished as to suffer stunted growth, mental retardation and early death in the Third World, North Americans spend $5bn annually on special diets to cut their calorie intake and reduce weight.

DECLINE IN THE FIRST WORLD
Increasing numbers in poverty

The most distinctive feature of the 1980s, particularly in the US and UK, has been the hardening attitudes of the ruling elites to their most disadvantaged fellow citizens. These have come to resemble more and more their well-established ruthless attitudes to the populations of most of the Third World countries. Their viewpoint has been 'every man for himself in a free-for-all market economy'; this was epitomized by UK premier Thatcher's notorious statement: 'There is no such thing as society - only individuals'. The result has been increasing polarization within First World societies. In the UK, for instance , between 1979 and 1989, the income of the richest fifth grew by almost 40%, while the income of the poorest fifth fell by 6%.[31] In a 1985 lecture to students, US financier Ivan Boesky reassured those who felt embarrassed by business activities, saying: 'Greed is all right, by the way, you can be greedy and still feel good about yourself.'

An *Observer* report, (15/9/91), states that:

Recorded UK crimes for the period 1979 to 1991 have doubled to 5m, but with only 27% recorded, the real current figure is around 20m crimes. During this period the government held out no hope for the poor, and if we now have an underclass with little to lose by committing crimes, this is partly because of the way its members have been taught to regard themselves. The increase relates to increased poverty and inequality, and to sharp declines in consumption levels among the worse off.

Around 10m. UK citizens live on less than the Council of Europe's 'decency threshold' of £168 per week, and one in every four children will experience poverty. The *Observer* (12/7/92) reported that tuberculosis, in the UK, increased by 10% from 1987 to 1991, and by 15% among young women in just two years from 1987 to 1989. A leading consultant was convinced that the cause was the increase in poverty and homelessness.

In the aftermath of apparently aimless rioting on a housing estate, the Northumbrian chief probation officer wrote in the *Guardian* (2/10/91):

> Here one can see - as in many of our cities - the crushing effects of deprivation, in housing, education, and employment amenities, with most people suffering from the effects of severe poverty. In such places there is a real sense of alienation for a minority within a society where the majority have been experiencing a kind of affluence. The creation of such separate minority groups in a society where the pursuit of money and possessions, the philosophy of self-sufficiency and the general absence of compassion, has led to the establishment of different norms and values in order to survive in an otherwise hopeless situation.

In the US, in 1985, 33 million people were living below the poverty threshold; 35 million had no health insurance at all; in one year 1 million families were refused medical care for financial reasons; infant mortality rates in inner cities ranked with the Third World; around 20 million lacked adequate nutrition and one-third of mothers on welfare were illiterate. *The Nation* (1/6/92) reports that *poverty kills 27 children every day in the US where 'home' has become increasingly a site of conflict and abuse*; where every year 1.5 m children run away from home, not because they want to but because they have to, even the streets being safer than the physical and sexual abuse they are running from; over 5,000 children every year end up in unmarked graves.

The primary cause of First World poverty has been unemployment caused by the skewing of national economies. For example, in the US, in the decade 1977 to 1987, production workers disappeared from the following industries: machine tools 50%, farm machinery 60%, turbines 43%, construction machinery 42%, mining equipment 60%, textile equipment 43%, and oilfield equipment 68%.

In the US, infant mortality rates have been increasing steadily; for example, in Los Angeles, from 12 per 1,000 in 1983 to 18 per 1,000 in 1989. Numbers of births without pre-natal care have risen from 1 in 10 in 1981, to 1 in 3 in 1990. The structures of urban civilization are simply falling apart under the pressures of drugs, crime, unemployment, and a spreading insidious poverty which is driving the hearts of US cities back to Third World levels.[32] A 1990 US National Commission on Children report pointed to 'the US producing underclass generations of illiterate, unhealthy, alienated and unemployable young people.' Malnutrition currently affects around half a million children in the US and 11 million have no direct access to a doctor. 1 child in 5 (1 in 4 in rural areas) lives below the poverty line and at least 100,000 are homeless. The racial divide is shown by 1987 poverty figures for children: Blacks 45%, Hispanics 39% and Whites 15%.[33]

In the US in 1990 there were over 2m homeless, including approximately 80,000 in New York and 15,000 in Washington. Some 75,000 in New York, referred to by the *New York Times* as 'Calcutta USA' were sleeping rough. In contrast to the 20m who go hungry, approximately one-third of all US males 'suffer' from obesity. The problems of day to day living in First World 'constant growth' societies have led inevitably to increasing consumption of tranquillizers, breakdowns, and high proportions of hospital beds used by mental patients.

Worsening conditions of living

In the UK, both young and older women in inner city areas avoid going out after dark because of fear of crime. A survey during the 1980s of 1,600 people in a typical North London area, resulted in the following concerns about neighbourhood problems: crime, vandalism, dirty streets, unemployment, poor housing, air pollution, inadequate facilities for the young, poor health service, street lighting, drug abuse, racial tension, sexual harassment, poor public transport, poor schools, police behaviour, poor working conditions.[34] A February 1990 *World in Action* survey found a third of all UK wives had either been hit or threatened by their husbands, and US researcher Denise Andrews found that 40% of men considered it 'normal' to hit their wives. *The Nation* has described US society as one 'where the poor are getting poorer and the rich are getting richer, a country with a million millionaires, and with professionals, executives, and specialists comprising 25% of the workforce, surrounded by swarms of franchise operators, medical entrepreneurs and real estate speculators.'

The *Guardian* (2/5/91) reported that a recent study based on interviews with 2,000 US citizens, found that '91% of Americans lie regularly both at work and at home; 31% of married people have had, or are having, an affair; 33% of Aids victims have not told their partners that they are infected; 72% do not know their next-door neighbour, and a majority will not look after elderly parents.' The authors of the study conclude that the truth about the US is that 'a pernicious rationalization has begun to take hold in all areas of our lives; if everybody's doing it why shouldn't I?' A leader in *The Nation* of 21/5/90 describes the current US situation thus:

> Standards of living and quality of life have been declining for most people for 2 decades. Public education is a shambles, health care is tragically inadequate, racism is rampant, corporate privilege is unrestrained, the environment is degraded, class divisions are widening, unemployment and under-employment condemn tens of millions to poverty; violence at home and in the streets is endemic, the criminal justice system is criminal and unjust. Profound cynicism...accounts for the rock bottom level of political participation.

An important indicator of societal health is job satisfaction or contentment at work generally. In this respect too, First World societies presently leave much to be desired. A report in *New Internationalist* (December 1986) cites the following:

> The average Canadian worker takes 3 hours 42 minutes weekly off work in various ways; industrial jobs in the US show annual turnovers of 35%; in Australia 1 in 5 'sick' days off are unrelated to any cause; a survey of nearly 10,000 US workers showed 28% involved in some form of property theft from their employers; the US Government estimates that between 10% and 23% of workers use dangerous drugs on the job.

The *Guardian* (12/5/91) reports that 'in the UK, the Samaritans received a record 2.6m calls for help in 1990, nearly a million more than in 1980, suicide being discussed in 72% of cases. As the number of long term unemployed grew in the eighties, so did the number of men between 15 and 44 taking their own lives. Suicides among under-25s, mainly teenagers, rose 31% from 1979 to 548 in 1989. It is feared the death toll will reach 600 this year.'

The stresses of growing up in the First World's leading nation are having similarly devastating effects on millions of young lives. According to an official of the Atlanta-based Center for Disease Control, about 1m US teenagers attempted suicide during a recent 12 month period, and an estimated 276,000 sustained injuries serious enough to require medical treatment. The Center further estimated that the suicide rate has risen from 2.7 per 100,000 teenagers in 1950 to 11.3 per 100,000 in 1988.[35] Social problems, generally, are exacerbated by increasing violence in society; for example, the most common cause of teenage death in Washington DC is from gunshot wounds. Bullet proof vests in appropriate sizes are now available for children to wear to school.[36] The *Guardian* (19/6/91) reported that the US has the highest jail population and it is growing at 13% pa. Prisoners totalled over 1m or 426 per 100,000 population, compared with (per 100,000) 268 in the SU, 97 in the UK, and 33 in South Africa. The total of 610,000 black men aged 20 to 29 in prisons compares with 436,000 black men of all ages in colleges, and the report notes that the current cost of the most expensive US college education at $20,000 pa is approximately half that of keeping a prisoner in jail. US judges are protesting at the imposing of mandatory sentences; for example, Chief Judge Donald Lay said 'the criminal justice system is a complete failure and a disgrace to a civilized nation.'

One of the most sensitive indicators of the growing instability of First World societies is the high and accelerating rate of divorces. In the UK, for example, the rate has increased five-fold since 1960; well over one third of all marriages now fail, with particularly harmful outcomes for the children concerned. The resulting dramatic increase in the number of individual households is putting a severe strain on the already short supply of homes.[37]

First World living conditions for the elderly have also deteriorated seriously. In the UK, for example, around one quarter of a million old people not only have to live permanently in residential 'homes', but often suffer abuse in them. A 1991 report by the Labour party health spokeswoman shows that such abuse includes: tying residents to chairs, residents sustaining inexplicable bruising and sometimes serious injuries, residents being left in damp smelly clothes, proprietors stealing from residents, insufficient provision of food and bad medicinal practices. A report on the problems of the elderly in New York City states that the 'war on poverty, the purpose of which was to uplift the poor, has been redesigned merely to contain them.' In one block 'grandmothers have been held hostage by their own drug-addicted grandchildren, who take over their apartments and their money…a notice gives the time of the weekly trip to the local supermarket when they can go shopping with a police escort.'[38]

Erosions of human rights

First World countries are almost invariably referred to as 'parliamentary democracies'. parliaments they certainly have;

politicians, lobbyists, and others whose careers depend on them see to that. Democracy is another matter. In the US for example, only half the population even feels sufficiently involved to vote at the occasional elections, and there has never yet been a political party even purporting to represent the interests of working people. Possibly the most significant contributory factor to the undermining of democracy has been increasing militarisation, including nuclear arming. Because of the lethality of plutonium (one-millionth of a gramme can produce cancer and 10 kilogrammes a bomb), it has been said that 'a plutonium economy and a free democracy are a contradiction in terms.' Leading UK and US legal experts state 'plutonium provides the first rational justification for underground intelligence gathering against the civilian population.'

As a result, First World countries are tending to become 'totalitarian democracies', within which official bureaucracies, police and other legal authorities have considerable power over individuals. Leaders are increasingly depriving people of those very liberties they are supposed to be defending. This is well exemplified in the UK, where decisions of terrifying gravity, such as spending around £30bn on the Trident weapons system, are increasingly taken by an inner caucus—not even the full cabinet—and certainly not after parliamentary debate. In 1968 West Germany set about re-creating a police state by legalizing phone-tapping, and with its 1972 'Berufsverbot' law, under which 3m trades unionists, peace activists, ecologists and other progressives have been investigated, and tens of thousands made redundant or refused jobs.

The US itself has one of the worst records of brutality and abuse of human rights on racial grounds, including the near-genocide of native americans, whose numbers have been cut from around 5m in the 17th century, to some 1.5m today. The US also has a bad record of spying on its own citizens. Corporations keep private security forces, in liaison with the CIA, and backed by vast resources to maintain dossiers on millions of innocent US people. The *Observer* (7/7/91) reports that 'US states can impose laws whereby federally-funded clinics are forbidden even to discuss abortion with patients; any doctor doing so, faces a 10 year prison sentence and a fine of $100,000'. In relation to its Central American 'backyard', the US has consistently rejected any suggestions that its military aid to right wing governments should be conditional on respect for human rights. In particular, for example, the White House continued to support the military elite running El Salvador, in spite of its having murdered many thousands of peasants, journalists, teachers, priests and others, over the years.

In the UK the right to privacy is abused by widespread phone-tapping.

The US National Security Agency has a tapping centre near Harrogate, with the capacity to monitor a quarter of a million phones. Many overseas call from the UK have been recorded, together with millions of internal calls, assisted by voice-recognition equipment. To store 'intelligence' information about millions of UK citizens, MI5 has an outsize computer with a 20bn character capacity, equivalent to 50,000 paperbacks. This cost the UK tax-payer £20m: but this type of expenditure can never be questioned, much less answered, because all questions in parliament regarding MI5 activities remain unanswered. Britain's record came under scrutiny at the UN Human Rights Committee in April 1991, particularly in respect of treatment of prisoners, telephone-tapping, political and press freedom, freedom of expression, and denial of full public access to facts on safety risks and accidents, to 'protect commercial confidentiality'.

The immensely well-equipped UK Government Communications Headquarters takes it upon itself to intercept an enormous range of commercial and other international telephone and telex messages, usually it seems, for no reason other than the need to justify employing numerous itchy fingers on dials and buttons. In June 1992, for example, the *Observer* revealed that the intelligence services had been spying on UK charities such as Amnesty International and Christian Aid, which are very concerned that recipients of their assistance could thus be endangered. GCHQ intercepts are regularly passed to US government agencies, which in turn pass them, for example, to extremists in Latin America, where local religious aid groups have been targeted by death squads.

According to a 1991 report[39] by the international monitoring group, Human Rights Watch, based in New York, there has been a 'marked change for the worse in the climate for liberty in the UK, with widespread erosion of civil liberties in the 1980s, in part due to the lack of a written constitution guaranteeing freedom of expression.' The group condemned Britain for detaining Arabs for deportation during the Gulf war, and explained its particular concern with Britain 'because many countries, particularly in the Commonwealth, justify their own repressive actions by pointing to the British example;…South African president Botha praised the 1988 ban on broadcast interviews with some Northern Ireland groups.'

In the last resort, the right of any people to elect a government of their own choice is compromised by the ill-concealed obduracy of the US elite. If, for example, any European country in particular, looked likely to elect a genuinely progressive, anti-establishment government, the US leadership would, in all probability, set in motion its contingency plan for such an unwelcome scenario. This could involve support by air-lifted US troops for counteractions by indigenous reactionary forces. The required, varyingly disguised but strong neo-fascist organizations already exist in major European countries.

In spite of occasional relaxations of dictatorships here and there, the world-wide trend is one of continuing domination by greedy elites. These almost exclusively unelected groups, with vital assistance from their compliant media, have the audacity to maintain their autocratic, life-and-death control over millions of fellow humans, and furthermore at their expense. The crowning indignity is provided by those elites managing to blanket a range of nefarious activities under the deepest secrecy, justified, if challenged, by 'national security'.

1 Third World Atlas, The Open University, 1983
2 The Creation of World Poverty, Teresa Hayter, Pluto,1981
3 Ditto
4 How the Other Half Dies, Susan George, Penguin, 1976
5 Ex-Services CND Newsletter No. 28, May 1990
6 Guardian, London, 23/1/89
7 New Internationalist, Oxford, December 1990
8 Guardian 4/3/91
9 Observer 9/12/84
10 Guardian 1/3/91
11 Ditto 24/2/89
12 Observer 23/12/90
13 How the Other Half Dies, Susan George, Penguin 1976
14 Observer 17/3/91
15 Guardian 21/10/89
16 Observer 21/10/90
17 Guardian 15/1/89
18 Ditto 28/9/90
19 Ditto 4/12/90
20 Observer 30/9/90
21 Guardian 28/9/90
22 Sunday Times 30/9/90
23 Guardian 27/9/89
24 Ditto 21/4/90.
25 A Fate worse than Debt, Susan George, Penguin, 1988
26 Ditto
27 Guardian 21/1/90
28 Observer 18/11/89
29 How the other Half Dies
30 Guardian 16/7/91
31 Ditto 28/3/91
32 Ditto 28/9/90
33 Ditto 28/4/90
34 Ditto 13/2/90
35 Ditto 21/9/91
36 Ditto 28/9/90
37 Ditto 24/8/91
38 The Nation, 72 Fifth Avenue, New York, 17/6/91
39 Guardian 28/10/91

Chapter 2

THE TYRANNY
OF MONEY

INTRODUCTION
Views of some of our forebears

'If you make money your God, it will plague you like the
Devil.'...Henry Fielding. 'Only when the last tree has died, and the last
river been poisoned, and the last fish been caught, will men realise that
we cannot eat money.'...North American Indian saying. 'Money has
become the predominant passion and excludes all really useful mental
pursuits. It has even infested the minds of men of cultivated
understanding whose opinions rule the opinions of all other
men.'...Thomas Edmonds, 19th century author.[1] 'It would have been
reason enough, had there been no other, for abolishing money, that its
possession was no indication of rightful title to it. In the hands of the
man who had stolen it, or murdered for it, it was as good as in those
which had earned it by industry.'...Edward Bellamy.[2]

In his famous *Utopia*, the great 16th century humanist and statesman Sir Thomas More wrote:

> There is no trace of equity or justice in any country which gives great
> rewards and fees to gentlemen, goldsmiths [bankers], usurers, and such
> like who do nothing or are merely the flatterers or devisers of vain plea-
> sures of the rich, and on the other hand makes no provision for the
> poor ploughmen, colliers, labourers, carters, ironsmiths, carpenters and
> other workers, without whom no commonwealth could exist. The lot
> of the working people is even harder than that of the beasts of burden;

poverty is the recompense of their toil when they are strong enough to be in employment, and destitution and misery when old age or illness renders them incapable of work. And the laws are against them. Keeping all this in mind, it is impossible not to perceive that what we call a commonwealth today, is but a conspiracy of the rich to procure their own well-being. Money and pride are the roots of all evil. All crime would die if money perished; indeed, poverty itself, which only seems to arise from lack of money, will disappear if money disappeared.[3]

Contrary to widely held conceptions, the renowned Adam Smith in the *Wealth of Nations* set out several quite radical views including:

People of the same trade seldom meet together, even for merriment and diversion, but the conversation ends in a conspiracy against the public, or in some contrivance to raise prices.

He also regretted that:

Workers, in their efforts to combine and improve their wages, were often singled out for uniquely adverse attention, whereas employers could combine against workers with no similar criticism.

He did not think at all well of joint-stock companies, now called corporations, and, indeed, regarded them with contempt.[4]

Money today

Money can be likened to a drug which has hooked humanity. Anthony Sampson writes that:

Our ancestors would be right to assume that money had taken over many attributes of a religion, providing the means by which people and nations judge each other. Like a religion it demands great faith, and involves a huge priesthood with rituals and incantations which few ordinary people understand. Like missionaries, the bankers and brokers travel the still unconverted parts of the world, seeking to convert still more desert and jungle tribes to their own faith in credit, interest rates and the sacred bottom line.[5]

Penelope Lively has written incisively of:

The unstoppable force of profit, of wealth flooding down decade by decade, a stream becoming a river, gushing through the city over centuries, bricks ripped down and rising again to the greater gain of Grosvenors and Bedfords, families fattening on houses and shops. People die, but money never does. Most people spend much of their lives thinking of nothing else; the stuff itself, indestructible, pours mindlessly onwards, throwing up streets and factories, obsessing both those who control it and those who crawl through stunted lives for lack of it.[6]

Granted the existence of money, the system most widely in use today for 'controlling' it is, of course, capitalism. The primary purpose of this system is to ensure that those already owning capital not only retain it, but accumulate more of it. Capitalism is not only evil because of its bias against the disadvantaged, it is also ridiculous in that the continuous cycles of booms and slumps it generates are largely unpredictable, and clearly beyond the control of those supposed to be running it. For example, the UK being forced off the gold standard in 1931 caused great consternation in the City of London, but business continued as usual and the pound hardly wavered. The Governor of the Bank of England at the time, Montague Norman, was so astonished at this that he remarked: 'I must confess that I do not understand money.' Commenting on this later, Bernard Shaw wrote: 'This was not surprising, for money apart from goods, and treated as a separate subject, is simple nonsense, and cannot be understood by anybody.'[7] More recently, the UK MP Sir Ian Gilmour pointed out: 'Last year the Treasury forecast that between 1988 and mid-1991, GNP would rise by 4.75%, with manfacturing output rising by 5.5%. The actual figures for the 2.5 year period were zero growth for GNP and minus 1.25% for manufacturing output. This a staggering discrepancy.'[8]

The vagaries of capitalism are perhaps best encapsulated by this comment from an economics forecaster: 'The truth is that we are a lot less scientific than we profess; not only can't we forecast the future— we can't even forecast the past.'[9] The *Observer* (26/1/92) notes that in 1979 a senior UK establishment figure suggested to Prime Minister Callaghan that the pound should be put into the exchange rate mechanism and was told that it was not low enough; after an interval he made the same recommendation to Prime Minister Thatcher and was told the pound was not high enough. In March 1992 a BBC *Panorama* TV programme on the current, severe recession was banned to avoid embarrassing the UK government by showing how the monetarist's 'economic miracle' had become a mirage. Excerpts from the programme, reported by the *Observer* (15/3/92), included a remark by the Government Press Secretary at the time, that the Chancellor of the Exchequer 'got to be too clever by half, and began to experiment in various ways'. At this the then Chancellor retorted: 'Well, errors are always made…but it's an illusion to suppose that, if mistakes are avoided, you won't have recessions…the economic cycle is a fact of life…one never knows what's going to happen.' That capitalism's global grip may not be so secure as it usually appears was illustrated by fears that the May 1992 collapse of the property developers Olympia and York, putting $12bn worth of loans at risk, might have endangered the whole international financial system. Further evidence of the rudderless drifting of capitalism was provided by Professor Ormerod, stating (*Guardian* 29/8/92) that: 'Economics [is] in a true crisis with no effective answers to key questions such as why unemployment had risen so strongly in many Western economies, what determines economic growth, or even what growth there will be,' and by a UK Whitehall official, referring to his colleagues (*Observer* 4/10/92), that 'you have no idea how much at sea these people are. They have no idea what to do next.'

An outstanding feature of the 20th century has been the abundance of scientific discoveries and inventions, which continue to proliferate at an accelerating pace. The terrible liability which market-dominated economics impose on societies is their inability to prevent private companies rushing in to exploit every new development, to maximize profits, before allowing sufficient time to assess their potential for harmful effects. In *World Facts & Trends* John McHale cites in particular PCBs 'which are used in vast quantities by industry because of their chemical stability, but which are bio-non-degradable. They are already found world-wide in fish and birds, and in human mothers' milk;…tolerance limits for these compounds have not been established, and tests for carcinogenicity, effects on reproduction, and other possibilities have not yet been done.'

Many pesticides, derived from Nazi nerve toxins after 1945, were found to cause cancer, nerve disorders or sterility, and were banned in the First World. However, US and other Western firms continued to export them to the Third World, with no control over their use; amounting to over $1bn worth from the US alone in 1981. The result: widespread poisoning of people, stock and crops. President Carter placed a restriction on such exports prior to leaving office; but the *Guardian* (24/7/82) reported that within a month Reagan lifted the order, describing it as 'excessive Government interference in business affairs.'

President Truman once said: 'All freedom is dependent on free enterprise.…The whole world should adopt the American system.…It can only survive in America if it becomes a world system.' Needless to say, for many decades US leaders have spared no efforts to achieve that end, which, following recent developments in the SU and Eastern Europe, they have all but managed. However, gaining more disciples does not necessarily vindicate the system. The drunken lurch of the US economy from world leading creditor in 1981 to leading debtor in 1991, owing over $4 trillion (and growing by $1bn daily) is hardly a good advertisement for capitalism.

The pros and cons of money

Of the 5.4bn people in the world, around two-thirds lack money altogether. These include women, young people, the unemployed and the millions working without wages in some form of slavery. Next, it has been estimated that around 1bn people who do have an 'income' earn less than £1 per week. Thus, around 80% of humanity either has no money at all, or so little as to be only meaningful in terms of purchases of bare necessities locally, and of no significance elsewhere. They have no savings, and banks are non-existent in their localities. So, for the great majority of humanity, money is either virtually unknown, or else available in such trivial amounts as to make its existence almost academic. Therefore, over vast areas of the world, the disappearance of the money system would hardly be noticed, provided it was replaced by arrangements such as those proposed in Chapter 11.

Under 20% of the world's peoples, in fact, live in societies in which banking is considered worthwhile at all. In the case of these, primarily First World societies, whose members are locked into the money system, the great majority have relatively steady incomes, comprising either wages, pensions or some form of state support such as unemployment benefit. At the same time, this group has relatively steady outgoings, made up of rent or mortgage payments, plus food, travelling, clothing and other expenses. *The significant, though unsurprising, factor concerning this large sector of humanity is the rough balance between income and outgoings, ie, in essence, the lifelong simple exchange of manual and brain power, for food and shelter. To arrange this basically simple exchange, the money system has evolved a vast and complex superstructure* of banks, building societies, speculative developers, rent or lease landlords, wholesalers, retailers, advertisers, insurers and a host of other financial paraphernalia. This whole superstructure is given the 'image' of providing services without which societies could not function, while in fact its primary, motivating purpose is to produce huge financial returns for those running it and their shareholders. Finally, at the apex of the world's money graph, there is a very small elite, with financial and property resources vastly in excess of normal human needs.

For those who use it, money does have the apparent advantage of flexibility over its predecessor, the barter system. While recognising this, it is contended here that the ill-effects of the very existence of money outweigh overwhelmingly that advantage. The all-important, fundamental feature of the money system is, of course, profit. At the same time profit is its Achilles heel, because it is mercurial, uncontrollable and thus anti-social; who is to say where profit ends and robbery begins? Virtually all activities within the money system involve profit-making; yet it is all but impossible for societies to decide what is a 'fair profit level' for any of them. And, even if they could, it would be academic, because any attempts to police such levels would inevitably be thwarted by the system's built-in protective mechanisms. The *Guardian* (13/3/92) stated: 'The British public has never been more exposed to the risk of being fleeced by its financial institutions, and the system of regulation designed to prevent this happening has been captured by the very interests it purports to regulate.'

Within the very loose parameters of the money system, many businesses, particularly smaller ones, make profits which broadly equate to their efforts; at times they suffer losses too, often through no fault of their own. At the same time bigger, and very big organizations, with their huge resources, can make exorbitant profits, often of an automatic, repetitive nature, which are out of all proportion to the original inputs involved; some of these are referred to in the 'A-Z' which follows. Without doubt, the profit system represents an amoral, chaotic and inequitable way of rewarding human endeavour. The world as a whole would be vastly healthier without it, and the money system of which it is the key ingredient.

AN A-Z OF THE ILL-EFFECTS OF MONEY

The following list, which is not intended to be comprehensive, aims to include those activities, occupations, happenings or malpractices, which could in many cases be eliminated, and in the remainder, be greatly curtailed, by the abolition of money. It is well understood that millions of honest and worthy citizens spend lifetimes working in some of the occupations mentioned, and no criticism of them is intended. It is considered simply that their abilities could be employed in many more rewarding ways, both to themselves and to society. With so many headings, it is impractical to include more than the briefest notes referring to the more evident societal problems or constraints related to each; in most cases additional aspects will undoubtedly spring to mind.

Accidents

Many accidents are caused directly by the 'human factor'; for example, by reckless or drunken driving. However, untold numbers of deaths and injuries, world-wide, result from owners or operators failing to spend enough on safety precautions. Terrible mining, industrial and transport disasters occur continually in the Third World; one of the worst ever, at Bhopal in India, was referred to in Chapter 1. Wholly preventable accidents occur in the First World too, largely because of the relentless pressures of the money system to eliminate 'inessential' expenses in pursuance of maximum profits.

Some idea of the carnage caused by hazardous working environments can be gauged by this report from *The Nation* (28/1/91):

> In the US, since 1970, some 200,000 workers have been killed on the job, and some 2m more have died from diseases caused by conditions at their work; that means 300 dead men, women, and children, per day. In fact, work kills more than Aids, drugs, drunk driving and all other road accidents. Also, since 1970, a further 1.4m have been permanently disabled by accidents at work. Not only do workers continue to die in staggering numbers, but often also in the most appalling ways: asphyxiated, electrocuted, blown up, cut to pieces, scalded, burned. Or they die after years of sickness from black lung, brown lung, cancer, or chemical or radiation poisoning. An Indianapolis fast food firm named Domino has a policy of reducing the price if its pizzas are not delivered within 30 minutes of ordering; the resulting pressure on its drivers to speed has, it is estimated, brought about the deaths of around 100 persons— drivers and bystanders— since 1980.

In the UK, 250 are killed annually in the building industry alone, many through falls from inadequate scaffolding.[10] The major oil companies are notorious for their narrow safety margins; the North Sea in particular has seen some horrendous, unnecessary disasters such as the Piper Alpha platform fire. In the different branches of transport, both passengers and crews are put at risk by skinflint attitudes to safety. In the UK, 'economies' in equipment and manpower on the railways have resulted in numerous fatalities. Also in the UK, the fact that the Civil Aviation Authority is responsible both for safety and for the commercial interests of the airlines—who finance it—leads inevitably to critical compromises. Glaring examples of cutting corners to maximize profits occur in the shipping world, where regulations are often either lacking, inadequate or ignored. Designs and specifications of vessels are tailored to minimize capital and running costs. The notorious capsize of a car ferry at Zeebrugge in 1987 with the loss of 192 lives, resulted, almost unbelievably, from a trivial initial cost saving on an interlock system which would have prevented the vessel leaving harbour with its bow doors open. *With what proved to become tragic irony, the ferry had all too aptly been named 'Herald of Free Enterprise'.*

The *Observer* (7/7/91) reported the replacement of well-established cross-channel hovercrafts (£50m new), with 'Sea-Cats' £10m new) which, the operating company said, 'make more sense in today's competitive environment.' Critics claim that the company is putting profits before passengers. Professor Rawson said 'the light, 750 tonne, aluminium Sea Cat would be crushed to half its size if it were in collision with a heavy ship.' The death rate among seamen is comparable with that of miners. This stems largely from various financial pressures involving, for example, employing inexperienced skippers, hastening turn-around port times thus curtailing maintenance, and proceeding too fast in fog. Ship-owners, in countries having regulations which they find onerous, resort to transferring registrations to 'flags of convenience' of small countries such as Panama, whose rules regarding navigation and safety are minimal. At least 22 'bulk carriers'—very substantial vessels—have been lost in recent years, resulting in the deaths of many seamen.

Finally, accidents in the home too often result from money pressures. For example, fires regularly cause deaths because of the lack of smoke alarms—comparatively cheap items, yet too expensive for many householders, and an 'unnecessary expense' for landlords, whether private or civic. Every year, in the UK alone, over 150 people are burned to death in house-fires.

Accountancy and auditing

The great majority of people cannot afford accountants; they have no option but to trust that the tax and other stoppages withheld from their incomes are correct. All sizes of firms, and individuals with above average incomes, use accountants to provide often legitimate guidance through the minefields of taxation and other financial legislation; but the built-in urge to enhance their clients' money supply exerts constant pressure to 'bend the rules'. This is particularly evident when accountants are involved in auditing. A mid-1991 report states:

> Accounting gymnastics and financial engineering are readily approved by auditors, desperate for business. The supposed 'watchdogs' are silent collaborators. Britain's top six accountancy firms audit nearly two-thirds of all quoted companies. The top ten firms have a fee income of nearly £2.5bn.

The police are investigating some £2bn of known fraud; public accounts described as 'true and fair' have often turned out to be meaningless. Nine major UK firms have all collapsed within weeks of clean audit reports.[11]

In spite of the astonishing saga of BCCI's multiple sins over many years, that bank's accounts for 1987, 1988, and 1989 were all described as 'true and fair' by UK accountants Price Waterhouse.[12] In fact, 'the fees for these audits run into millions, and nobody can recall the last time one of the Big Eight resigned an Account on grounds of fraud.'[13]

Advertising

Advertising ranks amongst the most extreme of all the wasteful, superfluous, indeed ridiculous activities spawned by the existence of money. It is a system designed to persuade consumers to buy products they were going to buy anyway, or that they neither need , nor want, nor could ever afford; or, in some cases, items which are actually harmful to them. Further, advertising is unnecessary because if someone wants something enough, he/she will find it; whoever heard of advertisements for narcotics? The gigantic expenditures involved are not covered by the product promoters, but, in the end, by the hapless consumers themselves through inflated prices. An unquantifiable number of consumers, in fact, reject advertisements by switching off the TV or turning a page - yet they still finish up paying for them.

Some indication of the rich pickings made by those running the advertising 'industry', for contributing nothing of value to society, can be gauged from the following few examples: in the UK, television advertising costs up to £6,000 per second or £1m per minute; luxury firms such as Chanel spend £20m to £30m just to promote a new highly-priced perfume. The business conglomerate, Grand Metropolitan, spends around $750m on advertising and marketing global brands, including $60m in the US alone launching a new cat food.

Art prices

Anthony Sampson encapsulates the relationship between big money and art, particularly paintings:

> It is in art that the rush of new money, as it circles round looking for recognition and reward, can suddenly visibly identify itself and take shape: where the competition for status reaches its peak. Art...is the

ultimate consumer product of our society. No other product can go from relatively no value to millions of dollars, maybe in twenty years....- Paintings became a safe hedge against inflation; collectors saw them as a currency in their own right, more reliable than pounds, dollars, or even yen....In 1988, New York dealers sold 1,404 works of art for $443m...in 1987 Christies in London sold Van Gogh's Sunflowers for £24.7m...*there was a bitter irony in the record sum paid for the work of an artist who had been close to starvation.*[14]

The prices of all manner of other 'objets d'art' have similarly been driven to astonishing heights. A mid-18th century piece of furniture resembling a sideboard, known as the 'Badminton cabinet', last changed hands for £8.5m. Not suprisingly, art is now the third most lucrative area of international crime, after drugs and arms trafficking. And so, like practically everything else, the most beautiful products of the world's artists and craftsmen have fallen victims to the raging torrent of money. Instead of being available for all to enjoy, increasingly they are hidden away in private mansions to serve as badges of privilege, and ranking in the wealth stakes.

Banks

The original thinking behind the creation of banks was the need for somewhere safer to keep spare cash than 'under the mattress'; this was soon amended when the bankers realized they could benefit from manipulating their depositors' funds. Voltaire once said 'if you see a banker jump out of a window, follow him; there's bound to be a profit in it.' In fact, after the 1929 Wall Street Crash, rumour has it that several bankers did jump, and that two jumped hand in hand because they had a joint account. Susan George has explained that: 'Bankers' clear philosophy is that profits accrue to them, but losses are a matter for governments (ie taxpayers). This was expressed pithily by Walter Writson, when chairman of Citicorp Bank: 'Our strategy is not one of making loans, our strategy is one of making money.' In 1985, profits of the 'Big Nine' US banks were $3.4bn, and of the 'Big Four' UK banks £2.6bn.'[15] In fact, in 1989, UK banks—Lloyds and Westminster—were able to set aside no less than £1.2bn and £575m respectively, out of their profits, to make up for Third World debt repayment failures. How much less aggravation there would have been all round if they had just given the money to the countries concerned in the first place!

The barely credible capacity of the banking system to generate fantastic assets, from comparatively modest start-up capital, is best illustrated by the Bank of Commerce and Credit International (BCCI) whose assets grew 10,000-fold from $2.5m in under 20 years. This golden-egg-laying-goose image of banking, not surprisingly, attracts many into its magic circle; there are, for example, still 12,230 separate banks in the US, despite the rising tide of failures.[16] Huge banking profits often stem from wheeler-dealings with wealthier clients' funds. These include such questionable activities as foreign exchange swaps, the use of 'offshore trusts' and phoney investment companies, 'back to back' loans involving lending his own money back to the client, 'futures trading', and so on. 'International investment banking is secretive, complex, and above all, in constant flux as the greedy and the crooked invent new ways of outwitting the regulators'.[17] Not surprisingly, these kinds of precarious, speculative activities sometimes go wrong, resulting in the total demise of the bank concerned. For instance, in the US, from 1950 to 1981, an average of 6 banks failed each year; in 1982, 45 banks collapsed; between 1985 and 1990 the failures ranged from 120 to 206 banks each year.[18]

In July 1991, BCCI finally succumbed to excessive overdoses of practically every evil activity imaginable, including arms trafficking, bribery, drugs, extortion, fraud, kidnapping, laundering, tax evasion, terrorism and so on. The exact extent of the resulting losses may never be known, partly because 'tons' of documents were shredded, its main computer knocked out, and its top executives given over $50m between them to keep quiet, before an inquiry team reached its headquarters. Estimates of the losses range around $5bn, involving many hundreds of significant accounts including numerous Third World governments, and some prestigious First World organizations such as the CIA, in total affecting 1.3m accounts and the livelihoods of 14,000 employees. The fact that 'disciplinary' action against BCCI was not taken years earlier, when its nefarious practices were already known, illustrates the deep reluctance of the world's financial elite to take any action which might cause a collapse of public confidence in major banks, and which would threaten the entire world financial system.

If other commercial organizations collapse financially they are left to fade away. Yet, if a bank totters or collapses through either malpractices or stupidity, the financial elite rushes to its rescue. Thus, in 1986 a US Congressional Committee concluded:

> The Reagan administration used US Treasury resources to preserve the solvency of the US banking system, and to shelter individual banks from the consequences of their ill-advised lending decisions...the

THE TYRANNY OF MONEY

Administration not only preserved their safety but ensured, and in fact promoted, their profitability. Thus, its management of the debt crisis has, in effect, rewarded the institutions that played a major part in precipitating the crisis.[19]

The US, in fact, has a special Government agency known as the Federal Deposit Insurance Corporation, whose specific responsibility is to use Treasury funds to bail out failing banks, big and small; its current obligations may well cost the US taxpayer $200bn.

Their psychological advantage, which banks have succeeded in getting the majority of the world to accept, is illustrated by the paradoxical relationship between them and their customers: *when a bank handles your money, it becomes, magically their own, as clients of failed banks know to their cost. But, when you borrow bank money, it remains bank money.* According to a BBC TV broadcast on 10/2/92, in the UK alone banks and building societies regularly 'earn' some £700m pa from their customers by reducing rates of interest on their investments without telling them. An employee who suggested that some form of advice about the availability of better returns should be made available to customers was told 'that would not be in the best interests of the bank'.

In keeping with this policy of preserving the system at all costs, the financial elite also adopts a flexible attitude to individual misdemeanours in the banking world. A West London BCCI branch manager said 'we knew fraud may have gone on in the bank, but we knew it went on in other banks as well'.[20] In an article by Marks and Hugill, they state: 'Fraud in banking usually involves some manager or accountant who has quietly salted away half a million or so.'[21] No less a figure than the former Governor of the Bank of England Sir Robin Leigh-Pemberton said to a UK Treasury select committee on 23/7/91 'if we closed down a bank every time we found one or two acts of fraud, we'd have rather fewer banks than we do now.'[22]

Bankruptcy

Bankruptcy is one of the most demeaning processes and very often afflicts totally innocent individuals who have fallen foul of the machinations of the money system, stripping them of all their assets and scarring them for life. *The Nation* (5/10/92) tells us that in 1991 almost 1m bankruptcies were filed in the US, while the American Bankruptcy Institute boasted of a 'decade of progress for the nation's insolvency professionals: lawyers, accountants, judges, liquidators and others. In the case of proceedings over six years relating to a large company's bankruptcy, these insolvency professionals garnered almost $150m in fees. In the UK, the Maxwell bankruptcy hearing fees were estimated by the *Financial Times* to be running at £325,000 per day.

Black markets

Black markets take many forms, all with the same base purpose of enriching the unscrupulous who have 'cornered a market' in a particular commodity which is either scarce or unobtainable in the normal way. They aim to meet the requirements of those with sufficient means to pay 'over the odds', encroaching further on stocks available to those in genuine need. During famines, black marketeers smuggle food into other areas, even other countries, for profit. Destitute, starving people have died on the pavements outside food shops with full windows. Countless thousands have perished, not for lack of food in their countries, but total lack of purchasing power.

Bribery and corruption

Bribery is one of the many inevitable results of the money system. For those with the means, it is just so easy to buy favours, or silence, or whatever other mischief they have in mind. Millions of acts of bribery will no doubt persist world-wide as long as money exists. Just three examples must suffice:

A former Senate investigator, Jack Blum, told the *Guardian* that BCCI officials had informed him that they paid out millions of dollars in bribes in the US over the past 10 years[23]; in the early 1970s, Adnan Khashoggi contracted a loan for Sudan guaranteed by Saudi Arabia, at double the interest rate offered by others. $10m was deposited abroad, for 'greasing Saudi machinery', of which $4m constituted Khashoggi's 'commission'[24]; the *Observer* (10/5/92) reported that an official enquiry into Britain's biggest arms contract—the £20bn Tornado deal with Saudi Arabia—concluded that the contract was structured in such a way that huge commissions running into hundreds of millions of pounds may have been paid by British Aerospace to Saudi and British middlemen; the issue was considered so sensitive that the UK Auditor General asked for the report to be suppressed.

As with bribery, so with corruption, the existence of which depends on money. Let one monumental example serve to typify corruption generally. As J K Galbraith put it: 'During the 1980s in the US, the government-insured deposits of the Savings and Loan Associations (equivalent to UK building societies) were squirrelled away by the most ignorant, reckless, feckless and felonious operators in all our financial history; a minimum of $500bn was lost or stolen.'[25] This 'financial earthquake', the greatest 'rip-off' ever, was reckoned by the *Wall Street Journal* to have cost the US more than World War Two. The inevitable Treasury bail-out, involving heavy borrowing charges over the next 30 years, could cost every US tax-payer over $3,000. Commenting on the world-wide growth in corruption in the *Observer* (26/4/92), Bruce Lloyd, head of the UK South Bank University Management Centre, said: 'If this trend is not controlled and reversed, the consequences for individuals, companies and even countries, will continue to be extremely serious. It can even lead to a crisis of confidence in the system itself.' A prospect can thus be perceived of the money system committing suicide through over-indulging itself.

Bureaucracy

As long as the system exists, money remains the lifeblood of all worthwhile, constructive activities, in the field of housing, health, education and the like. All too often, at the behest of governing elites, concerned to hang on to their unfairly large 'share of the cake', bureaucrats spend much of their working lives simply 'imposing economies' and thereby curtailing those very necessary social needs. Further, in keeping with what became known as 'Parkinson's Law', bureaucrats continually generate evermore procedures and paper-work and thus constantly increase their own numbers. For example, between 1986 and 1990 *the number of UK National Health Service managers increased by 1,800, while the total number of nurses fell by 7,000.*(*Guardian* 10/2/92). These managers, forever busying themselves with cutting every conceivable cost except their own salaries, have never been bound by the Hippocratic Oath and ride roughshod over ethical objections to consequent patient suffering. At a British Medical Association conference in June 1992, consultants deeply opposed money being the 'bottom line' in what is 'supposed to be a service' (*Guardian* 19/6/92) and complained that the vast numbers of new administrators 'have an almost childlike faith in the efficacy of the market system'.

As with almost every aspect of the money system—whether spendthrift or stingy— examples are legion, so the following from the UK must suffice. The *Guardian* reported:

> Council officers in the London borough of Wandsworth are being paid
> a bonus of up to 10% of annual salary if they meet performance targets
> set privately by the Council's Conservative leadership. Targets include
> achieving the lowest poll tax arrears in inner London, implementing cuts
> and closures on time, identifying possible economies, and minimizing
> the numbers and costs of homeless families.[26]

Charities

Within the severe limitations imposed by incomes dependent on
public whim, many charities succeed in assisting the alleviation of
various forms of evil. The achievements of such as Oxfam and
Medecins Sans Frontieres for example in the Third World, have
been of real value to those fortunate enough to have benefited from
them. However, charities epitomize the patronising attitudes of
elites towards the disadvantaged. They provide convenient alibis
for governments not prepared to spend adequately either on
emergencies, or on all manner of day-to-day societal needs.
Charities also enable millions of basically caring people to salve
their consciences, rather than take forthright political action to
insist that their own tax money is spent, officially, as it should be.

'Cheque book journalism'

This is one of the many examples of the way the money system
encourages greed. Simply through the accident of having witnessed,
or been otherwise connected, with some 'newsworthy' incident,
individuals are suddenly given access to often huge sums, by
auctioning their stories to the highest media bidder from the so-
called 'gutter press'.

Commercialisation of sport

Until around the middle of the 20th century, sports of all kinds
were engaged in, in a spirit of straightforward recreational
enjoyment and friendly competition, and this still holds for those
who accept they will never be more than amateurs. However, that
spirit has now been soured by the insidious intrusion of big money,
particularly in the fields of advertising, gambling, and sponsoring for

profit. Few sports remain untainted; football clubs are sold as investments for millions, snooker competitions culminate in £100,000 prizes, the Australian rugby team sign on a $7m deal with Castlemaine brewers.[27] A UK Independent Television programme *World in Action* (1/6/92) alleged that 'the modern Olympic Games are a circus in which greed, corruption, cheating and profiteering have starring roles'.

Instead of being able to simply enjoy becoming involved in any of the big name sports, youngsters are now tantalised by the possibility of making it to the top, with huge financial rewards. The attendant pressures result, for example, in the US Medical Association reckoning that 500,000 teenage sports fanatics are on steroids, and in two famous teenage girl Wimbledon players, Austin and Jaeger, becoming crippled by back injuries before reaching the age of 21.[28] Boxing provides the most damning indictment of the effect of money pressures. The Guardian (23 & 25/9/91) reported that: 'The world heavyweight title match may gross $100m....The fight game thrives among the have-nots, who reach out for the million dollar purse, encouraged and accommodated by the promotional factions who end up with most of the money, alive, and without brain damage...Since 1945 *there have been about 400 deaths...Promoter Hearn said...we are in business, and fighters are here to earn money.*'

The stranglehold of money on sport is further illustrated by an article in *The Nation* titled 'Big Buck Basketball'[29]:

> The business of sport is not only a big business, but one that is no longer the sole property of teams involved....At the Seattle coliseum, the scorer's table rotates new advertisements every five minutes...The players receive 53% of the revenue from television contracts and ticket sales, totalling almost $1m per player....Until recently, every player could expect to make over $30,000 pa merely from wearing whatever brand of shoes he was paid to endorse....Now the shoe companies pay huge sums to the high-profile athletes, while excluding those on the lower rungs....They begin wooing potential future superstars with bribes of free shoes and athletic equipment, to children not yet out of junior or high school.

Commodity price fluctuations

The distribution of virtually all, primarily Third World-produced, foodstuffs, minerals and other raw materials, is controlled by commodity brokers operating in the First World Exchanges, specialising in particular products. Their main concern—to maximise their own commissions—results in exceptional price contortions as they speculate and bargain around the world, with total disregard for a fair return for the producers. In the mid-1970s the price paid for sugar dropped from 64 to 6 cents per pound over 18 months; cocoa, per ton, fluctuated from $1,000 to $400 and back to $1,000 before dropping to $600. At the same time copper fell from $3,000 to $1,300, while an ounce of gold see-sawed from $35 up to $800 and then back to $380 in 1990. During just one day in July 1986 the price of cotton was slashed from 68 to 34 cents per pound; the resulting loss for the economy of Tanzania was likened by President Nyerere to the equivalent of a natural disaster.[30]

Compensation anomalies

The very existence of money demands that everything has to have its price, even life itself if cut short by accident or medical mistake. It is hard to conceive of anything more inhuman or degrading than the process of attaching financial values to human lives in compensation cases—a problem which all but the most hardened bureaucrats find impossible. In unedifying court battles, the wrongdoers struggle to knock down the plaintiff's claims. In the December 1990 UK settlement for 1,217 haemophiliacs who had been infected with Aids by contaminated blood clotting agents, each claimant (many were already dead) received a paltry £35,000, well below half of the sum called for.[31]

By contrast, prominent members of the elite fare incomparably better when suing for libel. Conservative MP Teresa Gorman was awarded £150,000 by the Court for an accusation of vanity, while Jeffrey Archer received £1.5m in respect of allegations that he was keeping questionable company. Thus ironically, an aggrieved, but alive and healthy author, is allotted around 40 times the sum given to a dead or dying haemophiliac.

Counterfeiting

Like a gold-rush fever, the temptation to print free money is resulting in all kinds of hardened criminals turning to the 'upmarket, white collar' field of counterfeiting. This is now facilitated greatly by the increasing availability of sophisticated equipment, such as laser colour photocopiers. And, conveniently, the most widely accepted currency of all, US dollar notes, is more easily faked than some others, such as pound notes. As so often in the harsh world of money, this practice is targetted at the less advantaged, and hurts them most. A counterfeiter has already pleaded in a British court that his activities were not intended to damage the UK economy, because they were only aimed at Third World countries.

'Creative accounting'

This somewhat innocent sounding term came into use in the 1980s, to describe what had always previously been known simply as 'cooking the books'. The practice is used in questionable ways by auditors. For example 'in September 1990, Price Waterhouse bid for the audit of Prudential, at a discount of £900,000; but the tender made absolutely no mention of shareholder protection, or the provision of meaningful information. They simply offered "constructive accounting solutions on how best to present results".'(32) Alternatively 'creative accounting' has, for example, been resorted to in desperation by UK local authorities, starved by central government of funds for essential social services. Regrettably, although motivated by the best intentions, this practice often resulted in borrowing, which only benefited the moneylenders and further impoverished the needy councils.

Crime

The great majority of all kinds of crimes are finance related. Some of the more sophisticated types, such as bribery and fraud, are mentioned elsewhere. Increasingly common, and more straightforward ways of augmenting personal money supplies include: burglary, extortion, mugging, pickpocketing, robbery and theft, with or without violence. The majority of these crimes are committed by individuals or small groups, in some cases no doubt motivated by genuine need. At the upper end of the scale, the Mafia have made big-money crime an international institution.

The relationship between crime statistics and divisions within so-cieties has been well established in the UK. Writing in the *Guardian* (4/7/92) Will Hutton points out that the more income inequality grows, the more crime grows. Britain in the 1980s had the most rapid crime growth in Europe. It was also the country where the top 20% had six times the disposable income of the bottom 20% in 1980, and by 1990 they had nine times more.

Hutton points out 'the crime wave is a symbol of the disintegration of civil society, compelling growing numbers to retreat to private laagers because the public domain is materially threatening and morally devalued. In the US there are now more private security guards than police officers and Britain is going the same way.'

A further *Guardian* report (17/8/92) states that professional crime is now the fourth largest industry in Britain and the fastest growing business, with an annual turnover of around £14bn. Crime employs, either as active criminals or in the law enforcement agencies, over 420,000 people.

Development for profit

This is one of the most pernicious, because so permanent, legacies which future generations will have little choice but to inherit from the money system of today. Throughout cities in both the First and Third Worlds, vast, demolition-costly monuments to the money culture have been erected; plus their pedestrian-unfriendly vehicle arteries and parking places.

These buildings provide offices primarily for banks, insurance companies, stock exchanges and commerce generally, and have been erected by speculators hoping, often vainly, for fast financial returns. They continue to be erected, with wanton consumption of building materials and other resources desperately needed for genuine societal needs—particularly housing.

These soulless developments have often been made at the cost of demolishing the familiar environments of thousands of local inhabitants, to the severe detriment of their whole lives. A classic example of this ruthlessness, the 1980s redevelopment of parts of London's East End, is well documented in David Widgery's *Some Lives*:

> In 1981, Conservative Minister Heseltine set aside 150 acres, and gave the unelected Docklands Development Commission the authority to act as planner and landowner, buying at artificially low prices and selling on to speculators. They, in turn, offset building costs against tax, and enjoyed a 10 year rates 'holiday', with no obligation to consider the needs of the long-term residents....The result is...a ghost city and a disenfranchised local community....To solve the resulting traffic jams an underground motorway is under construction at enormous cost which required the re-housing of 2,000 people.[33]

This wanton disregard for the day-to-day lives of the 10,000 or so local inhabitants, in the mad rush for profits, drove them, in desperation, to launch a claim for compensation which could total £100m., against the developers. The most persistent forms of disruption suffered have been the all-pervading dust, resulting in three-year-olds needing asthma inhalers, and such levels of noise that conversation becomes impossible.[34]

Divorce disputes

With around 1 in every 3 First World marriages failing, millions of couples, annually, become involved in more or less acrimonious attempts to divide up their money and possessions, and arrange maintenance payments, the main beneficiaries being the solicitors involved. A 1991 report on the problem by Gwyn Davis, of Bristol University, stated that:

These disputes over money and property are a battle—to secure information; to bring the case to court; to obtain a court order, and then to ensure compliance. In theory, the weak are protected, in practice, the more bloody-minded tend to triumph....One case took three years to resolve division of the proceeds of sale of the home, by which time the building society was trying to repossess the property which had become dilapidated; the wife, suffering a nervous breakdown, gave in and let the husband have what he wanted...*Many couples spent longer resolving disputes over money than they had ever spent together.*[35]

Drugs

It is unlikely that any corner of the world remains untouched by the curse of narcotic drugs. In the US, there were around 2.2m hardcore cocaine addicts in 1990—about 1 in 100 of the population. In 1988, in Italy alone, over 600 youngsters between ages 10 and 21 died from drug overdoses. The vast and varied extent of violent crimes generated by drugs cannot be quantified.

Since the great majority of narcotics are illegal almost everywhere, the plague spreads continuously for only one basic reason: the money-lust of the international 'drug barons', and the various 'finance houses' worldwide which launder their filthy gains without a care. The value of world trade in illicit drugs exceeds that of oil; annual drug-trafficking profits are estimated at around $50bn. About 25 million US citizens, together with millions of Europeans, spend approximately $120bn annually on drugs. The value of marijuana produced in the US, approximately $20bn, exceeds even that of corn. An ounce of cocaine, bought for $1,000, will net $7,000 when transformed (very easily) into 'crack' in the US, where there are an estimated 230,000 crack dealers.

Original cultivation for narcotics occurs mainly in Third World countries, where economies are skewed, and crime abounds because of the money involved. Many Third World farmers must feel saddened that their labours should be prostituted in bolstering the drugs-cash-culture, thereby stunting and killing fellow humans, rather than producing desperately needed foodstuffs. The relentless pressures of the money system leave them little option, as shown by the following: in Brazil, around 25,000 square kilometres, a quarter of the area of one state, is used for growing marijuana which earns farmers 200 to 300 times more per hectare than for beans or maize.[36] In Bolivia, a non coca growing peasant earns under $200 pa, a factory worker or miner around $600 to $800 pa, but a peasant growing coca for cocaine can earn $10,000 pa from just one hectare (or up to $50,000 if he also trades it). As a result, 300,000 are involved. Drugs bring in an estimated $4bn pa to the Colombian economy, three times the income from the main legitimate crop, coffee. Around one million Colombians benefit directly or indirectly from narcotics production.

To avoid the eventual certainty of being shot by the army, narcotics billionaire, Pablo Escobar, gave himself up, on condition that he could reside in some comfort in a specially built prison in Medellin, Colombia: from where he still controlled his world-wide, still expanding operations. The *Observer* (24/11/91) reported on the diabolical effects in the city of this money-crazed drug culture: nearly 10,000 murders pa (25 times the number in New York's Manhattan) and judges on indefinite strike after yet another assassination of a colleague for failing to acquit a drug dealer. In Peru, coca growing occupies around one quarter of a million hectares of farmland, produces nearly half of total export revenue and employs about 400,000 people. Narcotics-related crime is also exemplified in Brazil, where over 240 community leaders in Rio alone have been murdered in the past 3 years by drug dealers; the cities are becoming South America's leading drug-money-laundering centres; 1,000 clandestine air-strips in Amazonia are available to traffickers and cocaine is sold openly in Porto Velho.[37]

World-wide drugs distribution represents an industry in itself. For example, up to 200 couriers arrive at US airports every day with around $4bn worth of heroin inside condoms or balloons in their stomachs, meeting around 25% of the demand of the estimated 500,000 heroin addicts there. Some have been found to have up to 80 heroin-packed condoms; several have died when these have burst.[38] The lure of huge sums of money for smuggling drugs ensnares many, including teenagers world-wide, in spite of the drastic penalties, including death.

'Political window-dressing' attempts have been made by US Administrations, costing $20bn pa, to curtail narcotics consumption with little success. Subsidies offered to South American farmers to switch back to ordinary crops have been either inadequate, or outbid by the barons. Air-drops of bacteria by the US Drug Enforcement Agency to kill coca plants have also killed off bananas, tangerines, cassava and other crops.(39) Even if these or any other measures succeeded in reducing supplies from a particular source, the certain outcomes would be substitute sources, increased drug prices, and yet more crime as a result.

The chief UK Customs and Excise investigating officer has said: (*Guardian* 20/4/92):

> What is noticeable about today's smugglers is their increasing sophistication. The South American cocaine cartels now have their own aircraft and their own ships. They even have their own investigation units to find out what went wrong when a cargo is seized, and their own hit squads to kill unhelpful people. There have been cases of smugglers flying above the drug-carrying vessel to spot any possible interception. The amount of cocaine, the number of heroin addicts, and the number of synthetic drugs are all increasing. Enforcement alone can never stop the drug problem.

The world-wide drugs disaster, with its many financial ramifications, illustrates vividly the grip which the money system has on the world's well-being. Attempting to stem the flow of narcotics by any forms of policing can only be likened to persuading water to flow uphill. *Nothing short of complete eradication of the money system can break the stranglehold of drugs, and enable many millions of human beings to breathe freely again.*

Factory farming

Throughout the First World, the cult of maximising profits at all costs has spread from the cities and tainted the countryside. Animals, poultry and even fish, which used to roam naturally, now spend their whole, if often brief, lives in unnatural, cramped conditions. Instances of cruelty to domestic animals such as dogs cause immediate public consternation. The fact that appalling ill-treatment of millions of equally sensitive calves, chickens and the like is hardly questioned, underlines the extent to which the primacy of money-making has come to be accepted as overriding all other considerations.

In the 1980s and 1990s, a further profit-seeking distortion of nature took place when farmers were encouraged to buy artificial feedstuffs to fatten cattle, hitherto primarily herbivores. In some cases these products were contaminated by inclusion of ingredients rejected by both slaughter-houses and human foodstuff manufacturers. Inevitably, innumerable cattle developed the wasting disease, BSE. Tragically, thereafter, the poison entered the human food chain through consumption of 'burgers' and other popular beef products, resulting by the mid-1990s in a number of terminal cases of the inevitably fatal CJ disease. Unpredictable numbers will fall victim in years to come. Professor Lacey, formerly of Leeds University, has estimated that eradication of BSE can now only be achieved by mass slaughtering, finding fresh grazing territories and providing compensation, at an estimated cost of £15bn to £20bn (*Independent* 4/8/96) Thus terrible, unprecedented and totally avoidable diseases in both men and beasts were introduced by yet more despicable acts of market-driven money-grubbing.

Food mountains

This despicable saga of selfishness illustrates the extraordinary lengths to which First World governments will go to throw away their taxpayers' money in order to protect the profit levels of big business cronies. The *Guardian* reports that:

> By the mid-1980s, world grain harvests consistently surpassed 1,600m tons, which would have been enough to give over 3,000 calories daily to every one of the 5bn people on earth, but which drove down prices. On both the European and American continents subsidies are showered on big farmers while the smaller ones struggle to exist. In 1989, the Economic Intelligence Unit forecast that by 1995 the European community will be faced with surplus food which would cause dramatic falls in prices, and concluded that vast tracts of farmland should be forced out of production.[40]

In the US in the early 1980s, the government arranged storage for 140m tons of 'surplus' grain, which would have sufficed to give each of the 500m starving enough every day for a year. The special storage involved cost $12bn pa which exceeded, for example, the entire annual income of Bangladesh.[41]

To 'mitigate' the 'problem' of over-production, the US government persuaded farmers to take one-third of all US crop land, an area equal to the whole of Italy, out of production; in return they were given free grain from the stockpiles, which they could then sell.[42] Similarly, in the UK in 1984 for example, 160,000 tons of grain were stored at a cost of £128 per ton pa, to avoid depressing prices.[43] In Europe, the 'need' to maintain prices is met by an 'Intervention Board', to store surpluses which, in 1991, amounted to 20m tons of cereals, 750,000 tons of beef and 900,000 tons of dairy products.[44] Finally, the hollowness of the much-vaunted 1991 'victory' of the free marketeers in Eastern Europe was exposed by this report from Budapest. 'Meat and butter mountains, milk and wine lakes, have arrived with capitalism in Eastern Europe, alongside rampant inflation and unemployment. In Poland, Hungary and Czechoslovakia, the effects of this year's good harvest threatens to be as disastrous for farmers as last year's drought.'[45]

Fortunes

These extraordinary accumulations of personal wealth represent one of the wilder aberrations of the money sytem. Old and new fortunes have, in most cases, been made in a variety of questionable ways; for instance, in 1988, only 75 out of 400 individual UK fortunes, originated from manufacturing[46], where at least it could be argued that some effort lay behind them. The most obvious examples of totally fortuitous fortunes must be those, derived worldwide, from owning land under which oil or other valuable mineral deposits are later discovered. Fortunes confer on their owners totally undeserved privileges and power. Further, the astronomical sums involved bear no relation whatever to normal human needs.

The fortunes league table begins, as would be expected, with royalty and heads of state. The Sultan of Brunei probably leads the field with reputed assets of $31bn.[47] Despite recession in the UK, the Queen's personal wealth rose by 25% during 1990. With assets exceeding £6bn including castles, priceless jewelry and art collections she is the world's richest woman. Her investments, worth about £500m in 1991, are expected to rise to a value around £2bn. Her income from these shares is about £2m per week; on top of this, UK taxpayers contribute over £50m pa to keep her and other members of the royal family.[48] In the course of a BBC TV portrait of a year in her life the Queen clearly regarded her own massive state support as totally in order, while opining that 'Western democracies were bankrupting themselves with welfare payments'. President Mobutu of Zaire has a personal fortune which exceeds his country's foreign debts, which, in 1991, stood at $8 bn. Apart from royal families and heads of state, whose wealth is feudal or political, there are nearly

300 persons around the world worth over $1bn. Assets of the top 20 women range from £500m to £2.6 bn.

There were estimated to be over 1m millionaires in the US in 1990. The Rockefeller family controls over $300bn of corporate wealth in every major industry and country, including 5 of the 12 largest oil companies and 4 of the world's largest banks. In the UK in 1990 there were approximately 20,000 millionaires; the 200 wealthiest Britons own around £40bn worth of land, property, antiques and art. The Duke of Westminster's fortune of over £4bn is based chiefly on land in central London and elsewhere, including Canada, Australia and Hawaii.[50] Western Europe has over 50 dollar billionaires, including Giovanni Agnelli with around $4 bn. Contrary to widely-held assumptions, vast wealth does not necessarily lead to happiness. In January 1990, 18 year-old Frenchman David Hosansky jumped to his death from a Nice skyscraper, after telling reporters he wanted to be rid of his multi-million fortune which had brought him 'nothing but misery'.[51]

For those able to bear living with their fortunes, the almost insuperable problem arises of how to use up amounts exceeding even the wildest imaginings of reckless spending (other than gambling). Junk bond dealer Michael Milken's acquisitive skill netted him half a billion dollars in one year; he was then reportedly at a complete loss as to how to spend it. If, for instance, he had fancied a new car, say a Rolls Royce Corniche at its 1987 price of $183,500, he would have needed to buy 3,000 of them to absorb his year's income. The following examples indicate how the world's super-rich have attempted to make minor reductions in their bank balances: Billionaire Malcolm Forbes' 70th birthday party lasted from May-August 1989, involving ferrying 500 guests in both Concorde and 747 jets from New York to his private palace in Morocco, at a cost of $2m. Mobutu of Zaire spent part of his fortune on acquiring seven different chateaux in France and Belgium, palatial estates in Spain, Italy, Switzerland and Zaire, numerous ships, jet planes, and over 50 Mercedes cars.[52] The UK Queen achieved a minute reduction in her assets by commissioning a half-size replica of a Jaguar car for £60,000, as a present for a grandchild. The ostentatious wedding reception at the temple of Dendur for Jonathan Tisch and Laura Steinberg cost $3m. including $17,000 for the cake.[54]

Fraud

Fraud is a prime example of the widespread distortions of morality, not just made possible, but actually promoted, by the existence of money. It takes an enormous range of forms and dimensions, but all have the common feature of gainers and losers, the latter being usually the more vulnerable members of society. The UK 'fund management' group, Barlow Clowes, stole millions of pounds from their 11,000 investors, many elderly, to fund their millionaire life styles.[55] The UK office of Fair Trading has found that, each year, around 215,000 people lose £18m between them because they paid in advance for goods and services that were never actually delivered.[56] Credit and cheque card fraud rose to £150m in the UK in 1990, involving the theft of over 100,000 cards which now fetch £150 to £200 each.[57] Organised counterfeiters can produce an exact replica of a credit card in minutes [58]

That major City of London fraud is a 'growth industry' is shown by the following:

A joint CBI/Crime Concern report in 1990 estimated fraud in business at £3.3bn pa....There is a whole portfolio of frauds available: mortgage fraud, dealing fraud, share ramping, illegal share support, straight computer thefts transferring funds overseas. The rewards of successful fraud are so great that the temptations are irresistible to many. *The middle class graduate will see crime as a possible career as never before.*[59]

Fraud is of course as truly international a disease as money itself. Some of the more colourful examples have emerged in Japan, where, for example, Ms Onone, a restaurateur and spiritualist, managed to extract £1.5 bn illegally from a bank. An article in the Japanese weekly *Focus*, commenting on this extraordinary case, refers to a 'litany of consuming greed, shady connections and sudden downfall'. It highlights a score of politicians, tax evaders, greenmailers, stock speculators, corrupt lawyers and gangsters.[60]

The class-biased attitudes of official bureaucracies to fraud are exemplified by the following report:

The stark difference between Government's treatment of rich and poor is well illustrated by the UK figures for 1986, when unemployment and other social services benefit frauds cost £500m and resulted in 14,000 prosecutions, while tax frauds cost £5,000m and resulted in only 20 prosecutions. As one specialist tax accountant put it...'you have to be very unlucky, very stupid and very crooked to be "done" by the Revenue'.[61]

The *Observer* (12/7/92) reported the covering up by the UK Foreign Office of a series of criminal offences by British diplomats, including the export of heroin in a diplomatic bag and personal financial fraud; a confidential list of serious disciplinary cases covered high-ranking staff including at least two ambassadors, but there were no prosecutions. The same issue reported that nearly £2.5bn pa was being fiddled from the European Union's finances by false claims, misappropriations and fraud - equivalent to £20 pa for every employee in the EU.

The profits made by passing one export off as another, for example, are enormous, and the risks of detection negligible; but, no matter how many attempts at reform are made, the Court of Auditors agreed that there is no prospect of cutting down on EU malpractices. It is abundantly clear that, as with so many other spin-offs of the system, so long as money survives, fraud will inevitably continue to flourish.

Free trade zones

Around half of all Third World countries now have these zones. Their ostensible purpose is to attract First World investment, to create infrastructure and employment, by waiving taxes, duties and various regulations including such labour laws as may exist. The results, as would be expected, are gross exploitation of the local labour force and massive profits; for example, Honduran workers earning around 50 cents per hour take just 10 minutes to make a shirt sold in the US for $28.

Gambling

About two-thirds of all Britons part with £10bn annually on some form of gambling. Barely half comes back to the comparatively few winners, with £3.4 bn staying with the betting 'industry' and £1bn taken in tax.[62] As with fraud, the demeaning aspect of gambling is its use of the money culture to entice people with the prospect of enormous rewards, in return for virtually no effort. This may be of little concern for those with 'money to burn', but for the increasing numbers of families in the First World with inadequate incomes who could really benefit from 'windfalls', the usually unrewarded drain on their limited resources represents a further indictment of the money system. The *Observer* (10/11/91), reported that: 'Two-thirds of all school children gamble regularly, and that many steal, shoplift, and forfeit their dinner money for the chance of winning up to £4 on the "one armed bandits"...Several thousands each year become addicted; regularly playing truant to satisfy the urge.'

Genetic engineering

The following is from the *New Internationalist* (March 1991):

The new science of Biotechnology threatens to turn our world into a nightmare if not controlled, because we can now manipulate the inherited characteristics of any living thing and its future generations. Genetic engineering offers potential goldmines of billions; one technologist involved said "just imagining the profits can unhinge even a sane scientist". The main problem is that firms first applying to patent any living organism—ie trees, flowers, herbs, animals, even humans or parts of humans—become owners, able to decide their outcomes and exclude all others from influencing them. A wild tomato variety, taken from Peru in 1962, has contributed $8m pa to the US tomato-processing industry, but none of these profits has been shared with Peru. The 'raw materials' of the gene revolution are nothing less than all the microbial, plant, and animal genetic resources particularly abundant in tropical areas; the total contribution of wild species to the US economy is estimated at $66bn already.

Genetic engineering holds the potential for diagnosing and treating general ailments, improving food production and other useful tasks. However, it could do enormous harm by altering the structure of organisms in ways not always predictable. Once released into the environment, we could not control them as we do not know what they would do. At present a few multinationals control genetic engineering and their priority is profit. For example, it could be used to develop pest-resistant crops to improve agricultural production. Instead, chemical companies have developed herbicide-resistant seeds so as to increase herbicide sales, and hybrid seeds which do not 'breed true', to force farmers to buy more seed from them every year.

Approximately 400 companies, world-wide, are developing genetically-engineered products; by the year 2000 there will be over 1,000 new companies in the field, worth around $50bn in all.

The *Observer* (22/3/92) reported that American scientists attempting to patent the genes that control the human brain— even before they have been discovered—infuriated researchers throughout the world. Their action triggered off a tit-for-tat patent war on both sides of the Atlantic that could set back cures for certain psychiatric illnesses by many years. Dr D Rees, head of the UK Medical Research Council, commented that 'this is an attempt to use patent law as a method of extortion,…it is parasitic activity, based on very doubtful ethics'. The trend is all too apparent. In unbiased hands, genetic engineering could be approached with the extreme caution it deserves; then to the extent that appears safe, it could well be of great value to society. Instead, the regressive money system is already swallowing it whole. As a result genetic engineering could become the world's largest and most profitable industry, and its probable ill-effects will affect all our lives.

Golden handshakes

The whole momentum of the money system drives both rich individuals and rich institutions towards ever greater riches. From time to time, directors or other 'top brass' leave institutions they have been associated with, because of age, disagreement or because 'the grass in the next field looks greener'. On these occasions, it has, in recent years, become customary for their management colleagues to vote them increasingly enormous sums, which eclipse totally the value of whatever services they could possibly have rendered their respective organisations. Needless to say, these 'golden handshakes' also eclipse by far whatever redundancy payments if any, are made to humbler employees when their time comes up to leave. The suggested $32m pay-off made to director Akbar on leaving BCCI may well have been exceptional.[63] However, Sir Ralph Halpern retired from the UK firm Burtons in November 1990, with a golden handshake of £2m which equals four times the lifetime earnings of a low-paid worker.[64]

Human organ sales

One of the most repulsive activities promoted by the existence of money, is the organised sale of their kidneys or eyes by the desperately poor, to provide spare parts for the ailing bodies of the rich. In one village near Madras, where the average wage is around 300 rupees per month, several hundred 'donors' have sold a kidney, through a local tout, after seeing advertisements offering 25,000 rupees (approximately £700). The poor are also tempted to sell a live cornea for around $2,000, as the idea gains ground that 'you only need one eye'.[65]

When this terrible trafficking started in the early 1980's it is believed that a kidney fetched up to £20,000. But 'market forces' soon got to work, and the acceleration in both the trade and the desperation of the sellers led to the price falling to around £1,000.[66]

As if the trade just described were not diabolical enough, the lure of big money for healthy organs has led to even greater depths of bestial depravity, as the following report records:

> An investigation in 1990 by Interpol, and authorities in Italy and Brazil, revealed that possibly 1,000 Brazilian children sent to Italy for 'adoption' were in fact sold for between £6,000 and £12,000, and then killed for their kidneys, testicles, livers and hearts, which were sold for between £20,000 and £50,000. Such a trade was already known to exist in Mexico and Thailand.[67]

Income disparities

One of the most prominent features of the money culture is the dramatic contrast in remunerations between those of the vast majority of both manual and white-collar workers, who actually produce the wealth in society, and the tiny minority of directors who control their destinies. Further, wages in the various industries are relatively uniform, and generally only rise following union pressures, whereas top salaries vary considerably, and often rise rapidly for no apparent reason. A mid-1990 study showed there to be 14 directors in the UK earning over £1m pa including one on £6m. and some 70 others on over £0.5m.[68] Thus, many British 'top brass' receive over 100 times the average worker's wage. In March 1992, 133 senior executives in the UK were earning over £500,000 pa, while in the UK as a whole, from 1979 to 1987, real incomes for the top 1% rose by 72% while for the poorest 10% they fell by 7%. In the US, chief executives receive, on average, 70 or 80 times the income of a typical worker, and the gap has more than doubled in the past 15 years.[69] Although exceptional, 'junk bond king' Milken's bonanza could be repeated. In 1987, his 'wages' of $550m ($1,000 per minute) amounted to, for example, $90m more than the GNP of Guyana, and equalled the combined annual incomes of almost 79,000 people on the US minimum wage.[70]

A 1990 study of senior UK executives showed average salary increases of 33%: ie £2,400 per week, or over 90 times the pay increases given to workers on average earnings.[71] An increase alone in Lord Hanson's salary amounted to 20 times the UK average national wage. Although the retail price index rose by only 40% from 1985 to 1991, the average rises at the top of Britain's largest companies grew by 120%. Increases in directors' fees have been particularly noticeable in organisations which have become privatised; for example, British

Airways' Lord King's salary rose from £30,000 in 1986 to nearly £520,000 in 1990.[72] It can reasonably be asked, are the managerial efforts of all these directors really worth 100 times more than those of their employees? Certainly not, judging by the widespread malaise in both UK and US businesses.

When, in fact, a subsidiary investment department of NatWest Bank made a loss of £49m, its chairman, instead of being dismissed as might have been expected, was given a rise of 60% to bring his salary to nearly £1.5m.[73] Further, directors' duties are hardly arduous; being on a top company board has been described as a 'cushy deal', resembling, as Lord Boothby said, 'a perpetual hot bath'.[74] Both the busy and the idle rich need experts to look after their wealth, health and legal problems. Thus accountancy, medicine and the law became the 'top three' professions, with earnings of up to around £500,000 pa, which, again, contrast glaringly with, for instance, wages of essential employees such as nurses. The whole scenario of income disparities can be summed up in terms of financial elites looking after their own interests, at all costs.

Inflation

Inflation is another inevitable by-product of the money system. Being both unpredictable and difficult to control, it can create considerable, unnecessary anguish for whole communities, particularly the less advantaged ones. For example, Argentina, once the world's seventh richest country, suffered 5,000% inflation in 1990, reducing the local currency unit to 2,900 per dollar from 15 per dollar one year before. In such circumstances, naturally, all transactions become distorted, with day to day uncertainty about costs, and what wages will buy.

Influencing education

Financial institutions have often been involved in projecting their images in the academic world through sponsorships and the like. This process has been taken a stage further in the US. 'Media entrepreneur Whittle presented $50,000 worth of video equipment, and sufficient TV sets for most classrooms, to some 3,000 secondary schools, provided they show a minimum of 10 minutes news, and 2 minutes advertising per day. Mr Whittle says he has sold over $3m. worth of advertising for the first 3 years.'[75]

The John M Olin Foundation is pouring millions of dollars into Universities in an effort to re-shape the curricula, take the intellectual initiative, and give scholarly legitimacy to Reaganite social and economic policies. The 1988 report of the Foundation lists grants of $55m, most of which help underwrite programmes 'intended to strengthen the economic, political and cultural institutions upon which private enterprise is based'. The Foundation has also committed $5.8m towards establishing a course innocuously called 'Law and Economics'. The goal of this course is a society in which conflicts are resolved, not by Government rules or community values, but by unregulated markets that set prices on different activities, based on the assumption that human beings are inherently selfish.[76]

To underline the terrible threat to many millions of innocent, unformed young minds of these insidious, money-crazed perversions of education spreading world-wide, it is necessary to be aware that:

When business enters education, it sells something more important than the brand name of its products. It sells a way of looking at the world and at oneself. It sells predictability instead of critical capacities. It sells a circumscribed, job-specific utility. The principal of a corporate-sponsored high school in Chicago says 'I'm in the business of developing minds to meet a market demand.' In the private sector literature, students are described, and valued, not as children but as 'workers' and seen as future 'assets' or 'productive units', or else, failing that, as pint-sized human deficits who threaten our productive capacities— but not as human beings who have value in themselves. The package of skills the child learns, or doesn't learn, is called the 'product' of the school. Many plans use technology, along with low cost, non-professional classroom assistants, as a way of radically reducing the authority and presence of teachers. The teacher's desk will be replaced by an Electronic Teaching Centre. (*The Nation* 21/9/92)

Inherited wealth

The instinctive concept of 'inheritance' is the receipt of various greater or lesser riches following parental deaths. In fact, of greater significance for a child's development is the environment it is born into. And, following the blossoming of the money culture, the nature of that environment is determined more and more by the level of parental wealth. Thus, through their most formative years, millions of advantaged children world-wide, grow up believing that a larger than average 'slice of the cake' is rightfully theirs for life. A 1990 *Sunday Times* study of the 200 richest people in the UK, showed that the majority had 'establishment' backgrounds, and that 'new wealth is vulnerable, but old wealth is remarkably stable'.[77]

As with fortunes, royalty are at or near the top of the bequests league. For example, in the UK, the Duchy of Lancaster automatically passes to the Prince of Wales; it is currently worth £250m and yields profits of £2.7m pa. In the largest-ever published will, the 6th Marquess of Cholmondeley left £118m. The chance accident of many being born on the 'wrong side of the tracks' skews societies the world over, by depriving them of the undeveloped talents of the disadvantaged; and burdens them with self-perpetuating domination by often stupid elites. The traditional passing on of privilege was once described by R H Tawney as 'the social poison of inheritance'.

Insurance

In common with the other major activities in the world of money, consideration for the clients of insurance companies is secondary. The insurers' first concern is to ensure that they, and their investors, make handsome profits from the whole gambling operation, by continually reloading the dice in the light of their pay-outs. It is probably true that anything anywhere can be insured against, granted a high enough premium. But, as usual in a money-dominated world, it is the disadvantaged who miss out. Premiums to protect what little property they may have are likely to be discounted as luxuries. But, for example, badly wanted life insurance to benefit next-of-kin of the disabled, such as haemophiliacs, may well prove virtually unobtainable because they are considered 'bad risks'.

The topsy-turvy nature of the insurance system can be illustrated by the average First World citizen paying out, at a conservative estimate, say £1,000 pa on house, life, car, personal, travel and other premiums; perhaps £50,000 in a lifetime, and yet never once making a claim, or at least one of any significance. Over the years, his £50,000, invested, will be worth very considerably more to the insurance company. A survey of 61 Life Assurance companies reported in the *Observer* (9/2/92) showed that nearly a third of clients cancel their regular premium policies in the first two years, resulting in almost certain loss of all they have invested. These losses, estimated to total over £200m pa, stem from the practice of the companies paying most of the first year's premiums to the salesmen who had successfully pressured customers into signing on. One company boasted that each of its 160 salesmen had earned over £60,000 pa in commission.

The insurance system can be compared with the gambling or lottery systems. In gambling, comparatively small outlays are made from time to time on impulse, with the possibility of a handsome profit. With insurance, substantial and regular outlays are made, with a significant return only in the event of an improbable personal disaster, such as one's house burning down. It is hardly surprising that, amongst business people with 'adequate financial standing', there is considerable competition to become a 'member' of one of the more prestigious insurance firms.

'Laundering' dirty money

Just as 'fences' accept the problems of disposing of items of stolen property, so the banks, knowingly or otherwise, accept the problems of digesting the enormous hoards of cash amassed by assorted criminals, drug dealers in particular. *More than $85bn of narcotics money flows through the world's legitimate banking system every year, according to estimates.*[78] Cash surpluses at the Federal Reserve Bank branches in Los Angeles, an index of money-laundering, increased from $165m. in 1985 to $3,800m. in 1988.[79] In November 1989, an investigation by MPs blamed the UK banks for laundering at least £1.8bn. of drugs cash through London. BCCI was fined $15m. in a Florida court in January 1990 for laundering $32m. worth of drugs money.[80]

Loans and debts

One of the many curses of money, experienced by both institutions and individuals with money, is its built-in compulsion to make more of it. Thus, First World banks and other institutions, having burned their fingers lending to the Third World, have since been busy off-loading their ample surpluses nearer home, in all conceivable ways which offered profitable returns. The result has been an avalanche of tempting offers of credit on all manner of purchases, and a plethora of credit cards, extending even, for example, to invitations to four-year-olds to become American Express members. Not surprisingly, in 1991, the grand total of all debt in the UK stood at well over £300bn or £6,000 for every man, woman and child. According to a *Guardian* report (3/12/91) this was continuing:

According to Money Advice Trust, at least 1m, and possibly 2m families are now finding it difficult to pay their bills; debtors often take out new loans to pay off old debts; this can cause them to fall behind with payments to five or more lenders, including building societies, banks, credit card companies, HP firms, and electricity, gas and telephone companies. Even schoolchildren have been able to run up considerable debts, and over half of students in higher education were in debt by the end of their first year. Pawn-brokers have become one of the few expanding sectors of the economy.

The inevitability of combined capital and interest debts following loans has led to predictably disastrous outcomes, including foreclosures, bankruptcies, broken marriages and suicides. The most traumatic situations have arisen where individual loan sharks, charging 1,000% interest have pressured their clients to the extent of urging young mothers to become prostitutes to cover debts, smashing televisions and threatening violence to their children.[81] All too often, the loan-debt scenario is one of people's lives compromised and frustrated by endless worrying over how to extricate themselves from the stranglehold of the money system.

Lobbying

To the extent that people consider legislative matters at all, many must believe that issues debated by their parliamentary representatives are decided on their merits alone. Alas no; as long as money is available to grease the palms of legislators, then speaking and voting will continue to be influenced by 'lobbying'. And surprisingly big money is involved. In and around Westminster for example, some 50 lobbying companies, earning over £10m pa in fees between them, 'retain' over 200 MPs as 'political consultants' to promote the interests of their backers, who include merchant bankers, defence contractors and privatised utility companies.[82] The tremendous value to commercial organisations of access to the services of persons with the 'right contacts' is illustrated by the sudden jump of £90m in the Stock Exchange value of Barclays Bank when it was joined by ex-Chancellor of the Exchequer Nigel Lawson, in February 1990.

In the US, ex-President Carter once described lobbyists as being *'like a pack of powerful and ravenous wolves, determined to secure benefits for themselves at the expense of others'*. For $298 pa, US lobbyists can receive the guidance of *Lobbying and Influence Alert*, launched by the Global

Success Corporation. This newsletter provides 'inside tips, tactics, and techniques' for lobbying that will leave 'opponents speechless, or ineffectual, or both.' It includes 'nine ways to befriend bureaucrats;...how to maintain a privileged relationship with a legislator;...how lobbyists can cultivate influence by proffering unusual, but legal gifts, such as giving his kid a scholarship.[83]

A new Environmental Protection Agency regulation set limits on pollution by the 34,000 chemical plants, oil refineries, factories and power plants owned by large companies in the US. One of them, Eli Lilly pharmaceuticals, objected strongly to Vice-President Dan Quayle about this regulation, reminding him at the same time about their generous contribution to his senate election campaign. As a result, Quayle had the regulation countermanded, not just for those that had protested, but for all the regulated companies, permitting them 'to rewrite their own permits to allow unlimited increases in pollution double, triple or a hundredfold',[84] Sponsored lobbying sometimes takes the form of mass, rather than individual, pressure; either way big money is involved. For example, 'the pro-Israel pressure groups managed to produce 1,200 lobbyists in Washington last week; the bill for coaching them to the capital alone came to more than $15,000'.[85]

Market economics

Writing in 1982, billionaire Warren Buffet explained 'the market, like the Lord, helps those who help themselves. But, unlike the Lord, the market does not forgive those who know not what they do.'(86) The global sweep of present-day markets is described vividly by Anthony Sampson:

> The images of national power in the 1980s are not warships or armies; they are the abilities to control financial markets, to bid down producers, and translate blips on the screen into physical resources. The more global and instant the market place, the more effective and pervasive this power becomes, for, when everything is for sale, money can buy information, experience, influence. It can even buy the future.[87]

The phrase 'free market' is in fact a contradiction in terms, because all markets are fashioned inevitably by societal and political pressures. In particular, they represent poor links between producers and consumers because their primary concerns are prices and profits, rather than efficient, co-operative distribution.

In a letter to the *Observer* (5/6/88) A Phillips said: 'Human and social issues count for nothing before the freemarket juggernaut. Un-fettered competitive aggression, we are assured, is the only true engine. Loyalty, continuity, participation in community and consensual man-agement are desirable, but disposable.' He quotes Milton Friedman on the role of business: *'Few trends could so thoroughly undermine the very foundation of our free society as the acceptance by corporate officials of a social responsibility, other than to make as much money for their share-holders as possible.'* The chaotic, uncontrolled and unpredictable nature of the market economy can be illustrated simply by the following col-lection of headlines on a single page of the financial section of the *Guardian* for 2/1/90: 'Survey shows firms will fail at faster rate...A decade of squandered opportunities on computer front...Rising costs tighten High St pinch...Exports fail to dispel trade gloom...Bad debts and worse judgements...Foreign competition still hits hard...Britain may be glad of scraps from Germany's table...Finance and property firms feel chill as credit squeeze bites.' What a way to 'run' society!

Doctors prescribing a new drug in 1991 were offered money by the producers in return for information on its potential health hazards, an exercise termed post-marketing surveillance (PMS). The director of the Southampton University Drugs Safety Research Unit commented 'PMS is almost an act of desperation by companies, who know it is the only way they can sell a drug, because there aren't enough sick people to sat-isfy their marketing desires.'[88] The all-pervading malaise of the market has also degraded our built environment, which, in today's context of steel and reinforced concrete, once erected, is so desperately permanent. Speak-ing in March 1990, UK leading architect Richard Rogers described the 'appalling' buildings constructed since 1945, as the result of 'self-interested bargaining between business-men and developers, the logical products of a society where money has become an end in itself, and even buildings are conceived in terms of profit - and a quick profit at that. The public realm continues to be eroded by private greed. We need a world-wide strategy on the built environment.[89]

Annually, First World pharmaceutical companies continue to export $1.5bn worth of powdered milk to the Third World, with resulting enormous profits. They spend millions on marketing campaigns to popularise substitutes for breast-milk among doctors, health workers and mothers, although studies have shown that bottle-fed babies are 14 times more likely to die from diarrhoea than are breast-fed babies. As a direct result of this pernicious free-market activity, one million children die every year, from the world's most easily prevented ill-ness,'baby bottle disease'.[90]

Yet another of the innumerable ill-effects of money, as expressed through market economics, is the devastation of agricultural land. The UN Food & Agriculture report for 1980 explained that financial pressures drive farmers to use synthetic fertilisers, and to abandon crop rotation and fallow years. The resulting lack of natural rejuvenation of the soil results in 13 to 17 million acres of farm land being lost annually. It is not only in the Third World that the market economy leads to the exploitation of children. A report by the Low Pay Unit issued in March 1991, disclosed that of about 2m children employed in the UK, 75% are working illegally, 25% were under 13 years, the minimum legal age for employment, while 7% earned under 50p, and 25% under £1 per hour.[91]

Means tests

The criticism of capitalism by the World Council of Churches was quoted in the Introduction. The Pope added his specific concern about market economics in his 1991 encyclical. In this he said 'if the market is not circumscribed within a strong judicial framework, which is at the service of human freedom in its totality, then the church could not recommend it as a model of development. One of the objects of that framework is to secure a living wage for workers and adequate provision for those out of work.' And yet, in the UK in 1990, for example, an unemployed married claimant received benefit of only 27% of average earnings. Moreover, an increasing number of recipients were being 'means tested' to check their 'credentials'.[92] Means-testing is one of the more repugnant features of the money system, involving compulsory probing into the private lives of already distressed people, by often reluctant officials. Further, various forms of benefits controlled by means-tests can catch people in 'poverty traps', in which people find it is hardly worth trying to earn more because their income would barely increase, if at all.

Monetarism

'Regulation of the money supply as a method of controlling and stabilising the economy' may serve as a dictionary definition; in practice, those supposed to be 'in control' are themselves confused. That a clear explanation of the quicksilver nature of capitalist economics eludes even its own experts is illustrated by the following piece of double-talk by the prestigious London Business School, stating its 'strong rejection of the notion that money causes income or prices or even that it can be used to forecast prices....If there is a causal link then it runs from prices to money, rather than the other way around....A rise or fall in the money supply won't necessarily affect prices, but price rises may affect the money supply.'[93] The only outcome which is all too clear is that during the intense application of market economics and monetarism in the UK from the late 1970s to the mid-1980s, the proportion of the population existing below the official poverty line increased from 10.8% to 16.6%.

The astonishing growth in the whole culture of money in recent years is illustrated by the dramatic increase in the numbers employed in the UK's various financial institutions: banking, insurance, stockbroking, tax collecting and accountancy. *The total of all these employees in fact increased from 493,000 in 1955 to 2,475,000 in 1990.(New Statesman 29/5/92).* How much stronger and healthier all-round would the UK have become if those extra two million men and women had been employed usefully on creating factories, housing, hospitals and schools!

The mean-minded propensity for 'short-termism' of monetarists, is well illustrated by the UK Government outlawing free eye tests in 1989. It has been estimated that, as a result, 200,000 people in need of treatment will have been missed, including 9,000 cases of hypertension, 10,000 of diabetes, 20,000 of glaucoma and 20,000 of cataracts, all, inevitably, leading to eventually essential medical attention costing vastly in excess of the initial savings on the test, apart from the widespread trauma and fatalities resulting.[94]

In a First World society such as the UK, it is barely credible that the adequate supply of essential medical equipment should depend on the whims of private manufacturers. However, in early 1991, the business conglomerate BTR stopped producing critically important 'iron lungs', complaining of inadequate profit margins. Chairman Sir Owen Green, who raised BTR's profits during the 1980s from £42m to £819m by taking over numerous smaller companies, does not believe that companies have a social role. He said 'those educated post-war have been taught—brainwashed—that it is socially undesirable to make money...[they've been taught] that it is just as important to have a good personnel policy, decent factories, to play a significant social role. They blur the issues —the key is the bottom line.'[95]

Monopolies

Protagonists of market economies promote the illusion that 'free competition' between producers of goods and services results in minimum prices for consumers, and as such has to be a 'plus' for the system. In fact, in some industries, for various reasons such as scale of production, competition is a non-starter because there is only one producer anyway. In others, different producers have got together, willingly or through take-overs, to form monopolies and thereby agree to maintain all their prices at common levels well above the minima. Elites appreciate that monopolies tend to 'muddy the image' of the market economy. Thus, in the UK for example, a Monopolies Commission exists to give the impression of there being a barrier against these price-rigging activities. In some industries, the same effect as complete monopolisation results when one or more companies simply stifle their would-be competitors by their sheer size and influence. For instance, in 1990 a small UK airline tried, unsuccessfully, to introduce a return fare to Paris which would have undercut that of the giant British Airways and Air France by £100.[96]

Mortgages

Next to food and clothing, man's most basic requirement is housing, and the money system takes full advantage of this necessity. If young families, understandably, prefer not to rent, but to become owners of their homes then they become enmeshed in the mortgage syndrome. With this system, the borrower is faced with obligatory payments, combining capital with fluctuating interest, which are likely to amount, over the 20 or 30 years involved, to perhaps double the original cost of the house. Thus the lenders, building societies and others, are able to pay their shareholders healthy dividends, while avoiding any risks by retaining ownership until final payments are made.

Many borrowers with steady, reasonably-paid jobs may well live through complete mortgage periods without undue problems. On the other hand, for the many not so lucky, the constant threat of losing not only the home, but all the payments to date as well, naturally leads not only to worry and trauma, but to cutting back on other necessities including food. In 1981 to 1991, in the UK, mortgage repayments averaged one-third of earnings.

Research in 1991, by the UK housing charity Shelter showed that at least one in 12 borrowers had repayment problems. Actual repossessions in the UK averaged around 20,000 pa in the 1980s, rising to around 70,000 in 1991.[97] There is no reprieve for individuals unable to continue their payments: they lose everything. In stark contrast, property company debts are simply 'written off'. The *Guardian* (1/4/92) reports that 'the collapse of property values threatens to force banks to set aside up to £40 bn to cover loans which they made to developers in the 1980s but which will now never be repaid.

Multinational corporations

Mention has been made in Chapter 1 of some of the baneful activities of the mammoth multinational corporations, which spread their tentacles ruthlessly around the world and suck vast profits back home to their First World bases. The Vice-President of one US bank has said that, compared to making around 13% on US operations, he can easily 'earn' 33% on business in Latin America. In fact, average levels of profit from the Third World are probably even higher, since accountancy is more of an art than a science. In *The Creation of World Poverty*, Teresa Hayter quotes an assistant to the president of one large US-based MNC stating that it was 'no problem' to maintain real rates of return from 50% to 400% pa. The most lucrative extra-territorial activity of all is, of course, drilling for oil. The 1990 increase of $15 in the value of one of the trillion barrels in the total world stock in total alone represented 3 times the total US GNP. The *Guardian* (5/11/90) pointed out that the increase equalled a transfer of $300bn pa from 'unlucky people' (ie almost everyone except those 'in oil') to the lucky ones. Needless to say, abandoning the money system would drain away the life-blood of these spurious, multinational organisations, and free many regions to develop in their own best ways.

Overdrafts

These sometimes unintended bank 'loans' are yet another irritation of the money system. The *Observer* (6/9/92) tells us that 'the banks have a knack for getting on the wrong side of the public. Undisclosed fees, exorbitant overdraft charges and other arbitrary actions led the UK Consumers Association to denounce the banks for acting with "breathtaking arrogance" towards customers. NatWest increased its quarterly flat-rate fee for unauthorised overdrafts by 16% to £55, while Barclays charges 37% on unauthorised overdrafts.'

Pensions

Pension schemes represent one of the most complex and worrisome aspects of the money system, involving as they do so many imponderables spread over so many years. One of the unfortunate spin-offs of the whole pensions concept is the arbitrary setting of retirement ages for men and women. It is significant that the elite professions, notably judges for example, have never considered themselves 'past it' at any particular age. Yet, of the vast majority presently considered only of scrap value at 65 or 60, increasing numbers are proving their continuing, or potential, value to society into their 70s, 80s and even 90s. The average UK employee, for instance, changes jobs five times in a working lifetime, so it is not surprising that over £50bn worth of contributions, belonging to previous employees, remain in employers' pension funds, which are themselves invested. In view of all the uncertainties of the market economy generally, it is impossible to guess what proportions of such monies eventually revert to benefit their original contributors.

The *Guardian* (2 & 9/11/91) reported that:

> Pensions, intended to ease life in retirement, seem to be causing people more problems than ever...Most have no idea how much their pensions will give them—even when they are within twelve months of retiring....There are increasing complaints recently about employers' insolvency and the subsequent wind-up of pension schemes....The biggest fiddlers are those in small companies who combine the roles of director with trustee for their pension scheme....The Inland Revenue identified 48 different ways of fiddling to give huge benefits to the highly paid, one involving transferring £2.25m. to a fund for two directors and their children, another where the beneficiaries retired twice to obtain two tax-free lump sums.

A notorious example of tampering with employees'pension rights came to light with the collapse of the Maxwell empire in December 1991. The disappearance of £500m from the Mirror Group's pension fund meant that employees who had saved for their retirement for 40 years ended up with nothing; the money had been siphoned off to prop up the ailing Maxwell private empire. It was even doubtful whether pensions would continue to be paid to the 6,000 existing pensioners; the savings of around 16,000 employees in all were at risk.

The Guardian (5/12/91) reported:

> Pension fund managers have become the princes of the financial community, with £400bn of assets under their control (equivalent to 73% of the wealth created annually in the UK). These managers can decide the fate of companies during hostile take-over bids; have helped create the culture of high dividend payouts which has discouraged investment in industry, and can cause stampedes in and out of stock markets....With the high inflation levels of the seventies, share value rises in the eighties

and the many takeover bids, many pension funds have built up large surpluses. These surpluses, which might appear to belong to the pension contributors and the trustees supposedly acting on their behalf, have, in fact been used for multifarious purposes.

Alternatively, or additionally to employers' schemes, the thriving market in private pension schemes is promoted by persuasive salesmen and free gifts on joining. As with insurance, the companies involved constitute an 'industry', whose priority is their own profitability. Either way, pension schemes are plagued by actuarial gobbledegook, including, for example, added years...buy-out bonds...contingent spouses' pensions...death in service benefit...final salary arrangement...home reversion schemes...investment bond schemes...limited price indexation...roll-up schemes...transfer values. Little wonder that M McKee, pensions manager at Family Assurance, said: 'Savers are confused and bored by pensions and it is the industry's fault. Our research clearly shows that on retirement most people will face a cut in income by more than a half, leaving nowhere near the Government's recommended 'two-thirds of final salary' figure. Joanna Slaughter warned: 'Those who do not place pensions on their financial action list will pay the price in their old age.'[98]

Pharmaceutical profits

In the eyes of the money men there is nothing special about the issues of human life and health, which simply constitute another sphere for profit-making, and on a very substantial scale at that. Unlike a number of other industries, pharmaceutical production has always been in the hands of private companies, who have become well entrenched in the process of providing for one of society's most essential needs. The *Guardian* reported:

Branded drugs can cost up to nine times more than generics; many cost double, and all except about 30 of the thousands on the market could be substituted by unbranded ones; but a proposal to save the NHS £175m pa (at 1982 prices) was defeated by the pharmaceutical industry, which made £300m pa profits in the early 1980s.(30/12/82)

The compulsive quest for profits by the different pharmaceutical firms involved has compromised scientists' efforts to develop the highly complex vaccine against malaria - which threatens 2bn people and is spreading rapidly. The leading firm involved, Genentech, has stated 'we are a profit-oriented outfit like any company, and need restricted rights to keep ourselves in a competitive position'.(6/2/83)

Nine pharmaceutical firms found by the Public Accounts Committee to have made excess profits totalling £30m on sales to the NHS have not been obliged to repay the money.(15/7/83)

Wellcome, the drugs firm best known as the manufacturers of Retrovir, used to treat Aids, has been making nearly £8m per week. Of every £1 spent on Wellcome products, 25p was profit. Their total profit, at £402m., was 28% higher than the previous year.(15/11/91)

In their haste to get newly-invented drugs on the market, the companies go one better than trying them out on animals, by trying them out on humans. The *Observer* (1/10/89) reported that 'Unemployed and others, for example students, desperate for cash, approximately 15,000 of them in 1989, accept inducements of up to £1,000 to act as human guinea pigs, testing new drugs by pharmaceutical companies.' Millions of children die unnecessarily in the Third World because companies promote their anti-diarrhoeal drugs, which are far less effective than the unprofitable Oral Rehydration Therapy (ORT). This is a simple solution of salt and sugar which can save a life, for just 7 pence. Wide use of ORT would severely dent the profits of the £300m anti-diarrhoea industry, whose products, according to the World Health Organisation, are mostly useless. The *Guardian* (26/11/82) reported that:

Medicines which are either banned or carefully prescribed in the West, are sold without prescriptions by village chemists in the Third World, who receive frequent visits from drug company salesmen. *Oxfam states that medicines are sold, not because they are needed, but for profit, and that they are often dangerous to health; yet they carry claims to safety and efficacy which are forbidden in the First World.*

An exceptionally clear example of how elites contrive to smooth the way for their business friends to make vast profits as easily as possible is provided by a report from the UK National Consumer Council:

Patients are facing unnecessary risks because the government refuses to expose the pharmaceutical industry to open regulation....New medicines are approved in secret tests by government appointed experts who are often in the pay of drug companies....The Department of Health has an 'in-built conflict of interests' because it has to promote the industry's well-being as well as regulating its products...and thus fails to prevent allegedly dangerous drugs from reaching the market.(*Guardian* 9/12/91)

The whole pharmaceutical scenario shows up the spurious nature of the money system. Once a drug or other product has been researched and produced, it is marketed repetitively year after year, with returns totally eclipsing the cost of its original development.

Poaching of flora and fauna

'When there are animals to kill, we'll find ingenious new ways to make a profit out of them' commented environmentalist Mowat, in the TV film *Sea of Slaughter*. Some idea of the scale of this problem can be gained from the Lausanne-based Convention on Trade in Endangered Species. This organisation lists 8,000 highly-endangered species in which trade is banned, and a further 30,000 species in which only carefully controlled trade is permitted. The scope for ruthless poaching is clearly immense - with commensurate rewards.

Thus the traffic in flora and fauna, dead and alive, worldwide, has become yet another vicious by-product of the money system, worth about $5bn pa. Africa's elephant population, for example, fell from 1.3m in 1980 to 624,000 in 1989, as poachers fed the ivory markets in Hong Kong, Japan, Europe, and the US.[99] The sheer scale of that traffic can be gauged from an estimate that just 120 dead elephants were needed to produce the 330 pounds of ivory— valued at over £500,000 —found by Johannesburg police in 1991.[100]

In the twenty years up to 1991, 85% of the world's rhino population was lost, mostly slaughtered by sophisticated teams of poachers, armed with Kalashnikovs, who can earn more from the sale of a single horn than an African farmer's annual wage.

African rhino horn fetches $20,000 per kilo, Asian horn $60,000 per kilo —more than the price of gold. Taiwanese are increasingly buying rhino horns as an investment, like works of art.[101] A TV programme provided this information about the ape trade.

First they shoot the mother. Then they bundle the live babies into crates, often with no food or water, with ice round them to slow down metabolism. After a bumpy, noisy, terrifying journey, the one in six babies which survives will be lucky to end up in a zoo. More likely, it will be bought as a pet by someone who saw its cousin being cute in a TV ad, or a cabaret act. When it grows, as it will, to human size, it will be dumped or killed. Such are the prospects for the shy, endangered Orang-outang at the hands of primate smugglers.[102]

Every year, about 3m exotic and in some cases almost extinct birds are trapped in the jungles of Africa and South America. They are then sent, with terrible losses, to the First World to satisfy the demand for caged pets, and the greed of the traffickers. In 1989, of 184,600 birds imported into the UK, 4,000 were dead on arrival and a further 19,500 died in quarantine. Further, many birds are known to die during both capture and transportation.[103]

Illegal trafficking in rare plants can be as destructive as ivory poaching; at least one plant in every 2,000 is basic to certain medicines. As with fauna, poaching flora can be immensely profitable; just one UK importer of illegal Asian orchids is known to have made £3m. In South Africa, the world's rarest plant, the cycad, has become an investment commodity; some 700, worth millions, are known to have been exported in 1988. In Arizona, the illegal trafficking in Soara cacti is worth over $1m annually; these giant cacti, sometimes 200 years old and weighing 10 tons, are rustled to decorate city shopping malls.

Pornography

The prominent feminist, Andrea Dworkin, believes that pornography is the major cause of abuse against women, that it is no more or less than 'technologised prostitution', and that its basic assumption and message is: 'No matter what you do to a woman, no matter how much you hurt her, she will like it.' The pornography 'industry' is a shameful blot on self-styled advanced societies, and the vast, degrading profits made by its publications are both encouraged and made possible by the money system.

Privatisation costs

The wholesale de-nationalising which took place in the UK in the 1980s illustrated the lengths to which free-marketeers will go to promote their philosophy of eliminating the least hint of 'socialism' in their economies. There can be little doubt that if the vast sums— said to have totalled towards £2bn—wasted on marketing and under-pricing losses, had simply been ploughed into the respective nationalised industries, they could have been improved well beyond the capacities of any private purchasers. Shares offered in British Telecom and the Trustee Savings Bank, for example, were so under-priced that purchasers profited immediately by premiums of 80% and 70% respectively. Around £50m was spent on advertising the sale of British Gas, a sum about four times greater than that spent on warning the public about the danger of Aids. In their anxiety to be rid of the nationalised Rover car company, the UK government accepted £150m despite a National Audit Office valuation of £200m and bids of around £400m from two other interested companies. The selling off of UK industries, companies, land and council houses produced some £80bn for the government. This was not applied to critically-needed capital works such as infrastructure, schools and hospitals but instead was used for politically-popular income tax cuts. These resulted in vast increases in spending on mostly foreign consumer goods, leading to a £6bn trade deficit.

Private education

The opportunity for the better-off to buy a privileged future for their children through private education is a flagrant example of the imbalances inherent in the money system. In the UK for instance, around 93% of all children attend free, state schools, while the remaining 7% receive private education. For those attending boarding schools, the fees amount to around £8,000 pa per child— more than the total annual income of many of their fellow, adult citizens. The tangible returns for such heavy outlays include smaller classes, and more congenial academic and recreational environments. The intangibles include the upper-crust atmosphere into which children of the entrenched elite gravitate naturally, and which provides the first rung on the ladder for those aspiring to join the elite-that-matters when they are older.

Private medicine

Understandable desperation by individuals to spend whatever they can afford, in order to preserve their health or lives, has meant that the money system has always spawned a tendency bordering on blackmail in the field of health care. The most extreme example of that influence is to be found in the US, which spends vastly more than any other country on health, yet has an infant mortality rate no better than that of Turkey, and 40 million citizens with no health cover at all. As with so many other activities based on market economics, health schemes relying on private 'enterprise' suffer terminally from profit-seeking having priority. In the context of UK governmental pressures in the late 1980s to privatise health care, Dr D Naysmith, President of the Socialist Health Association, said 'freedom of choice is the freedom to wait up to two years for an operation, or have it done by the same consultant within a month if the patient can pay...the private sector is parasitic on the National Health Service...it bears none of the costs of training...concentrates on low-risk, high reward areas...avoids the more expensive conditions...and when things go badly wrong the NHS is there, often conveniently near, to pick up the pieces.'[104]

The UK College of Health reported in 1991 that some surgeons exaggerate the times patients will need to wait for operations in order to steer them towards lucrative private treatment. Another report revealed that Britain's 2,400 highest paid consultants each earn over £95,000 pa from private fees.[105]

The money system prompts professionals to indulge in gerrymandering more commonly associated with confidence tricksters. A UK group of 'budget-holding' family doctors set up a private company to sell surgical services back to itself. The GPs, who control a £1.8m budget, are the company's directors, one of whom performs the operations. They are free to keep any profits the company makes. A loophole in the NHS 'reforms' not only permits this, but would also allow the 'marketing back' of almost any other medical service.[106] The profit motive is even resulting in unnecessary surgery being performed. The Journal of the American Medical Association has reported that 'proprietary hospitals, with the greatest incentive to maximise reimbursements, had the highest repeat Caesarian rates, costing an average $7,186 as against $4,334 for vaginal births. In California, Caesarian operations were performed approximately six times more often in private than in public hospitals.'

The *Guardian* (8/1/92) reports that:

> Officials in Texas are investigating widespread fraud at the psychiatric division of National Medical Enterprise Incorporated, the country's second biggest hospital company, in a medical world where clinical successes tend to be reviewed in the financial press more than in academic or medical publications. The graver allegations include paying bounties as high as $1,200 to people like probation officers, policemen and teachers, to bring in patients, including schoolchildren, for psychiatric treatment that can be charged to health insurance plans, keeping patients against their will, billing for services never offered, and grossly inflating charges. America is confronting a medical care crisis as millions of citizens are denied insurance while others go bankrupt trying to pay their bills.

The Nation (23/3/92) reports:

> *Experts have estimated that 100,000 deaths occur annually in the US because people cannot afford health care. Lack of health care causes three times more*

deaths than Aids. In 1990 56% of the population and 75% of the working class indicated that they had problems paying their medical bills. The overwhelming majority of Americans, poor and non-poor, do not have comprehensive health coverage, nor cover for long-term care for which the average annual cost is $27,243.

Property dealing

Since the money system has resulted in charging man for every inch of his own earth, and everything beneath it, and even the waters upon it, little wonder it is so often asked, 'can air be far behind?' World-wide, humanity is plagued by self-seeking elites controlling ever-increasing proportions of land. Astronomical rises in land and property values have undermined whole societies, exalting owners and driving non-owners to the wall. How can a young Japanese person fare when the price of a tiny patch of Tokyo land equals a whole estate in the West, and the 'value' of Tokyo City equals the 'value' of the whole US? To the money men, there is nothing sacred about mother earth— she is just another commodity for lucrative dealing. The *Guardian* (1/11/91) reported that UK Lord Beaverbrook (by coincidence, Treasurer of the Conservative Party) made a £50m profit inside 5 months by purchasing a huge tract of rain forest. A consortium headed by the 39 year old Lord, paid £9.7m for the Guyanese national timber company and sold it for £60m.

The Highlands of Scotland have become one of the world's most sought after areas by the property dealers because of their valuable 'sporting' potential for the ultra-rich. In January 1990, wealthy would-be buyers were queuing up to pay from £12m to £15m for a 30,000 acre deer forest with salmon fishing in the Highlands. The *Guardian* (29/3/91) reported:

> In 1989, the alleged second richest US citizen, fast-food billionaire John Kluge, purchased the 77,000 acre Mar Lodge estate for £3.3m so that his wife, a former nude model, could rub shoulders with the Royal Deeside neighbours at Balmoral. Like the other private landowners of the Cairngorms, Kluge prefers to breed the marauding deer for foreign shooting parties rather than cull them to save the native forests. The essential conflict is between the short-term profit from a sporting estate and the long-term value of nature conservation. It is money versus nature, and so far money has always won.

Across the world, owners controlling huge tracts of land not only deny its use to millions, but also misuse it themselves, so that often irrevocable damage results. In the UK, the Nature Conservancy Council paid out around £60m 'compensation' over 10 years to stop wealthy landowners who were threatening to ill-use sites of special scientific interest. The *Observer* (24/11/91) reported that Lord Kimball was demanding £3m for allowing the world-important peat lands on his estate to remain unspoilt.

The whole precious, multi-faceted integrity of our billion-years old earth is now at risk because the free enterprise system gives precedence to the property dealers. In *The Midas Touch*, Anthony Sampson has said:

> The problem is that the world's money system is unable to take account of resources that cannot be commercially valued. *It is therefore in preserving its own earth that human ingenuity faces its final challenge; for however much money can multiply material prosperity and wealth, it cannot multiply the land itself. As Mark Twain said 'They aren't making it any more'.*

Prostitution

The cruel indignity of prostitution is yet another miserable by-product of the money system. While money remains, humans will continue to sell their bodies, if that appears to be the only recourse left to them against poverty or destitution. World-wide, countless hundreds of thousands are involved, some individually, many recruited and controlled by pimps or sex syndicates, who grow fat on their substantial cuts of the takings. An April 1991 report states:

> At the Eros Centre in Cologne, the 70 girls pay the building owner £70 per day plus fees to the pimps...one network was exploiting 400 West Indian girls in France and Germany...another recruited girls from the bush in Nigeria, and talked them into agreeing to owing debts of £10,000, supposedly for their air fares, then forced them into prostitution in Italy and 'repayments'. Of 6,000 prostitutes in Paris, 2,000 were foreigners, mostly African.(107)

Apart from the demeaning nature of their occupation, prostitutes face increasingly serious life-threatening risks. In Thailand, for example, where cheap sex has become an explicit selling feature by Western travel agents, a government minister fears there could be between one and two million HIV positive cases by the year 2000.[108] In the UK 'every week a new influx of young, naive girls whose hopes of careers in modelling have turned to dust— or whose rent needs paying— go on the game. Each of them will be severely beaten several times before they learn the ropes...one says: "I need the money"...another says: "I know the dangers, I've been raped at gunpoint; but I need the money and I couldn't do anything else; it's my life".'[109]

Recessions

The world-wide recession of the early 1990s can be seen as typical. In the US, Alan Greenspan, chairman of the Federal Reserve, admitted that the credit system was not working well, adding that 'the distress signs are evident: rising unemployment, stagnant personal income, a sharp drop in industrial production, a moribund construction industry, weak car sales, and lay-offs because of city and state budget deficits.'[110] In Japan, the most successful of the major economies in the post-war period, 1990 saw the beginning of a recession that they had still not recovered from in 1996. In the Third World, all existing problems and suffering are aggravated by recession in the First World. In the UK, in 1991, there were around 40,000 business failures, and unemployment was costing £21bn, or 10% of total Government spending. There have, in fact, been seven severe recessions in the UK since 1950, and each has left higher unemployment than the previous one. However 'going out of business is not the end of the matter; with insolvency practitioners themselves under pressure, dealing with the sheer numbers of failures, even going bust can be a long process.'[111] But even for those that survive 'many small firms could find the effects of recovery more painful than recession itself. Some will see their businesses swept away, as they discover they do not have the funds to finance renewed demand from customers..'[112]

The UK business information group Dun and Bradstreet commented sadly 'this is a similar picture to the one we recorded during the last recession...the number of business failures continued to rise sharply for two years after the onset of recovery in 1981. The rate of business failures and rise in unemployment continues after any recession.'(113) The effects of recessions are distressing enough in terms of failures of individual businesses, into which owners and others have put years of effort; but when large industrial plants such as mills or mines close down, the disastrous effects are felt by whole communities. The life-warping stresses, which recessions, over the years, impose on the unfortunate millions caught up in them, can include: bankruptcy, bad debts, bank charges, cash-flow stoppages, corporate debt, depression, divorce, heart attack, home repossession, overdrafts, personal debt, loss of car etc, receivership, tax demands, unemployment, voluntary liquidation and suicide.

A monetarist definition of recession is said to be 'a period when growth is negative'. There can be little doubt that millions suffering the ill-effects of recessions would gladly settle for no 'growth' at all, just remaining steady, rather than put up with the regular bouts of recession suffered by the money system which play such havoc with their living standards.

Writing in the *Observer* (1/12/91) William Keegan commented that 'It is rather unfortunate that capitalism should have celebrated the collapse of communism by arranging a crisis of its own…as the chancellor reminded us last week— even when there is a recovery, it is a long time before people recognise it, or know there has been one. The message is still pretty terrible and even those who claim the bottom has been reached are not all certain about the route out of recession—let alone the timing…sections of British industry are desperate…there are even rumours (surely unfounded) of firms that want to go bankrupt while their banks will not let them.'

Apart from the very real suffering endured by the worst hit victims of recessions, it is thoroughly demeaning for millions of intelligent citizens throughout much of the world to be completely at the mercy of a volatile system which even its own alleged experts do not understand. The money system is like a rudderless ship, drifting from one disaster to the next. There are many counts upon which the money system can be indicted, but the one which applies most forcefully in the context of recessions is the utter stupidity of a culture which can spawn such aberrations. *Abandoning money is the only alternative to the degrading and soul-destroying scenario of boom/slump, boom/slump, which has become routine during the 20th century, and which no free marketeer has attempted to explain, let alone control.*

Renting

The provision of rented housing is one of the most valued activities of public authorities in many countries, particularly because they constitute reliable landlords with sufficient resources for essential maintenance. However, the high levels of rents they are obliged to charge, usually due to central government fiscal pressure, result at times in terrible predicaments for their tenants. In the UK, in 1990, out of some 5m mortgages or tenancies under local authority or housing association control, a total of 91,839 eviction orders had to be issued.[114] More generally in the First World, rental accommodation is obtained privately. As a result, the basic need for shelter becomes a puppet of free market economics. A chronic shortage of housing, world-wide, enables property owners to take advantage of scarcity to maintain highly profitable rental levels.

Apart from high rents, which may increase at short intervals according to the market, private tenants also suffer from insecurity. In the UK in 1990, for instance, Home-Lets, one of London's largest agents, crashed with debts of over £1m. About 2,000 tenants lost their deposits, some over £500. According to the Association of Residential Letting Agents, 'there are some 10,000 letting agents throughout the UK with no professional basis or standards of conduct whatsoever.' Also, it is not uncommon for tenants to return home and find that the locks have been changed, after the property has been repossessed because of the landlord's mortgage arrears. In such cases there is virtually no protection for the tenant.[115]

Sects

The world-wide money culture, with little room for worth-while cooperative activities, is wide open for cranks to dupe the young and the gullible, anxious for some cause to espouse. Churches of all denominations have always invoked reverential superstitions about various deities in order to garner financial support. However, the leaders of the latter-day sects or cults, Pentecostal, 'Born Again' and the like, with millions of adherents, have made money-raising into really big business, with few doubts about the destination of most of the proceeds. As would be expected, the US leads the field, with around 1,000 'religious' radio stations having an annual revenue exceeding $0.5bn. In the mid-1980s, the Rev Falwell's 'Moral Majority' and 'Clean up America' crusades depended largely on the 'electronic church'—a vast TV and radio marketing operation reaching about 100 million US homes weekly. In the UK in 1991, David Rubin, son of the Rabbi of Sassow, the living saint who is rabbi and leader to the Sassower Hasidic sect, disappeared owing up to £150m invested by fellow Hasidim, some of whom have been ruined.[116]

Smoking

It is now established, and accepted world-wide, that smoking causes emphysema, chronic bronchitis, aortic aneurisms, ulcers, strokes and heart attacks, apart from cancer. These dire results can also affect 'passive smokers', that is non-smokers including babies and young children who are frequently in the company of smokers. Smoking causes six times as many premature deaths as road accidents, all other accidents, suicide, murder, fires, drug abuse and Aids put together.[117] In the UK, deaths from smoking total 300 per day. At the same time, every day 300 children start smoking: 1% of 12 year olds, 12% of 14 year olds and 23% of 15 year olds, particularly girls. At any one time, about 9,500 hospital beds are occupied by those laid low by smoking, costing the National Health Service £437m pa.[118] It is reported that 3.6m years of life are lost annually through smoking in the US, where only 25% of the population continues to smoke.

In the world as a whole, the annual death toll from smoking is now around 3m. The cumulative world total of smoking-related deaths can be equated with the total numbers of all deaths in the First and Second World Wars, together with those resulting from all the other wars of the 20th century. Barely credible though it may seem, this organised mayhem continues to be perpetrated by the tobacco industry, in full possession of all the gruesome facts about the inevitable results of its activities. This enormously profitable industry is well-entrenched in many countries. Its products are all too easy to obtain, and all too difficult to reject; and their sales provide governments with dependable and easily collectable taxation revenue. Thus governments, the only bodies in a position, indeed with a moral obligation, to curtail tobacco sales, have a vested interest in promoting them. In the UK, for instance, the Government spends £5m annually on health warnings, as against £100m by the tobacco industry on promoting their products. In the US, the Administration subsidises tobacco farmers with $100m pa.[119]

Some idea of the mammoth scale of the tobacco menace can be gauged from estimated world total production being 5,000bn cigarettes pa; that is, 1,000 cigarettes pa for every man, woman and child on earth. British American Tobacco, responsible for 10% of world output, made a trading profit of £966m in 1990.[120] If the manufacturers of the remaining 90% of cigarettes are as efficient as BAT, then annual global profits from cigarettes can be estimated at approaching £10bn which exceeds, for example, total annual UK expenditure on public education. To maintain demand and resulting profits, the tobacco giants indulge in ruthless promotion tactics. Imperial Tobacco Ltd of Canada included 12 to 17 year olds in its target groups for Player's filter brand.[121] Imperial's marketing plan for 1988 was marked 'Personal and Confidential' on every page. It stated: 'If the last 10 years have taught us anything, it is that the industry is dominated by the companies who respond most effectively to the needs of younger smokers.' The plan continued 'TV guides, sports/youth publications, posters and beetleboards will be used to support Player's Filter...these vehicles offer a more youthful approach to reach the younger smokers...the best explanation for success in the young smoker's market is long-standing sponsorship of sports events.'[122]

Advertising in all its many forms is of course the most important of all the tobacco promotion methods. In Europe, however, some countries ban tobacco advertising already, and an EC proposal to extend the ban has been bitterly opposed by the tobacco lobbyists. They have marshalled the support of some newspaper publishers, who risk losing millions of pounds in advertising revenue if the ban is imposed.[123] At present the numbers (chiefly children) taking up smoking roughly balance the numbers dying from the effects of it. However, since smoking is gradually becoming less acceptable in the First World, the manufacturers are accelerating their promotion drives in the Third World. Smoking deaths in the First World are pitiful enough; but promotion in the Third World involves persuading under-nourished, impoverished people, totally ignorant of the proven dangers, to purchase products which their manufacturers know full well are even more likely to kill them, being less fit, than their First World addicts. This activity represents the ultimate in callous, free market commercialism, where profit rules supreme. One estimate of the possible outcome has suggested an increase in the global total of deaths from smoking from 3m to 10m pa by 2020.

The actual growing of tobacco represents 1.5% of global agricultural production, takes up 4m hectares of precious farm land and nets annual profits of $3bn for its producers. Further, tobacco plants ruin the soil, taking out 11 times more nitrogen, 24 times more potassium and 36 times more phosphorous than most food crops. Annually, 1m hectares of forests are felled and burned just to cure tobacco crops.

In January 1990, J D Reynolds, chief of a highly successful tobacco conglomerate, jumped to his death from a Florida hotel, apparently overburdened by the guilt of having lived off the profits of an industry responsible for untold numbers of deaths.[119] That dramatic act of conscience-salving clearly made no impression whatever on his colleagues, who have continued unperturbed with their death-dealing activities. *The tobacco industry is an outrageous example of how the money system hooked humanity into accepting without protest that 'business is business', no matter how destructive the product may be. As with the arms industry, the tobacco industry is not only thoroughly evil, but totally surplus to the world's requirements.*

Stock exchanges

Stock exchanges are at the core of the money system; they are like private casinos, with guaranteed winnings, for the exclusive use of the financial elite who can afford to be members; in New York membership costs $400,000, in Tokyo $6m. The free market 'system' of buying and selling stocks, shares or bonds, has as its driving force the brokers' commissions, made on both selling and buying. These dealers do little more than watch blips on screens and make money out of money, by gambling with other people's funds, doing business with people they never meet, using instant world-wide communications penetrating numerous different economies.

Anthony Sampson has said:

> Financial deregulation, technology and world markets have made it possible for people to speculate on a huge scale with very little of their own money committed. Since such speculative returns were greater than if you had to go to work and build a factory, the so-called financial industry became the biggest growth industry in the world.[124]

Some idea of the size of the trough from which rich pickings can be taken, can be gauged from just one part of the action in London— the Foreign Exchange Market, which turns over around £180 bn daily. The lure of such big money has even skewed the destinations of University leavers. A report states 'a new form of "brain drain" now results in fewer graduates going into UK industry than into the City of London, where the chance of getting away with financial crime has never been so good.'[125] Particularly in the mid-1980s, there were numerous young men in their twenties or thirties, earning $50m or $100m pa in New York, or £100,000 pa in London, just trading money, but risking a health 'burn-out' after 3 or 4 years.

At times, to augment their already substantial 'legitimate' earnings, brokers indulge in 'insider' dealings. These involve using privileged, inside information about a company to make money from some imminent secret development, and are considered, in UK parlance, to be definitely 'not cricket'. In 1986 an eminent New York financier, Ivan Boesky, used confidential information to invest in stocks prior to advantageous mergers. He had paid huge sums for the information, including $700,000 in used notes to a banker in a Wall Street alley.[126] In mid-1991, the Bank of England considered investigating the role of the money brokers who steered millions of pounds towards the collapsed

Bank of Credit and Commerce International. 'The affair has spotlighted the usually obscure workings of London money brokers, who marry large-scale lenders with borrowers. They are entitled to receive commission payments from both parties and in a typical deal, neither party knows what brokerage rate the other is paying. There are no limits on the amounts brokers charge, but negotiation of these can be fierce.'[127]

A feature of stock exchanges is that in spite of all their brain-power and expertise, brokers cannot predict or control the wild fluctuation in the markets. During the 1987 crash the 'value' of US companies alone dropped by over $500bn in one day, yet they continued working normally as if nothing had happened. Again, on one day in October 1989, the UK stock market plunged £40m because of fears of a Wall Street panic, then recovered when US investors unexpectedly drove prices up instead of down, and left dealers and analysts stunned. A *Guardian* headline for 23 February 1991 read: 'Blind optimism of the financial markets ignores unpredictable outcome of Gulf conflict and fragility of the economic cycle.' A 1986 report stated that foreign exchange dealing has made speculation respectable, although a senior Bank of England expert declared 'it's a mystery to me how the pluses and minuses work out,' and Lord Lever said 'although the turnover is enormous it is virtually all self-balancing froth and contributes absolutely nothing to GNP.' A dealer is quoted as explaining that the market is 'like a predator, it looks around for a vulnerable currency and strikes it unmercifully, like a cobra; a currency is vulnerable when the market decides it is, and small countries fare worse than big ones.'[128] Market crashes occur from time to time, whether in spite of or because of the stockbrokers. They occur ostensibly because owners of securities sell as their values fall, in order to preserve something of their assets. This scenario has now become automated by computers programmed to sell at certain levels, so a domino-fashion crash has become more likely. No one understood the cause of 'Black Monday' in 1987, when £50bn was suddenly wiped off share values. This represented a 23% drop in one day, and it was said that the world financial system almost collapsed. Anthony Sampson commented that 'the mania and crash of 1987 showed many signs of mob psychology, and even Friedman, though he had predicted a fall in the stock market two weeks earlier, conceded that "nobody knows what causes these panics".'[129]

Ultimately, the machinations of stockbrokers and their like affect the future of both industries and society as a whole. The stock market scenario provides yet another vivid example of the unstable, unpredictable nature of the money system as a whole. Without that system, mankind could be significantly closer to control of its own destiny.

Takeovers

The whole 'takeover' scenario illustrates well the ruthlessness engendered by the money system. Would-be purchasers aim to grab the ownerships of companies often operating in totally different fields from those of which they have any previous experience, purely as playthings to further inflate both their egos and their existing fortunes. The effect their actions may have on the welfare of the hundreds, or even thousands, of employees involved is clearly of no concern to them. Paradoxically, would-be purchasers often even gain from losing a takeover battle, because, in order to shake off their unwelcome bids, the companies they try to buy into, themselves buy back the bidders' investments, resulting in huge profits for the bidders. Many of the more drastic 'scorched earth', 'poison pill', and 'golden parachute' defence mechanisms, triggered by US managements in opposing unwelcome bids, are open to abuse and conflict of interest. It has been said that 'jungle law prevails on Wall Street, where only the fittest survive.'

One-time takeover expert Sir James Goldsmith, then known as a 'ruthless predator', once stated 'business needs the stimulus of constant competition; sharks don't go after dead but live meat.' His attempted takeover of Akron Rubber was foiled by the local residents' petition bearing 36,000 signatures; however he sold his newly acquired shares back to the company, making a $94m profit. During the 1980s in the US, around $1.3 trillion was squandered on mergers and buyouts, amounting to about one-third of the total amount invested in new plant and equipment over the same period. No less than $13bn went on fees for simply arranging these deals, a sum 45 times greater than the US government's annual outlay on protecting workers' health and safety.[130]

Taxes

In the free marketeers' ideal world everything would be initiated and run by private enterprise, and there would be no need for taxes at all. But their ideal could not be realised, chiefly because they wanted armies, navies and police forces, which even they conceded could not be privately run. Also, activities like education and health provision for the mass of the population gradually became, together with certain other social services, so widely accepted as communal responsibilities that they could not demur. And so taxation became inevitable.

However, as with most other aspects of the money system, the elite have always managed to organise taxation so as to favour themselves. For example, in the UK, the pre-1979 higher rates of income tax were reduced so dramatically in the 1980s, that if reintroduced today, they would bring in £27bn pa or nearly sufficient to fund the entire UK national health service. Furthermore, these reductions in direct taxation were only made possible by almost doubling Value Added Tax, which affects the poor much more than the rich; by cutting the scope and real value of social security payments; and by utilising the proceeds of widespread privatisations of nationalised industries which had been the property of the whole nation.

Probably the most astonishingly inequitable tax system ever devised was the UK Thatcher Government's attempt at a 'Poll Tax', to bear equally on all, regardless of income or status. The only previous introduction of such an iniquitous tax, in 1380, led to the Peasants' Revolt under Wat Tyler. During the first year of the recent Tax in the UK, people again revolted and over 2 million individuals faced summonses over failure to pay at all, some receiving prison sentences; as at April 1991, over £1.6bn remained uncollected. Not suprisingly the Tax was soon to be replaced, but in the meantime around 1 million UK citizens lost their right to vote, since the Tax was seen to be related to the electoral register.

Not content with rigging the tax system in their favour initially, elites further contrive to evade their obligations to pay at all, in various ways. Low tax jurisdictions such as Panama, Switzerland or Hong Kong.enable companies or individuals to maintain investments, or branches, so profits can surface in amenable environments. Also, 30% of all international trade takes place within multinational corporations, which encourages financial manipulations and enables corporate income to show up in those countries with the most favourable tax arrangements.[131]

Two small countries specialise in acting as tax havens: Liechtenstein and the Cayman Islands. The former has tax rates which are miniscule by international standards, as low as 0.1% in some cases; company law makes it possible to set up corporate structures whose beneficial ownership is impossible to ascertain. Not suprisingly, estimates suggest over 50,000 companies are registered in Liechenstein, exceeding the number of its population.[132] The Cayman Islands, splitting from Jamaica in 1962, became a British dependency and invented new banking laws. The bankers came, and the population grew from 17,000 to 28,000. Their laws prohibit financial institutions providing information about their clients; they demand no taxes and have no exchange controls. They even relieve tycoons of the trouble of actually going there, by providing directors, offices and nominee shareholders. In particular, they point out that 'the Inland Revenue will never know what you are worth.' The Caymans invite you simply to choose your management company, or approach one of the 535 banks.[133]

Finally, the UK Royal family went one better than their financial elite, by paying no taxes at all. Queen Victoria, in fact, paid her taxes in full, without question. Edward VII also paid, though he tried to avoid them. Then, reflecting the self-seeking dynamic of the money system, George V lobbied Parliament around 1910 and was granted his first tax concession.

Others followed, until, 40 years on, the Royal family had progressed from full tax to no tax. A file, recording the whole story, always kept secret, was finally destroyed in 1977. In the early 1990s, agreement was reached that the Queen should, in fact, contribute a proportion of her tax liability.

Taxation is inevitably a highly controversial and vexatious subject: how to arrange it equably, how to collect it, how to avoid evasion, and so on. There can be no doubt, eliminating taxes would be one of the most welcome reliefs following the abandonment of the money system.

Unemployment

Along with food, clothing and shelter, man's most natural need is meaningful work. The driving force behind that need is the fact that man is intelligent, creative and energetic: he/she needs to work to occupy time and talents constructively, and preferably enjoyably, in the interests of society. *Work is so important, as the foundation of all human well-being and progress, that it follows as a natural right, for it to be organised by society as a whole, and allocated to everyone according to their ability.* Instead, it has for long been accepted, almost worldwide, that numerically tiny elites are entitled to usurp that societal right and act as sole, domineering employers. The money system has distorted the constructive, co-operative function of work by substituting the negative concept of labour as simply 'breadwinning'. Further, the human right to work is as ignored as is the right to sustenance and shelter; almost half the global population are either unemployed or under-employed. In recent decades, the jobless have increased fourfold in the First World and eightfold in the Third World. The elites utilise their 'hire and fire' advantage to control pay levels, because however poor wages may be, they are better than none, which can mean starvation.

Populations as a whole are never consulted about which jobs they would like to perform, nor where or how. It is left to the whim of those in a position to initiate an enterprise, to do so where and in a manner it will be most profitable for them. The money system, through ubiquitous credits, enables industrial and agricultural enterprise owners to install as much expensive machinery as they wish, which in turn promotes profits for the makers of such machinery. Thus, even in the Third World, with its invariably huge labour surplus, employers install automated, energy-consuming production equipment. This fulfils their preference for highly predictable outputs and profits, rather than having to deal with fallible human beings. This inevitably exacerbates unemployment.

On average, numbers needing work in the Third World are growing four times faster than the number of jobs. What little development does take place is usually in the urban areas, leaving the majority rural populations with minimal prospects. Apart from the human trauma involved, the tragic irony of unemployment in the First World is that governments spend billions of their taxpayers' money on welfare payments to their jobless, simply to keep them alive during their enforced idleness. For example, the cost to the UK exchequer in 1992 of unemployment in terms of benefit and lost revenue was estimated at over £20bn. Such money could instead be constructively invested, for example, in much needed public housing construction, which would also provide employment. However, such a logical course of action would run against the grain of free market economics.

Unemployment robs society of the often highly trained potential of millions, who are condemned to years, even life-times of soul-destroying inactivity, often culminating in health breakdowns or suicides. The money culture would have us believe that unemployment is a fact of life; inevitable, even advantageous. In fact it is one of the most damning indictments of a system which cares nothing for society as a whole, but gives priority to elites making profits as and how they please.

'Warehousing' the elderly

Particularly in the First World, a combination of medical advances prolonging life, and the growing demise of the extended family, has led to large increases in the numbers of older people requiring accommodation in homes. These have already become a target for big business, known in the US as 'granny farming', where the interests of the elderly will become secondary to those of the private shareholders involved. Old peoples' homes will soon become 'warehouses of the elderly'.

Already in the UK, hundreds of millions of pounds have been invested in buying up existing and potential old people's accommodation, by multinationals, breweries, merchant bankers and the like.[134] In the UK from 1981, the number of people in private residential care grew by over 300% to 150,000 in 1991, while numbers in publicly provided council homes dropped by 4% to 109,000. Moreover:

> People with criminal records are being allowed to run private homes where elderly residents suffer unacceptable conditions; in many private homes defenceless people are abused , neglected, humiliated and degraded; for many 'community care' has meant swapping the grim inhumanity of the large institutions for the grim inhumanity of the small institutions.[135]

It seems clear, at the moment, that long-term care of the elderly is doomed to be dominated by private sector organisations, increasingly privately funded. Following a legal decision in 1991 in which the maximum number of elderly persons in a particularl home was fixed at 16 rather than the requested 23, the owner protested that 'the court's decision is going to be devastating for the whole industry.'[136] It is entirely in keeping with the money culture that caring for pensioners at the end of their lives should have come to be termed an 'industry'. Yet again, it can be seen that no aspect of human life, however unlikely, is secure against monetarist predators concerned only with 'a quick buck'.

Waste, and profits

The money system engenders numerous forms of waste, both human and material. Many of the A to Z items listed above involve tragic wastage of human lives, through death, disablement, unemployment or inappropriate employment. Because it was never planned, but just 'happened', the free market system inevitably results in duplication of effort, mistaken activities, competitive secrecy, gluts and crises causing interruptions and idle labour, and endless cycles of booms and slumps. Over-production is signalled by price crashes, wage cuts, redundancies and bankruptcies. A superfluity of merchants, retailers, traders, agents, commercial travellers and middlemen of all sorts contrive to produce enormous numbers of different versions of the same consumer article or foodstuff, leading to highly wasteful duplication. Similarly, products made by a firm say, in the south of a country, may be dispatched to outlets in the north, whilst near identical products are transported south.

The money system results in prodigious waste of raw materials. Since planning is alien to market economies, trading of timber, metals, petroleum products and innumerable other natural resources rushes profitably on, without regard for the consequent critical depletion of world stocks.

The trade in actual noxious wastes themselves has revived, with a vengeance, the 19th century British catchphrase 'where there's muck there's brass'. Disposal of such wastes has become very big business indeed, and the increasingly common practice of shipping them to some other country weakens any incentive for the originators to 'clean up their act'. World-wide, deaths, diseases and discomfort result from toxic industrial processes and products, which bring maximum profits under minimum controls. A 1988 report on the disposal of highly inflammable chemicals, corrosive toxins and carcinogens like polychlorinated biphenyls (PCBs) around the world pointed out that 'the dangers caused by the lack of regulations and safe disposal facilities are made worse by the shadowy nature of the trade itself. Like drug smuggling and arms dealing, dummy companies, forged documents, secret deals and the bribing of officials are commonplace'.[137]

Italy produces around 70m tonnes of waste annually but has authorised disposal facilities for only 16m tonnes p.a. As a result, the police say rubbish now approaches drugs as a criminal money-spinner, with the Mafia controlling the transport operations from executive cars having phones, two-way radios and fax machines. Astronomical profits arise from expenses of only 30 lire per kilo, as against charges of 1000 lire per kilo for ordinary waste and 7000 lire per kilo for toxic waste.[138]

Even richer pickings can be made by taking advantage of Third World countries' desperate needs for hard currency, to use them as receptacles for hazardous wastes. In keeping with the various other fields of money-grubbing, the situation has even thrown up a new breed of entrepreneurs: waste brokers. These individuals sense the prospect of huge profits by using cheap bulk shipping to dump in the Third World countries for trivial charges, compared to paying £1000 per tonne for high temperature incineration in the First World. Arrangements are even made to 'swap' less bulky waste from Third World factories for really lethal First World waste, relying on bribery, which is so widespread as to have prompted calls for execution as a penalty for it. Many millions of tonnes of toxic wastes are shipped annually to the Third World at rates of up to £5000 per tonne. In 1988 the disposal rate in West Africa was $50 per tonne as against

$1000 in Europe; Guinea-Bissau was offered $120m pa for accepting waste, a figure exceeding its annual budget.

Instead of paying $2000 per tonne to dispose of PCB waste in Europe, an Italian company persuaded a Nigerian farmer to accept 2500 tons of that lethal cocktail on his land for a 'service fee' of $100 per month, thus making a $2.5m profit.

The wasteful, ruthless, get-rich-quick philosophy of the money system was epitomized by the Brazilian company Electronorte, following their building of the Tucuri hydro-electric dam. They were so anxious to complete the contract that they did not wait to clear the forest before flooding the area, abandoning nearly 3m hardwood trees to rot underwater having first sprayed the whole area with the notorious 'agent orange' defoliant (dioxin). In doing so they mislaid several drums of the poisonous dioxin, which could easily burst under pressure from the reservoir water, which becomes the main supply for Belem, a city of over 1m people.[139] Waste is also referred to in Chapter 4.

Weapons

Every one of the millions of death-dealing devices from hand-guns to atomic weapons owes its very existence in large part to the money system. The vast profits to be made from arms manufacturing—referred to further in Chapter 7—have resulted increasingly, and worldwide, in disputes quickly deteriorating into terrible violence. As with all the other particularly evil products such as narcotic drugs, elimination of money would rid the world of the hideous deformity of weaponry, and all its horrific results.

1 A History of British Socialism, Max Beer, Spokesman
2 Looking Backward, Edward Bellamy, Penguin
3 A History of British Socialism, Beer
4 J.K. Galbraith, Observer 15/7/90
5 The Midas Touch, Anthony Sampson, Hodder and Stoughton
6 City of the Mind, Penelope Lively, Penguin
7 T Widdicombe, Guardian 18/6/90 (letter)
8 Observer 24/3/91
9 Ditto 16/6/91
10 Guardian 3/7/91
11 Ditto 14/7/91
12 Ditto 14/7/91
13 Observer 21/7/91
14 The Midas Touch, Sampson
15 A Fate worse than Debt, Susan George, Penguin
16 Guardian 16/7/91
17 Observer 21/7/91
18 The Nation 25 /2/91
19 A Fate worse than Debt, George
20 Guardian 9/7/91
21 Observer 21/7/91

22 Guardian 24/7/91
23 Ditto 29/7/91
24 New Internationalist, Oxford, June '91
25 Observer 15/7/90
26 Guardian 29/7/91
27 Ditto 31/7/91
28 Ditto 23/6/90
29 The Nation 17/6/91
30 A Fate worse than Debt, George
31 Guardian 12/12/90
32 Observer 14/7/91
33 Guardian 7/7/91
34 Ditto 2/9/91
35 Ditto 24/7/91
36 Ditto 12/7/91
37 Ditto 10/6/91
38 Ditto 19/11/90
39 Ditto 13/5/91
40 Ditto 2/10/89
41 Ditto 29/3/83
42 Ditto 28 & 29/3/83
43 Ditto 5/8/84
44 Ditto 10/7/91
45 Ditto 18/8/91
46 The Midas Touch, Sampson
47 Observer 15/9/91
48 Guardian 4/2/91
49 Observer 6/10/91
50 New Internationalist, June '91
51 Guardian 10/1/90
52 A Fate worse than Debt, George
53 The Henderson Anthology of Money, K.Weinstein, Curtis
54 The Midas Touch, Sampson
55 Guardian 3/7/91
56 'Moneywise', Readers Digest
57 Observer 28/4/91
58 Ditto 15/9/91
59 Guardian 6/3/91
60 Observer 25/8/91
61 Ditto 23/10/88
62 Guardian 25/7/91
63 Observer 1/9/91
64 Guardian 16/11/90
65 Observer 7/7/91
66 Guardian..26/4/90
67 Ditto 24/9/90
68 Ditto 2/8/90
69 Ditto 14/6/91
70 New York Times 3/4/89
71 Guardian 5/8/90
72 Ditto 13/6/91
73 Observer 7/4/91
74 Guardian 14/6/91
75 Ditto 7/3/90
76 The Nation 1/1/90
77 New Internationalist June '91
78 Guardian 1/10/91
79 New Internationalist October '91
80 Observer 7/7/91
81 Guardian 10/5/90
82 Observer 29/9/91
83 The Nation 16/9/91
84 Ditto 29/7/91

85 Observer 15/9/91
86 Ditto 25/8/91
87 The Midas Touch, Sampson
88 Observer 10/3/91
89 Guardian 9/3/90
90 Ditto 8/3/91
91 Ditto 8/3/91
92 Ditto 24/6/91
93 Ditto 25/2/91
94 Ditto 2/4/90
95 Observer 19/5/91
96 Ditto 21/4/91
97 Ditto 4/8/91
98 Ditto 25/8/91
99 Ditto 12/4/91
100 Ditto 25/8/91
101 Observer 21/4/91
102 'Inside story' BBC 8/4/91
103 Observer 4/8/91
104 Socialism & Health, Socialist Health Association, October'91
105 Observer 25/8/91
106 Ditto 7/7/91
107 Guardian 5/4/91
108 Ditto 26/3.91
109 Observer 25/8/91
110 Guardian 28/2/91
111 Ditto 1/7/91
112 Ditto 1/10/91
113 Ditto 30/9/91
114 Observer 18/8/91
115 Ditto 25/8/91
116 Ditto 4/8/91
117 Ditto 17/11/91
118 Guardian 10/7/91
119 Observer 25/2/90
120 New Internationalist July '91
121 Observer 10/11/91
122 The Nation 6/5/91
123 Guardian 11/11/91
124 The Midas Touch, Sampson
125 Observer 14/12/86
126 'How is it done', Readers Digest
127 Guardian 12/7/91
128 Observer 19/1/86
129 The Midas Touch, Sampson
130 The Nation 25/2/91
131 New Internationlist June '91
132 Guardian 10/8/91
133 Ditto 8/8/91
134 Observer 26/11/89
135 Guardian 9/7/91
136 Ditto 7/12/91
137 Ditto 15/7/88
138 Ditto 4/10/91
139 A Fate worse than Debt, George

Chapter 3

POLITICAL
ABERRATIONS

Nation states; clinging to 'sovereignty'

One of the more retrograde traditions hampering man's progress is the concept that it is normal for the world to be divided up into such an astonishing variety of independent sovereign states, which may, customarily, make war on each other to settle their disputes. In such states, citizens' natural affinities to their local cultural/economic regions are compromised by chauvinistic seduction to the 'centre' however distant it may be. As Guy de Maupassant said: 'Patriotism is the egg from which wars are hatched'. Leaders of nation states thrive on confrontations as a means of uniting many of their peoples, and distracting attention from their endemic domestic problems; witness Margaret Thatcher's flamboyant excursion to the Falklands/Malvinas, and President Bush's evident loss of direction following termination of both the Cold War and the Gulf conflict.

When asked what they used to call North America before the Europeans arrived, a Native American replied 'Ours'. Overseas empires came and went, in name at least. But, over recent centuries, local groups of populations world-wide have been dragged together into vast, unwieldy conglomerates by domineering elements, ambitious for ever more power. In Africa, some 80 different ethnic and language groups were coerced into the 45m strong Ethiopia; Lincoln welded together the independent US states, whilst Bismarck did likewise with the German provinces, and there are all too many other examples.

The most obvious, dramatic feature of the world's nation states is the bizarre variation in their sizes by population, comprising approximately,

30 with less than 1m, 120 varying from 1m to 10m, and 50 varying wildly from 10m up to the billion level. By contrast, within states, efforts are usually made to sub-divide populations into roughly equal groupings for administrative purposes. Faced with the task of setting up any organisation, can it be imagined that anyone would create a hotch-potch of departments with some being 10, 100 or even 1000 times larger than others? Little wonder that the UN, set up with such high ideals after World War Two, should have become, all but inevitably, the 'Disunited Nations'. For the UN regulation, allowing the Security Council to override all other countries, makes a mockery of its own rule of 'sovereign equality of all members'.

In some instances, not even the full Security Council, but two or three of its most powerful members, have usurped the moral authority of the UN to cloak their own particular bellicose activities. Regrettably also, by underpinning the concept of the sanctity of national sovereignty, the UN has actually done a great disservice to many unfortunate millions, by condoning 'non-interventions', when interventions could have prevented, or alleviated, tragic cases of famine and genocide.

Separatist movements

Evidence of the widespread resentment of localised cultural groups against their forcible inclusion within nation states is demonstrated by the many separatist movements across every continent. These vary from armed reactions opposing brutal repression, to peaceful pressures for various forms of regional autonomy. 1991/92 saw the onset of the breaking up of both the USSR and Yugoslavia, and the re-emergence of some of their original constituent republics. Several of these themselves however, still contain significant would-be-independent groupings. *In spite of the legitimate and understandable pressures for independence by so many minorities, the world has yet to witness any nation state agreeing willingly to subdivision— their leaderships are invariably too concerned with maintaining their own dominance.*

Since world leadership is in the hands of the major nations, whose leaders are allergic to changes which might diminish their own powers, a noticeable bias against separatist movements exists world-wide. This is exemplified by the following February 1991 report:

> The US is anxious to avoid the disintegration of Iraq, which is extremely difficult to govern at the best of times because of its disparate ethnic groups. There are many forces...Muslims, Communists, Nasserites

and Kurds…but none is able to control the country by itself. The Kurds constitute about one quarter of the country's population…but they are not Arabs and could hardly lead the rest of Iraq.[1]

But why should they, and why should all the others be 'led' by them anyway ? It is hardly surprising that the state of Iraq is 'difficult to govern' in view of its having been a totally artificial creation by the British, as recently as 1921, with scant regard for the aspirations of the various groups of tribesmen involved. Those aspirations, as of millions of others world-wide, for full regional, cultural independence remain submerged beneath the bolstering by the great powers of that particularly brutal example of national sovereignty.

Increasing erosion of frontiers

Many world citizens undoubtedly accept the existence of sovereign states simply through having grown up with them and known nothing else. In fact, as with other forms of organisation rooted only in tradition, they are totally inappropriate in today's world. John McHale comments:

> The nation state today is, at best, a laggard partner in the global community, often contributing more to the disorder than the control of world events, through clinging to its illusions of earlier physical and sovereign autonomy. In effect, though we continue to talk and act as though it were indeed possible, no single nation today, however large and powerful, can 'go it alone'. If all access to transnationally sustained networks such as postal services, telecommunications, airlines, world weather and health information and the like, were cut off, no developed nation could survive more than a few days.[2]

That nation states are anachronisms is illustrated by the ways frontiers are both breached conveniently in some circumstances, and act as irritating obstacles in others. For example, states do not hesitate to discharge toxic products into the atmosphere for dispersal over the territories of their neighbours. Businessmen do not hesitate to transmit their funds across frontiers to wherever they sense opportunities for maximum returns; there are over 600 Japanese companies in Southern California alone and UK investment in the US totals $120bn. In a unilateral decision on 3/11/89, the US Justice Department did not hesitate to decree that members of either US Forces or the FBI have the 'legal right' to arrest any drug dealer, in any country, without the consent of that country. When this astonishing ruling, to give US agents the 'right' to kidnap and forcibly abduct foreign nationals from their own countries for trial in the US, was challenged in the Supreme Court, it was endorsed by a majority of 6 to 3. The ruling so exasperated Mexico that it withdrew its co-operation with the US against drug-trafficking.

The *Guardian* report (17/6/92) continued: 'Other countries are also expected to refuse to accept what amounts to a US declaration of legal supremacy over other national jurisdictions'.

Even nations themselves, at times, attempt to rationalise their separate identities by diminishing, but not eliminating, frontiers, as exemplified by the protagonists of the European Economic Community. A glaring example of the innumerable obstacles created by state frontiers is provided by the chaos resulting from national airspace boundaries, threatening to strangle the international air transport network. An August 1991 report states:

> There are 31 different air traffic control systems in operation in Europe, using computers from 18 manufacturers with 22 independent program languages, using different designs and methodologies, leading to further incompatibilities, resulting in half having significant deficiencies and 24 percent having major deficiencies. National sovereignties are preventing the extension of radar boundaries, and there are fears that national pride will prevent governments using technology readily available in the US;...politicians view the creation of a co-ordinated European aviation authority as a threat to national sovereignty![3]

The ill-effects of nation states impinge chiefly on their ordinary citizens, who have to put up with the many resulting restrictions on their lives, including trading and exchange problems, inhibitions on travelling, and varying degrees of political repression, together with the obligation to pay taxes to maintain unnecessary armed forces. *The financial elites however, are able to adopt a more pragmatic approach to national sovereignty—they ride roughshod over it when it suits them, but expect support of all kinds, even armed, from 'their' country, if required, to protect or further their interests.* That the really powerful in the world have scant regard for nation states today is illustrated by the following quotation from George Ball, former US Secretary of State and chairman of Lehmann Brothers International. 'Working through great corporations that straddle the earth, men are able for the first time to utilise world resources with an efficiency dictated by the objective logic of profit. By contrast, the nation state is a very old-fashioned idea and badly adapted to our present complex world.'[4]

'Parliamentary democracies'— executive control

The great majority of First World countries pride themselves on being parliamentary democracies. In Third World countries, where any forms of popular representation exist, they too, usually adopt the same approach; for example, former members of the British Empire tend to favour the 'Westminster model'.

Parliaments relate to nation states and these are, in the great majority of cases, far too large to be amenable to truly democratic governance. A serious flaw in the theory of parliamentary democracy—widely recognised but rarely questioned—is that in virtually all cases real power is wielded by executives, not parliaments, resulting in whole populations of very many millions of highly educated and articulate citizens being controlled by a handful of cabinet members. This scenario naturally suits top elites admirably, for the simple reason that it is easier to influence six people than six hundred. Judging by the prominence regularly accorded to Presidents or Premiers of most nations, whether medium or vast in size, as though they truly reflected all their citizens' aspirations, it can be assumed that the plague of executive control is widespread.

A report on *Civil Liberties in Modern Britain* by Ewing and Gearty (Oxford University Press, May 1990), asserts that, despite the rhetoric of Liberalism, there has never been a true democratic culture in Britain. They point to executive (ie Prime Minister's) proposals quickly becoming law via a quiescent Parliament, without sufficient scrutiny or debate and without the possibility of subsequent challenge.[5] Speaking in the House of Commons on 17/5/91 Tony Benn MP said: 'We are always boasting that we are the mother of parliaments and that the whole world envies our system of government. But the truth is that, under the cover of a mass of ritual and tradition, this House has become a shell, concealing its political impotence against the executive under a cloak of panoply, and has surrendered, one by one, rights which earlier generations wrested so painfully from the authorities of their day.'

That the 'Westminster model' parliament represents a hollow form of democracy is illustrated by an excerpt from the memoirs of Fernando Moran, Spain's Foreign Minister from 1982-85. During an interview regarding Gibraltar with Mrs Thatcher, Senor Moran's attempt to introduce other British views on the sovereignty of the Rock came to an abrupt halt when Mrs Thatcher suddenly roared: 'They can say what they like in the House of Commons. It's not in the Commons but here [at Number Ten] that foreign policy is made.' After protests from Senor Moran there followed a pause, after which Mrs Thatcher said: 'Very well, let's make a deal. You forget everything I've said and I'll forget everything you said.'[6]

To guard him or her against serious disagreement either close at hand or countrywide, a British premier has exclusive control over the secret intelligence service MI5, with 2,300 staff and a £300m pa budget, which may not even be discussed by Parliament. A UK premier also has the support of powerful statistical and publicity departments which have become adept at 'cooking the books', so as to present figures which maximise the achievements of the executive. For example, in the late 1980s, of some 25 alterations in the presentation of statistics of unemployment, 24 showed it to be falling; of 380 vaunted new hospital projects, 80 were not due to start for 3 years and the total was further inflated by devices such as including nine separate subcontracts for the same hospital; the boasted new 17,000 odd hospital beds ignored the loss of some 20,000 already; and so on.

The domination of parliaments by executives is clearly 'not in the public interest', but even if executive powers were curtailed, twentieth century experiences world-wide have shown that parliamentary systems cannot provide genuinely popular democracies in their present contexts. A 1991 poll showed two-thirds of UK citizens dissatisfied with their political system; in the US, at least half the population is totally unconcerned with electoral politics; never voting, and ignorant even of the names of prominent politicians or the party in power. In his memoirs, ex-President Carter says: 'Knowing how confused and fragmented the system is, how intense the forces are that tend to induce ill-advised decisions, and how fallible are the leaders that serve in public office, it is almost a miracle how well our nation survives.'

A further flaw in the theory of parliamentary democracy lies in the continual emphasis placed on the 'multi-party' characteristic. The mass media portrays single-party states as, by definition, non-democratic; whereas states having two or more political parties are held automatically to be democratic. This applies even where the differences between the policies of the parties concerned are all but impossible to detect. For example, the US, self-styled leader of the 'free world' has never had a political party even pretending to represent the interests of the mass of working people, and both the Democrats and Republicans stand unashamedly for the interests of the moneyed establishment. In the UK, the loyalties of so many voters to 'their' party, regardless of policies, means that elections are largely a formality in many constituencies which are 'safe' for one party or the other, leaving real contests only in the 'marginals'.

The issue of voting systems, at the occasional elections held within parliamentary democracies when any citizen-input is involved, has been the subject of endless debate over decades. All conceivable systems from 'first past the post' to the many variations of proportional representation have been tried out in nations world-wide, but none has ever been claimed to be totally satisfactory and popular.

Even if dominating executives did not exist and parliaments were completely their own masters, and the perfect electoral voting system were to be devised, parliamentary democracy would still not represent real democracy, *because the ratio of around 100,000 citizens to one parliamentarian is clearly absurd. With very few exceptions, all modern states are vastly too large for existing forms of parliamentary representation to be democratically meaningful.* At the close of the twentieth century, the bitter proof of the failures of parliamentary democracy is the widespread rise of extreme right, even fascist movements —the very outcome which, from 1939 to 1945, countless millions died to prevent happening again.

Politicians

When asked for the cause of his relative failure as a politician, Lord Rosebery replied that he had gone into politics as a 'chivalrous adventure', and instead found himself in 'an evil-smelling bog'[7], which few will find surprising. However, the nub of his reply was that he 'had gone into politics', just as he might have chosen to go into banking or a hundred and one other careers. This underlines another fatal flaw in current world 'order', namely that, instead of being recognised as unique in that it involves the clearly impossible task of properly representing every aspiration of 100,000 fellow citizens, a career in politics is ranked no differently from any other. This serious anomaly is well illustrated by a 'Job Suggestions' leaflet issued by a UK county education service.[8] In this list of some 400 possible careers to choose from, barely credibly, 'Politician' appears between Public Relations Assistant and Air Steward/Stewardess!

Developments world-wide in recent years have strengthened the belief that the one job that should not be a job at all is being a politician. As nearly as possible, every citizen should be involved in democratic politics, which affect every minute of their lives; putting an X against the name of a total stranger every five years is a travesty. Treating politics as a job has, in most cases, had the predictable outcome that a politician's priority—as of any employee— becomes not only to retain the job but also to exploit whatever potential it may hold for his/her advancement. The urge to maximise popularity, particularly with constituents, results in politicians supporting 'quick fixes' rather than more carefully planned longer term solutions. For instance, to generate short-term employment locally, they may support developments which are potentially damaging to the environment.

Referring to two front-runners in the 1992 US presidential election campaign, Andrew Wilson said 'both are creatures of the political system that dictates they will say and do what they need in order to get elected.'[9] This indeed was borne out by President Bush himself in a TV interview: 'I am certainly going into this as a dog-eat-dog fight and I will do what I have to do to get elected.'[10] This is echoed by Bill Moyers, once Lyndon Johnson's press secretary. Describing Bush as 'the most deeply unprincipled man in American politics today' he went on to say 'I have watched him for almost 30 years and have never known him to take a stand except for political expediency.'[11]

It is perhaps in character that Bush chose Dan Quayle as his Vice-President, a man whose gaffes were so frequent and profound that a publication was founded just to record them all, known as the 'Quayle Quarterly'. Returning from a tour of Latin America, Quayle told a Congresswoman 'the only regret I had was that I didn't study Latin harder in school so I could converse with these people'.

World-wide, the care-free attitudes of 'parliamentary democracies' towards their politicians' activities is best exemplified by the financial rewards collected by the less scrupulous, normally right of centre MPs. In the UK parliament, out of 650 MPs, nearly 400 have commercial interests, either as consultants or directors, with average fees of £8,000 pa, so that with three extra 'jobs', their parliamentary salary can well be doubled. MPs' activities, promoted by the nefarious and growing lobbying 'industry' (see Chapter 2) are of course designed to benefit whoever sponsors them, certainly not the MP's constituents. Yet MPs were requested but not required to disclose to anyone what they 'earn' for promoting various interests and causes; if any embarrassing allegations were ever made, they were only investigated by fellow MPs. Little wonder that so many debates in the UK House of Commons take place before virtually empty benches.

Because of the constant ferment of financial wheeler-dealings amongst leading parliamentarians, corruption scandals keep emerging with monotonous regularity. In Toronto in September 1991, 13 prominent politicians were charged in court with everything from obstructing justice to taking bribes and peddling influence. They included one Minister, three former Ministers and a former provincial governor, all close colleagues of the Canadian premier.[12]

Japanese politics are particularly expensive, involving daily gifts by MPs to retain their constituents' support of around £50 at hospital visits, £100 at weddings and £150 at funerals. A Tokyo bribery case listed payments ranging from £3m to £49m to some 200 politicians, and at times it has been customary for established MPs to 'buy' a cabinet post for around £100,000 in cash.[13]

A group of rich business people wished, in 1945, to replace the sitting pro-Roosevelt Californian congressman with someone more to their liking, so they advertised: 'Wanted: Congressman candidate with no previous experience.' An unknown young lawyer called Richard Nixon applied, and, after a ten-minute interview, was chosen; whereupon the group's whole resources were thrown behind him. A year later he entered Congress and subsequently, with the same backing, costing over $60m, became President. Hundred of clandestine, illegal donations were made, some in expectation of future favours; a suitcase stuffed with $100 notes appeared to be a standard contribution.

The same elite business group subsequently sponsored Reagan's climb to the White House, using a different routing via the Californian Governorship, but the same promotional techniques. After his election, with astonishing disregard for that sponsorship, Reagan said: 'I'm not quite able to explain why I'm here, apart from believing it's part of God's plan for me'.

Reagan's philosophy was 'what I want to see above all else is that this country remains a country where someone can always get rich; that's the thing we have and that's the thing that must be preserved'. Of the 13 members of his cabinet, 8 were millionaires and 3 all-but millionaires. During the 1980s, 55 senior officials appointed by Reagan either resigned in disgrace, or were caught in corrupt dealings involving millions of dollars.

Little wonder that an opinion poll in the US revealed that only used-car salesmen are mistrusted more than politicians.

A senior US congressman spends 3 to 4 hours of each day fundraising for his election campaigns; if he does not raise thousands of dollars daily he is doing badly.[14] A former assistant to two US senators points out that 'any member of Congress who says donations don't influence him is lying; all of them are corrupt. The only question is the degree of corruption. Campaign money has to influence even the most incorruptible because people don't give away money for nothing.'[15]

Expenditure on propelling candidates into 31 Senate and 435 Congress seats in the US in November 1990 was $777m. Shortly after collecting $10m for his re-election fund, in May 1992, four of President Bush's leading donors and fund raisers were indicted by the federal regulatory authorities for their roles in failed Savings and Loans institutions which cost US tax-payers over $3bn. Total electoral expenses in the US were expected to exceed $1bn.[16]

That politicians and even presidents are too often only puppets of their wealthy elites is borne out forcefully by the wealthy US citizen, Frederick Townsend Martin, quoted in *Labor's Untold Story* (Boyer and Morais, New York, 1970), who said :

> It matters not one iota what political party is in power or what President holds the reins of office. We are not politicians or public thinkers; we are the rich; we own America; we got it, God knows how, but we intend to keep it if we can by throwing all the tremendous weight of our support, our influence, our money, our political connections, our purchased senators, our hungry congressmen, our public-speaking demagogues, into the scales against any legislature, any political platform, any presidential campaign that threatens the integrity of our state... The class I represent cares nothing for politics. In a single season a plutocratic leader hurled his influence and his money into the scale to elect a Republican governor on the Pacific coast and a Democratic candidate on the Atlantic coast.

Political parties

Within each 'parliamentary democracy' the existence of several political parties has become the norm; in the March 1992 elections in Thailand for example, 15 parties were vying for seats. The attraction of the possibility of power evidently outweighs the obvious difficulty of thinking up so many distinctly different policies for solving a country's problems.

To the very small extent that parliamentary representation is meaningful at all, political parties have in fact become barriers between people and parliaments, because of the virtual impossibility of a citizen representing his or her fellows unless sponsored by a party. In effect, two-tier representation results. First, each party elects its leaders by more or less fair means. They then hold conferences of such supporters as are elected and/or able to attend, who, by majority votes, create party policies. At times however, party leaders take it upon themselves to renege on these democratically arrived at policies. For example, for several successive years from 1989, the UK Labour Party Conference voted, by large majorities, for Britain's military spending to be reduced to the average level of other West European countries, and to allot the resulting £7bn pa saving to housing, health and education. However, in spite of the party's own constitution stating that two-to-one majority conference decisions must automatically become Labour policy, the leadership consistently refused to implement it.

Political parties adopt parliamentary candidates, acceptable to the leaders, who, if elected, may well remain MPs for a considerable time. Thus the average voter's chances of having his views even considered in Parliament for translation into law are problematical to say the least, depending on whether those views are in tune with the party's, with its leader's, with the MPs, and whether his favoured party wins power anyway. And that in turn, depends, to varying extents, on the financial support given. If his party's policy runs counter to the elite's, that support is likely to be severely restricted. If on the other hand, he supports the status quo, his chosen party can fare very well indeed. For instance, prior to the 1987 UK election, 333 companies paid over £4.5m into Conservative Party funds, which subsequently benefited further by £2m from a Greek shipping magnate, by £440,000 from a business man awaiting trial for theft and fraud, and by large sums from Hong Kong and Middle Eastern elites.

1 Guardian 27/2/91
2 World Facts and Trends, J McHale, Macmillan, New York 1972
3 Guardian 3/8/91
4 The Race for Riches, J Seabrook, Marshall Pickering 1988
5 Guardian 10/5/90
6 Ditto 25/10/90
7 Observer 18/11/90
8 Leaflet AC6 Shropshire Education Careers Service, Dec 1988
9 Observer 26/1/92
10 Guardian 6/1/92
11 Observer 8/9/91
12 Ditto 15/9/91
13 Ditto 26/1/92
14 Ditto 25/3/90
15 New Internationalist, July 1984
16 Guardian 14/5/92

Chapter 4

ENVIRONMENTAL CRISES

During recent centuries the world has begun to suffer a variety of assaults on its ecology, but in recent decades these have become acute. The likely results of the current terrible abuses of our planet can be compared to those which overtook the world 65m years ago when the dinosaurs vanished, except that those extinctions took place over thousands of years and these are happening at a breakneck speed. 'Just as canary deaths once alerted miners to the threat of gas underground, so the current world-wide extinction of amphibians could be a warning that rising pollution is beginning to take serious effect; today the toad, tomorrow mankind, runs the reasoning.'[1] A poll of 400 climate scientists by Greenpeace found almost half believe a 'runaway' greenhouse effect to be possible, with global warming feeding back on itself, melting the ice caps and the tundra beyond a point of no return and freeing even more carbon dioxide and methane trapped in frozen ground, further accelerating world warming. The poll also found more than 10 percent of the scientists believed the runaway scenario to be probable.[2]

In an unprecedented step, the two most prestigious scientific bodies in Britain and the US, the Royal Society and the National Academy of Sciences, issued a joint warning of the catastrophic outcomes of population growth, consumption of natural resources and destruction of the environment, stating: 'the future of our planet is in the balance, the next 30 years may be crucial.'[3] Two main reasons stand out for this traumatic threat hanging over humanity: first, the insatiable, mindless selfishness of the monied members of the First World, particularly in the US where around 3% of mankind produces nearly

127

25% of all carbon dioxide through their profligate use of cars, heating, air conditioning and the myriad other appurtenances of de-luxe living. The US Government has refused even to consider cutting carbon dioxide emissions, whereas Germany has actually put such cuts into effect. Second, that same chronic, shortsighted selfishness translates into totally distorted economic attitudes to the crisis.

For example, Maurice Strong (secretary of the UN conference on Environment and Development) has estimated that the total cost of correcting the world's environmental problems would be about $625bn pa, a mere 3% of the world's total GNP! Yet no contributions have been made, nor even appear likely. Kevin Watkins points out that, in essence, the World Bank/Gatt view is that the environment is just a mass of raw material to be processed and marketed, preferably through the international trading system, to increase GNP. In their view, all trade is, by definition, good trade and any obstacle to its expansion an unmitigated evil. However, some economists are now revealing the total inadequacy of conventional national income accounting, which records changes in wealth only when they pass through the market. In this distorting prism, a forest left standing, providing food and employment for its inhabitants and a defence against flooding and soil erosion, has no value whatever. But if it is cut down and sold as timber, the country appears to grow richer. In fact, over time, the annual market value of its edible fruits, cocoa and rubber exports would be worth six times as much per hectare as if the entire forest were felled in a single year.[4]

Of the following eight sub-headed issues, the first four are seen as being almost equally vital to mankind's survival.

Wanton destruction of forests

The great rainforests of Latin America, Africa and Asia are arguably one of the world's most precious assets. They are home to around a half of the earth's genetic heritage and provide irreplaceable resistance to global warming by generating oxygen and absorbing carbon dioxide. Yet they have been allowed to fall victims of the pernicious free market system resulting in their mindless decimation for short term gain. Apart from the destruction of around one million species of plant and animal life, in Brazil for example, the indigenous Indian population has been reduced from around 8 million to under 0.5m. Devastation results from loggers extracting only the 15 or 20 species of commercial value, and leaving 90% of the trees to rot in tangled wasteland. Replacement planting amounts, at very best, to one sapling for every 12 trees felled; natural regeneration time is estimated at 400 years. Felling removes the vital shield between tropical rains and fragile soils which results in erosion and landslides, and endangers water supplies for many millions.

George Monbiot reports that there is no ecologically sustainable timber operation in the Brazilian Amazon. The great majority do not replant at all, preferring to exploit the forests until they are exhausted, then reinvest in another industry, such as mining. Because of the haste and carelessness with which wood is removed from the forests, damage caused is out of all proportion to the amount of timber taken. When just 2% of trees are taken, over 50% of the canopy is destroyed, resulting in the forest floor becoming exposed to sunlight. After six days without rain, the leaf litter may be dry enough to burn, thus generating conditions for massive forest fires.[5]

The driving force behind all this mayhem is of course, as usual, money. The world uses 3bn cubic metres of timber annually, of which 55% is hardwood, mostly taken from the rain forests; the total value of timber trading is around $7bn pa. Polly Ghazi reports that negotiations to save the rain forests are in deadlock over the First World's refusal to provide aid for the countries concerned, who need compensation if they are to curb the loggers. Further, the 27 countries which contain 97% of the remaining rainforests, owe $630bn, half the Third World's total debt and are under tremendous pressure to sacrifice their hardwoods to satisfy Western bankers. This deplorable scenario is even being underpinned by the World Bank itself, which is planning to fund logging operations in the world's second largest rainforest, making a mockery of its 'green' forestry policy. The UN lending institution pledged in 1991 not to finance commercial logging in the vanishing jungles 'under any circumstances'. But confidential internal documents reveal that the bank has been offering loans to the Congo, which owes huge debts to the West, to boost its foreign earnings through an increase in timber exports. [6]

Beside the plunder of mahogany and other hardwoods, other forms of forest felling take place. First, vast areas are cleared to make way for crops or livestock—mostly cattle to satisfy the popular demand for beefburgers. In the process, half a million tons of good timber annually are lost simply by burning. After clearance, the soil may support cattle for up to a maximum of ten years, but soon becomes eroded, dusty and invaded by uncontrollable weeds; thus enormous areas become unuseable and worthless. Second, around 12% of all timber felled is used to cure tobacco. Third, of all timber felled worldwide, including soft woods, half is used as fuel, the great majority for cooking in the Third World, where approximately one ton pa per person is used, and supplies are fast running out.

The total area of rainforests has been decimated to around one-sixth of the earth's surface, from about one-quarter before mega-scale logging began, and an area bigger than Scotland is still being destroyed each year. Clearly there is a desperate need to pressure those First World elites who are well able to put a stop to this devastating destruction. If it is allowed to continue at the present rate, then it is estimated that by the year 2000, Malaysia, Nigeria, the Ivory Coast and Central America will be stripped bare, *that by 2020 total destruction of Brazilian rainforests will be complete, and that by 2025 all accessible forests throughout the Third World will be extinct.*

World-wide soil erosion

A nihilist might argue that mankind could manage without rainforests, but man could definitely not exist without topsoil, the most basic resource of all, being vital for food production. Yet the world now faces the appalling threat of the near extinction of top soil by roughly the same doomsday as the forests, 2025, unless steps are taken to reverse current trends. The 1984 Worldwatch Report pointed out that, unlike earthquakes, eruptions or other natural disasters, this man-made disaster is unfolding quietly but persistently, and concluded 'what is at stake is not merely the degradation of the soil, but the degradation of life itself.' That that is no exaggeration, but the terrible truth is underlined by the fact that nature requires 100 to 400 years to regenerate one centimetre of top-soil, or 3000 years to renew a spade's depth.

Topsoil is carried away by both wind and water, both hazards having been seriously magnified by man's interferences with the natural covering and binding properties of trees, shrubs and grasses. Without trees, a single tropical rain storm can strip 75 tons of precious soil from one acre. But men have also been guilty of what amounts to rape of the earth, by turning away from well-tried husbandry to large-scale, intensive, monocrop agriculture, spurred on by various financial inducements such as market upturns or subsidies, and pressured by salesmen of machinery, fertilisers and pesticides. In 1988, Worldwatch President Lester Brown presented a strategic report on the state of world farming, pointing out that increases in food outputs had ground to a halt largely because of soil erosion.

Following the doubling of grain prices in the early 1970s, US farmers expanded grain areas by nearly 25%, by ploughing millions of highly erodible acres, resulting in the loss of six tons of topsoil for every ton of grain produced. World wide, farmers were losing around 24bn tons of top soil yearly, roughly the amount covering all the wheatlands of Australia.[7]

Throughout North America and Europe in particular, intensive farming has resulted in a 7% depletion of world topsoil each decade. In the US alone, some 3bn tons of soil are lost annually and an area of farmland twice the size of California has been ruined. One third of India's farmland has been lost through erosion, water-logging or salinity, and another third degraded due chiefly to deforestation. Apart from it stealing away the nutritious top soil, the additional curse of erosion is that the displaced earth inevitably finishes up at the lowest points, silting up irrigation ditches, canals, estuaries, harbours and reservoirs. For example, sedimentation has halved the useful life of the Ambuk Lao dam in the Philippines, restricted entry for larger ships into the Panama Canal and impaired hydro-electric power output in many instances.

In its final, all-but irreversible form, soil erosion becomes desertification. Africa is particularly badly affected, having poor soil to start with, erosion rates have increased twenty-fold over recent decades and one quarter of the continent suffers moderate to severe desertification. Annually, world-wide, an area of originally productive land equivalent to the size of Ireland, is said to become desert. *At a time when 50% of humanity is either starving or malnourished, over half the earth's land is believed to be in possible danger.*

Fertility of soil depends not only on rainfall, but also on microbes within it, which are lost when topsoil disappears owing to excessive ploughing or stocking of herds. Thus begins the desertification process, which is already affecting China, central Asia, and about 10% of all US land, besides Africa.

Desertification already affects a quarter of the earth's land surface and puts well over one billion people at risk. The *Guardian* (10/6/92) reported that an inter-governmental panel of 300 scientists at the Rio de Janeiro conference concluded that, as the result of climatic changes, 'the Sahara desert could extend across the Mediterranean to Spain, Sicily and Greece and encompass the Middle East'.

In his excellent *Dictionary of Environment and Development*, Andy Crump provides invaluable data on this and other issues touched on in this chapter.[8]

Climatic horrors

Those in command of the world, notably US Presidential entourages, have a notorious capacity for ignoring scientific warnings. Perhaps they think, if they think about it at all, that if crops requiring soil become extinct, then mankind could subsist on fish. But food of any kind is superfluous if the world's atmosphere is inimical to life. Not surprisingly, calculations and forecasts about the exact extent of climatic changes and their effects continue to fluctuate, but what is never in doubt is the terrible reality of terminal dangers to humanity, even within many existing lifetimes. Over the last two centuries or more, world-wide, man has been pouring poisons with total abandon into the air, the rivers and the earth, for the same old familiar reason—cheapness. Because of the throttle-grip that the money culture has on humanity, it has been almost universally accepted that it is 'too expensive' to curb pollution.

For quantitative scientific details of atmospheric pollutants it is necessary to refer to sources such as the *Dictionary*[8] already mentioned. The three main horror groups, all susceptible to human restraints are: 1) Carbon Dioxide, from fossil fuel emissions by generating station and factory chimneys, now nearing double the concentration of the 19th century. 2) CFCs, from Aerosol sprays, refrigerators and air conditioners (less in quantity but 20,000 times more damaging). 3) Carbon and Nitrous Oxides, from rockets, super- and sub-sonic planes, lorries and, above all, continually increasing numbers of cars which are responsible for 20% of CO_2 emissions, 40% of acid rain and 90% of airborne lead. Car engines, capable of 80 m.p.h., spend many, many hours pouring out exhaust gases in city traffic jams world-wide, averaging 10 mph, a leisurely cycling pace. These various pollutants have already seriously damaged our atmospheric environment in two main ways: First, they have created an invisible 'ceiling' over the earth which prevents cooling and thus creates the 'greenhouse effect'; this is forecast to produce average world temperature increases of 1 degree centigrade by 2030 and 3 degrees centigrade by 2070, resulting in the hottest conditions ever known. Second, they have punctured the 'ozone layer', a shield some 15 to 30 km above us which protects earth against ultra-violet radiation from the sun; each flight by the US space shuttle destroys 10 tons of ozone and 300 more flights would destroy the entire protective shield.

Although both earth and skies have shown incredible resilience, they have clearly been grossly overloaded, possibly beyond their point of no return. For example, for many years observations of the ozone layer over Antartica showed no changes, then suddenly a threshold was reached and it snapped. A disastrous 20% rupturing of the ozone layer occurred also, for the first time, over Northern Europe in early 1992, as reported in the *Guardian* (8/4/92), leading to a 40% increase in ultraviolet radiation.

Dr Farman reports that 'the atmosphere is in such a sensitive, critical condition that it will not take much to cause catastrophic damage.'⁹ Those air-borne pollutants which do not reach as high as the ozone layer, also wreak terrible havoc world-wide as 'acid rain', by poisoning forests, lakes, and flora and fauna generally.

The most potentially deadly outcome of the 'greenhouse effect' is the inevitable rise in the level of the oceans due to thermal expansion and the melting of polar and glacial ice following quite modest temperature rises. Estimates of possible sea rises have gone as high as 4 metres by 2100, *but even a 1m rise would inundate one quarter of Egypt, one third of Bangladesh and make 300m homeless; up to 60% of the world's population could be at risk.* Polly Ghazi reports on research at the US University of Maryland, pinpointing Alexandria, Shanghai, Bangkok, Hong Kong, Tokyo and Rio de Janeiro as being at high risk of submersion. They warn that for several cities, subsidence caused by coastal development and the draining of underground water supplies are likely to more than double the effects of predicted sea level rises from increasing temperatures alone. These nightmare scenarios are certain to be exacerbated by the increasing numbers of typhoons, cyclones, hurricanes and floods which have already, in the 1990s, increased sixfold over the 1980s, according to the Worldwatch Institute.

Both the direct and indirect effects of atmospheric pollution on human health are already horrendous and will inevitably worsen. Millions of lives will be at stake from ultra-violet radiation, including 200,000 deaths expected in the next 50 years in the US alone. In Chile, skin cancers never seen before illustrate the grim reality that Third World countries, too, are inevitably going to suffer from sins committed almost exclusively by the First World. A February 1992 report from the UN predicts that damage already done to the ozone layer will cause 300,000 more skin cancers world-wide. It also suggests, for the first time, that ozone decay may help the spread of the Aids virus by damaging human immune systems, as well as causing massive damage to agriculture and fisheries.[11]

Over 20% of the world's population are already breathing air which is so polluted that it breaches internationally accepted safety limits. City conditions are naturally worst; breathing in Athens, Mexico City, London, Madrid or Bombay has been compared to smoking ten cigarettes daily. Poison-laden air is estimated to cause 50,000 deaths and cost $40bn in health care and lost output annually in the US. The UK has seen a startling increase in asthma, which has risen to 1 in 7 children, the most vulnerable section of the population. At the University of South California, scientists performed autopsies on 100 youths who had died as a result of violence, accident or other non-medical causes.

Their discovery was shocking: 80% had 'notable abnormality in lung tissue', 27% had 'severe lesions'. The pathologist concerned, Dr Sherwin, said the youths were 'running out of lung'. In fact, by the age of ten, thousands of Los Angeles children have already suffered permanent lung damage. Of Los Angeles' airborne toxins, 14% are carcinogenic, 27% destroy reproduction ability, 11% cause acute disorders (many fatal) and 48% cause chronic disorders. Without improvements, air quality is projected to lead to 100,000 deaths pa in Los Angeles alone.[12]

An indication of the desperate gravity of the situation is provided by a February 1992 warning from leading scientist, Professor Schneider, who said that 'risky, impractical and unethical schemes' to interfere with the earth's atmosphere might be needed to counter global warming if carbon dioxide pollution is not stopped very soon. He confessed to having taken part in studies of 'Jules Verne-like' schemes he would rather have ridiculed, intended as 'quick-fixes' to cool the planet. These included 50,000 100-kilometre mirrors in space, choking the stratosphere with soot from deliberately inefficient aircraft engines, using lasers to break up chlorofluorocarbons in the atmosphere, and dumping iron filings in the oceans to stimulate the growth of plankton which absorbs carbon dioxide.[13]

If any such, or similar measures ever had to be adopted as a desperate last resort, at least their incalculable, astronomical costs would bring it home to all concerned how much more preferable it would have been to have prevented the emissions in the first place.

Techniques do exist, for example, for alternatives to CFCs and for minimising chimney emissions of CO_2 by using 'scrubbers'.

Hitherto, First World countries have been extremely slow to introduce them themselves, and have also quibbled about paying into a fund to promote ozone-friendly technology in the Third World. For example, the US Government reluctantly agreed to contribute $20m, which represents a mere 2% of the $1bn revenue it had received in taxes levied on chemicals involved in pollution.[8] The extraordinary extent to which the money system has distorted priorities worldwide, is illustrated by the proposal tabled by some Third World countries for 'tradeable emissions'.[14] Their need for finance is so desperate that the proposal, in effect, condones the continuation of pollution by suggesting that those in the First World who 'over-pollute' should pay compensation to those who, pro rata, 'under- pollute', instead of insisting that all avoidable pollution, everywhere, be stopped. For example, in early 1992, 'environmental pricing' has led to countries with vast forest areas, such as Brazil and Indonesia, demanding payments for 'carbon absorption services'.[4]

Water crises

Men and women may survive for weeks without food, but without water, the metabolism falters in hours, and minds and bodies collapse. Humans need about 5 litres per day to survive, and about 80 litres per day for tolerable lives. Currently, daily personal consumption varies from 5 litres in the poorest parts of the Third World to 500 litres in the US. Globally, water use proportions are approximately 70% agricultural, 20% industrial and 10% domestic, with ever-increasing demands from the first two sectors pressuring the third. Approximately 2bn people lack adequate, permanent and pure water supplies, and 3bn lack sanitation completely. The situation is particularly acute in rural areas, and at least ten African countries face virtually total water loss by the year 2000. Third World city-dwellers commonly need to spend from 10% to 50% of their incomes buying water. One hospital bed out of four is occupied by patients suffering from water poisoning, which accounts for 10m deaths annually. Meanwhile, in the First World, 100,000 gallons are used to produce a car, 1,000 gallons to produce one pound of beef, and each household flushes 100 gallons to waste daily.

A significant proportion of demand is met from groundwater, but supplies worldwide are being exhausted at very alarming rates. For example, in India, the water table has dropped 30 metres over the last decade; in China, 50 cities face acute shortages with the Beijing water table dropping 1 to 2 metres pa and one third of the city's wells already dry; in Mexico City pumping exceeds natural re-charge by 40%. Further, groundwater is being increasingly poisoned by industrial, agricultural and sewage pollutants which sink through inexorably and are extremely difficult to purify out.

Most of the balance of water demand is met from rivers, and again, horrendous problems are involved. First, chiefly because of massive de-forestation, river flows have become erratic, resulting in flooding, silt-ing, and sedimentation which seriously deplete supplies for humans, crops and livestock.

Second, weakened rivers need to supply vastly increased popula-tions; for example, the Ganges must now support over 500m people, as against 200m in 1950. Third, nationalism rears its ugly head again, because, as some 200 great rivers are shared by two or more countries, so anarchy will inevitably result in many regions, as people divert water for their own use. Supplies taken from the Ganges, Brahmapu-tra, Euphrates and Zambesi have already caused serious conflicts. Egypt's 55m people depend entirely on agriculture irrigated by the Nile which is being increasingly depleted by Ethiopia, where it originates. In 1985 Egyptian foreign minister Ghali forecast that 'the next war in our region will be over the waters of the Nile'.[15]

Since the lion's share of the world's water is used for agriculture, it is critically important that irrigation should be efficient. In many parts of the world, care of the land has not been improved by the introduction of 'Western' methods, as, for instance, the magnificent irrigation systems of the Incas, in South America, were rejected by the incoming Spaniards. Of the world's 1.5bn hectares of cropland, about 250m (one-sixth) are irrigated, but 500m (one-third) could be. Around 35% of all water drawn off for irrigation is wasted in storage or distribution. Further, bad design and poor management result in large areas of irrigated land becoming waterlogged or excessively salinised. Again, use commonly exceeds supplies; for example, in the US 20% of all water withdrawals for irrigation are in excess of aquifer re-charge.

Finally, for better, or more usually for worse, rivers mean dams. In keeping, regrettably, with so many ill-conceived progeny of the money system, huge dams have been built worldwide, far too impulsively, before their full impact could be assessed. Their construction has stemmed from pressures from the big banks to invest their surpluses, from governments and investors expecting massive returns and prestige, and from civil engineering firms and foreign suppliers, anxious for the lucrative contracts involved. In the early 1980s, hydro-electric projects sponsored by the World Bank resulted in the uprooting of nearly 500,000 people, often left to themselves without compensation.[16] An October 1991 report states that some 300 dams over 15 metres high, are completed every year, and of dams 50 metres high or higher, the truly big ones, 70 are under construction, and some 85 are planned. The World Bank, the largest single international funding source for dams, is behind 25% of the biggest dams, but even the smallest projects pit the people affected against some of the world's most powerful funding institutions.[17]

The same report describes the severe ecological and other problems caused by the indiscriminate spawning of these huge structures.

Water impounded in reservoirs does more than flood productive and sensitive lands; by pressing down heavily on those lands, it can create seismic hazards. And, slowed in its passage, it stagnates, breeds algae and interacts with submerged vegetation and soils to produce toxins that infect the food chain. Subsurface decomposition of plants also releases copious amounts of greenhouse gases. And slowed river flow drops silt into permanent tottering waterfalls: the muddier the river, the sooner the dam is disabled. Acidification and algae growth corrode and foul both dams and turbines and then move on to damage fisheries, estuaries and deltas.

In spite of the now well-understood dangers, disadvantages and inevitable displacements of hundreds of thousands of powerless people, dam projects continue world-wide. In Brazil, the first Carajas project, which has involved the destruction by deforesting and flooding of an immense area in order to supply Europe with cheap iron ore, has been described as 'one of the greatest man-made ecological disasters this century'. Not to be outdone, the even bigger 'Grande Carajas' project is costing over $62bn, covers an area of 900,000 sq km and flooded an area equivalent to that of Europe.[18] In India, the Narmada project would be the biggest ever, involving 30 major, 135 medium and 3,000 lesser dams, displace one million people and submerge 2,000 square kms of fertile land and 1,500 square kms of forest. Hundreds of small, local irrigation schemes could achieve the same objectives with minimum disturbance, while the mega-project will enable the rich farmers to intensify cash-crop production while impoverishing the up-stream farmers, who will get less water than ever. In China, a proposal to inundate the world-famous 'Three Gorges' of the Yangtze at a cost of £6bn and displacing one million people is arousing heated controversy.

Misused resources

World consumption of natural resources continues to be profligate in the extreme. So long as profit is to be gained from extraction or use, consumption careers on as if there were no tomorrow. The US, for example, has already used up more minerals and fossil fuels during the past 50 years than all the rest of humanity since history began. On average, every single US citizen personally owns over 10 tons of steel in cars or households. Oil is arguably the world's most precious resource since it currently provides for 40% of all energy. It is estimated that at the present, increasing, rates of consumption, known oil reserves will be exhausted by around 2030, yet it is unusual to hear even a mention of this potentially catastrophic event.

Transport accounts for one-third of all energy used, most of it in the world's 400 million cars which pump 25bn tons of pollutants into the air, and kill one-quarter of a million people annually. In the US alone, road transport vehicles annually consume 20m tons of steel, 2m tons of rubber, 1m tons of plastics and paints, half a million tons of glass, half a million tons of lead and nearly one quarter of a million tons of copper. Just one motorway interchange uses 25,000 tons of steel and

250,000 tons of concrete. Traffic jams involving huge fuel losses cost £10bn pa in London alone; at any one time in the US around 2m horse-power is idling at traffic lights.

Sending goods by road rather than rail uses vastly more fuel and results in 25 times more accidents; roads occupy three times more land than railways. In 1929 there were 20,000 trains in the US making daily intercity runs; in 1990 there were barely 200. Killington, Vermont in the US boasts the world's largest artificial snow system, using water pumps and compressors; to cover its ski runs it uses 20,000 kilowatts of electricity, or considerably more than the energy used to heat and light the entire town in the valley below.[20] World-wide, paper consumption represents a further drastic waste of natural resources; US demand for newsprint amounts to 6m tons and the felling of around 3,000 square miles of forest annually. Weight for weight, a US citizen's demand for paper uses as much timber as a Third World person's firewood.

Flora and fauna losses

At least 140 plant and animal species are being exterminated daily throughout the world; one in ten in every species could disappear in fifty years. Tropical forests contain over 80,000 edible plants, none of them as yet cultivated. At present, just 16 plants provide 90% of the world's food, and any one of those 80,000 might provide much needed substitutes. Also, the forests contain untold numbers of medicinal species and others with potential industrial applications. At the present rate of destruction, 10% of the 250,000 flowering plants will be extinct by 2000.

A 1991 report tells us that scientists have discovered that from Brazil to Australia, and from Europe to the Rocky Mountains, millions of frogs and toads are vanishing. Animals that have been around since the dinosaur era are now threatened with extinction or already have become extinct. Apart from the risk of losing dozens of precious amphibian species, their demise could also be the first sign of a wider, more pernicious ecological threat to the globe. In the past three years, in the UK, the populations of the common frog have plummetted to below 30% of their former levels. *Dr Mary Swan, amphibian expert, explained: 'Frogs are not in fact sensitive indicators of environmental problems, they are insensitive ones, being quite hardy. If they are suffering, and they are, something very serious is happening to our environment.*[21]

In the run-up to the Rio conference, the *Guardian* (6/6/92) provided some basic 'biodiversity' statistics. In the decades ahead, species are likely to become extinct at an accelerating rate; only about 1.8m have been described and named, yet there may be from 8m to 80m altogether and half of them could have disappeared before we even knew of their existence. By 2000, one million animals and plants are expected to be extinct, and by 2050 half of all species alive today could be lost forever.

The loss of one plant species can cause the loss of 30 animal and insect species that depend on it. Only about 1% of all the world's plants have so far been assessed for their medicinal potential. An indication of the wonderful possibilities of that potential is provided by two examples: a chemical extracted from the skin of an Ecuadorian frog proved to be 200 times more powerful than morphine as a painkiller, and the Madagascan rosy periwinkle was found to provide two different anti-cancer drugs.

Numerous 'non-governmental' bodies world-wide, supported only by donations, such as Greenpeace and the Worldwide Fund for Nature, struggle to stave off these and all the other environmental crises mentioned in this chapter. The only official body concerned is the Convention on International Trade in Endangered Species of Wild Flora and Fauna (CITES). Although 112 governments have signed the convention, fewer than 30% of them have legislation which would give protection to endangered animals and plants. The convention either bans or severely restricts trade in no less than 2,500 animal and 35,000 plant species. Yet world wildlife trade is worth $5bn pa and CITES has a secretariat of a mere 10 staff to monitor it.

Concrete jungles

The physical development of built environments around the globe during the 20th century has been, with some honourable exceptions, a catastrophic disgrace to humanity. Passing through towns and cities in both First and Third Worlds, it is difficult to believe that such widespread ugliness can co-exist with the great architectural heritage models to be found the world over. The disastrous situation has been compounded by several factors: *private ownership of land has inhibited controls, developments have too often been motivated by profit-seeking, and the unregulated whirlwind pace of building has been too fast for the planners to gather breath, assuming that they or any plans existed at all.* In the Third World particularly, failure to maintain vitality in rural areas has led to dramatic demographic changes: in Peru, for example, the ratio of 70% rural to 30% urban population in 1940 had been reversed by 1980. By 2000 it is expected there will be over 60 cities with populations exceeding 4m. Annually, over 10,000 square kms of prime agricultural land is being lost to development. World-wide, roads and other car demands have become major land users; in the US as a whole nearly half of all urban areas are occupied by roads or parking spaces and in Los Angeles it is two-thirds.

A further negative feature of so much of 20th century developments is that reinforced concrete is so terribly permanent; at least unsatisfactory brick buildings could always be readily demolished. However, when eventually Third World families can be offered proper housing, demolition of their existing dwellings, if any, will present no problems. The anarchic nature of Third World settlements is highlighted by the fact that one-third of all shelter—inevitably lightweight and shoddy—is put up illegally on seized sites, and around 50% of rural and up to 80% of urban families have just one room. In cities such as Bombay, up to half a million people are born, live and die on the pavements without ever seeing the inside of a dwelling. Multi-storey blocks and highways give an impression of sophistication to many Third World cities, but within their infrastructure there is a woeful lack of drainage systems; three-quarters of Third World populations have no sanitation. In Mexico City, where 60% of the inhabitants live in illegal shanty areas, three million people lack sanitation and pollution kills 1,000 people daily.

The earth's integrity is not only being violated by the very obvious concrete jungles. Increasingly today, First Worlders, with money to spare and the itch for travel and sport, are leaving their marks world-wide in hitherto totally unspoilt rural and mountainous areas. In the Alps, fast becoming one of the world's foremost ecological disaster areas, farmers are abandoning their fields, and landslides and avalanches are increasing under the impact of 50 million tourists each year.

For the winter Olympic Games in 1992, massive environmental damage was done, amongst other things, by carving an artificial 'piste' in a mountainside, and building a ski jump in unnecessarily massive, inevitably permanent reinforced concrete, when a lightweight removable steel structure would have served perfectly well.[23] Similar reports of depredations of the natural world by tourists, propelled by the ever profit-hungry travel agencies, are heard from West to East and from the Himalayas to the Antartic.

Toxic and other wastes

Up to the 20th century, waste disposal was never a major problem because nature looked after the residues of natural products. But in the 1930s, scientists discovered synthetic alternatives to natural products which were cheaper and more convenient for production processes, and thus their output increased at breakneck pace, so that there are now over 60,000 of these artificial compounds worldwide. Because of the distorted values of the money system decreeing that initial cheapness is the only criterion, little if any thought was given to the Frankenstein being created in terms of the problems of disposal of the innumerable resulting toxic wastes, already amounting to over 400m tonnes pa worldwide, and increasing.

Naturally, these poisonous wastes originate almost exclusively from industries in the First World, where their dumping is highly unpopular, so instinctive reactions turn to offloading them onto the unsuspecting Third World. Thus the US, Germany, Holland, Switzerland and Scandinavia are now exporting millions of tonnes a year of hazardous wastes to countries with weak laws or administrations that are unable to monitor or tell the difference between raw materials and toxic waste. Further, they are ill-equipped to handle the waste safely, leading to long-term health and ecological problems, so that the whole process can only be described accurately as 'waste colonialism'.

The whole disreputable, high-handed process of taking advantage of Third World countries in this way has received the blessing of the World Bank. A report in March 1992 tells us World Bank Vice-President and chief economist Lawrence Summers said 'I think the economic logic behind dumping a load of toxic waste in the lowest wage country is impeccable'. A Harvard econocrat, Summers believes religiously that money is the final measure of value, that happiness is a growing GNP, that legal issues can be solved as competing economic claims, and ethical decisions can be translated into dollar terms, with the cheaper alternative always preferred. He was applying 'cost-benefit analysis' which measures human life by the stream of wages remaining to it. Summers continued 'health-impairing pollution should be done in the country with the lowest wages...if a pollutant is likely to cause prostate cancer, a disease of old age, why not dump in countries where people aren't likely to live long enough to get it?'. Following the inadvertent leaking of Summers' frank opinions, he offered to resign. The report continues:

> It makes no sense for him to resign; he expressed his bank's logic perfectly. It's a bank and acts like one. It may preside over a steady erosion of Third World incomes relative to First World ones, but it makes big money. Last year, after paying $7bn in interest and fees to investors and bankers, the World Bank had a $1.2bn surplus and a rate of return that commercial banks would envy.[25]

The disposal of ordinary waste in chiefly First World, 'throw away' societies has also become a major problem impinging on natural environments. It has been estimated that an urban population of one million produces around 5,000 cubic feet of refuse in one day. In the US even in the 1970s, for example, household wastes amounted to about 200m tons annually, which, combined with industrial, commercial and agricultural wastes, totalled 3.5bn tons of paper, 48m cans and 26,000 bottles.[26]

Many US authorities already spend more on rubbish disposal than all other municipal services combined. New York's possibly last landfill site extends to 3,000 acres and refuse will build up to 500 feet high; many NY districts are paying $100 per ton for carting rubbish several hundred miles away. Mention was made in Chapter 2 of the money being made out of waste disposal. Also, as long as the money system encourages profit-making from the manufacture of bottles, cans, packagings and so on, the incentive to promote 're-use', rather than 'throwaway' will be blunted. 'Re-cycling' of various containers is preferable to nothing, but in fact is an alibi for inefficient distribution and inevitably consumes energy.

Nuclear madness

No modern industry has proved more difficult to control than nuclear power. It began in secrecy, in the arms race that eventually lumbered the world with 50,000 nuclear warheads.

Civil nuclear power to generate electricity only developed later, but in close parallel with the military programmes.

Secrecy, inadequate accountability, distorted industrial priorities, profligate research, a misguided eagerness to reprocess reactor fuel that created a world surplus of plutonium, complacency about the resulting radioactive waste; they were all characteristics of the first three decades of civil nuclear power and they can all be traced back to the mentality of the bomb-makers.[27]

The threat of further diabolical disasters involving severe radioactive contamination of millions more human beings and their environments will persist until both nuclear installations and weapons have been de-commissioned world-wide, and all wastes successfully neutralised. A start has been made on destroying some of the vast stockpiles held by the major powers, but they show scant signs of abandoning

nuclear weapons altogether and their proliferation among smaller countries continues alarmingly. In spite of the proven risks of nuclear power
stations, whether caused by bad design, accident, sabotage or being
targetted during warfare, ambivalence towards nuclear energy persists.
In the US, the terror caused by the near melt-down at Three Mile
Island was sufficient to put a stop to all further nuclear power projects.
By contrast, the actual, appalling disaster at Chernobyl has hardly affected proliferation of nuclear generation elsewhere.

In common with all nuclear explosions, the terrible effects of the
1986 Chernobyl disaster will persist for years and years. To date, it
has already caused around 10,000 deaths, 50,000 radiation sickness
cases, and the need to monitor a further 340,000 people. The death
rate is still rising, from cancer, asthma and diseases of the heart and
blood vessels. The reproductive rate is falling and 2.2% of babies are
deformed at birth. Half a million people had to be evacuated from an
area of 1,000 square miles. Chernobyl's cloud passed over most of
Europe and dispersed over the whole northern hemisphere. The overall toll of suffering through illness, worry, abnormality and disruption
of life and livelihood is beyond estimation.[28]

*The nuclear energy saga should be a stern warning to mankind of the dire
need to think through impetuous new ideas thoroughly before applying them.*
The originators of nuclear power, falling over themselves to satisfy
First World greed for energy, announced that their electricity would
be 'too cheap to meter'.

A few years later, construction and other costs were soaring from
estimated millions to billions, and, after 'useful lives' of only 30 years,
reactors are proving all-but impossible to de-commission. Seventeen
US nuclear plants are so radioactive that estimates for closing them
down amount to around $150bn.

In 1987, Lord Marshall, chairman of the UK Generating Board
who had for long ardently promoted nuclear energy, admitted that it
was not, and never had been economic in comparison with other
sources of electric power.[29] The routine waste products from nuclear
generation remain radio-active for at least 25,000 years, and, to date,
no totally fail-safe method of disposing of it has been developed which
would guarantee it never entered water courses, nor the sea or land to
poison the food chain.

The inevitable by-product of nuclear generation, plutonium, remains one of the deadliest known substances for half a million years;
the 'tailings' from the original uranium mining operations will continue
to emit deadly radon even after the sun has burned out. Nuclear plant
explosions, fires, leaks and 'normal', apparently uncontrollable wastage

of 2% to the ecosphere have already lodged some plutonium in every human body on earth. Because of the 20 to 30 years time lag in cancers manifesting themselves, the true horrors of what may be termed 'less direct' radiation are now evidenced by the plight of the US and UK servicemen who attended the early nuclear tests, as distinct from the direct effects on the tragic thousands still dying following the agonies of Hiroshima and Nagasaki.

1 Observer 15/9/91
2 Guardian 10/2/92
3 Ditto 27/2/92
4 Ditto 6/3/92
5 Ditto 3/5/91
6 Observer 25/8/91, 26/1/92
7 Guardian 15/7/88
8 Dictionary of Environment and Development, A Crump, Earthscan 1991
9 Observer 21/7/91
10 Ditto 29/3/92
11 Ditto 9/2/92
12 The Nation 17/9/90
13 Guardian 10/2/92
14 New Internationalist, April 1992
15 Guardian 14/8/87
16 A Fate worse than Debt, S George
17 The Nation 21/10/91
18 Guardian 6/12/91
19 Ditto 4/4/92
20 Ditto 20/12/89
21 Observer 15/9/91
22 Guardian 2/3/92
23 Observer 9/2/92
24 Guardian 14/2/92
25 The Nation 2/3/92
26 World Facts and Trends, J McHale
27 Guardian 24/4/92
28 G. Hutchinson, British Peace Assembly News, Winter 1992
29 Guardian 14/10/87

Chapter 5

POPULATION EXPLOSIONS

We have seen, in Chapter 4, that the pathologically selfish First World elites currently controlling humanity consistently ignore unmistakeable warnings of total environmental collapse around one quarter way into the twenty-first century. By insisting on debt repayments, and failing to provide economic support to Third World peoples, those same ruthless attitudes have perpetuated the population explosions, which have been proven to result from the pressures on poorer groups to have large families. And in turn, population explosions exacerbate the various environmental crises. Population increases are naturally high in poor countries where children are seen as the most obvious insurance for parents as they grow older, particularly in the context of infant mortality approaching 4m pa, and where literacy levels are so low as to drastically hinder introduction of birth control programmes. Although average numbers of children born to each mother are falling, this is offset by the surge in fertility caused by nearly 40 percent of world population being under 15; the median age for all Africa is just 17 years. China's one child-per-family programme has failed, thus 120m more children than desired are expected by 2000.

That birth rates are inextricably related to living standards is illustrated by the World Bank's Table of Demographic Indicators, which shows a remarkable correlation between statistics for Deaths and Births. In country after country, a fall in the death rate has been followed by a fall in birth rates, on average to double the extent of the former. World population increased from 2.5bn in 1950 to 5.3bn in 1990, and is, at present rates of increases of around 100m pa, expected to reach over 6bn by 2000 and 8bn by 2025. However, even these totals would be exceeded unless the current birth rate of 3.9 children per mother is reduced to 2.1 by 2010.

The bloated mega-cities

Over half the world's population is already urban; by 2000, 75% of First World, and nearly 50% of Third World citizens will be living in cities. Impelled by deteriorating rural conditions, and slender hopes of better prospects, urban populations tripled from 700m to 2,100m between 1950 and 1990. City numbers rose, on average, by 2.5% pa, over 3% in poorer countries and by 4.8% pa in Africa. In Latin America, for example, only a bare 20% of people remain in the country areas; Lima's population of 175,000 in 1920 is now 3m and rising by 1,000 daily. By 2000, it is forecast there will be one hundred cities having over 2m inhabitants, sixty with over 4m, and twenty with over 10m, including Mexico City with over 25m.

Particularly in Third World cities, this human stampede has, not surprisingly, overwhelmed such essential urban infrastructures as water supply, drainage, communications and social services as may have already existed. Millions have shown incredible courage, initiative and ingenuity in creating their new living areas out of nothing: makeshift appendages to the parent cities, which can offer little except possibilities of scraping a living in increasingly polluted, often earthquake-prone zones. In the context of the huge numbers flooding in, it has even been forecast, if circumstances do not improve, that in some cities, particularly because of water supply and drainage problems, the inhabitants could die as fast as they are replaced from without.

An indication of how realistic that terrible prognosis may be, is provided by this report from Victoria Brittain, describing Kebelle 41, a district of Addis Ababa where 30,000 people share living space averaging 1 sq metre per person:

> The children walk in shit, play in shit and wash in shit; the pathways are tiny and crowded with children paddling in shit; the communal lavatories are open holes in the ground which flood during the rainy season shifting tons of shit through the tiny wooden shacks surrounding them. I met one lady who lives in a 10 foot square hut, which had fallen to an angle of 45 degrees; she has no bed, just a box on which she sleeps, sitting up, at night.
>
> There is a latrine on the hill above her which tips its waste daily into her home, and a latrine in front of her which stinks; she has lived there

for ten years. Another house had an indoor toilet; it was in the kitchen. The house is 15 square metres in size and three families live in its two rooms, sharing the same facilities. The people living at the back of the toilet in the wet season get the leakage and seepage, so for four months of the year they are living in the middle of shit.[1]

The terrible public health dangers are not the only hazard facing the teeming millions cramming into the mega-cities, where extremes of poverty and wealth co-exist in ever closer proximity. Arnold Toynbee has spoken of the danger that *'the whole of the world's additional population is going to silt up in urban slums of one kind or another, with the risk of a consequent cold war between rich and poor easily becoming a shooting and killing war.'*

Birth control

We have seen in Chapter 4 that humanity faces terminal collapse during the first half of the 21st century unless essential steps are taken to avert it. If forecasting population growth is not to be academic, it is necessary to assume that these steps will indeed be taken, because even assuming universal, unrestricted availability of birth control, world population will inexorably continue growing beyond 2025, before steadying at approximately 10bn around 2050. The world's long-term, critical need for family planning is self-evident. Immediately, particularly in the Third World, contraception is desperately needed to reduce the suffering of women, who not only have to bear the children but also take most of the responsibility for raising them. Also, it is estimated that, besides some 300,000 live births, well over 100,000 abortions take place daily, resulting in the deaths, or maimimg, of some quarter of a million women annually. We have seen also, in Chapter 1, the continuing horrific practice of infanticide, which can only prove unbearably traumatic for the mothers involved.

Happily, there have already been some birth control successes in the Third World which prove how eminently achievable they could be world-wide. Particularly over the last 25 years, dramatic reductions in family sizes have been made in several countries in each of the continents, including Colombia, China, Cuba, Dominican Republic, Jamaica, Sri Lanka and Tunisia. For example, in 1969 in Thailand, women had, on average, 6.5 children, and only one in six used any form of contraception.

In 1970 the Thai government launched a nation-wide family planning programme, making contraception freely available, even in remote rural areas. Non-specialists were trained to supply contraceptives and the programme was supported by a mass media campaign. Within just 20 years, the proportion of Thai people using contraception jumped from 14% to 68%, the number of children per woman fell from 6.5 to 2.2, and population growth fell from 3% pa to 1.4% pa.[2]

There are three main—readily surmountable— obstacles to universal birth control. These are: poverty—involving a need for children to support parents and replace those dying in infancy; illiteracy—preventing the assimilation of knowledge regarding contraception; and bigoted religious opposition— chiefly Roman Catholic. The latter has been been described by Brenda Maddox as follows:

> Around the globe the Catholic church's ban on artificial contraception is a virulent force for ignorance, repression and suffering. The Church's conservative hierarchy, bolstered by the equally conservative Catholic medical profession and the right-wing political organisation Opus Dei, are hard at work to stop the spread of family planning and sex education. By their efforts they are hampering attempts to control soaring population growths. By their opposition to condoms, they are contributing to the spread of Aids. Hundreds of millions of women lack even the basic information to space and limit their children; they want contraception and, where they can get it, they use it. Contraceptive ignorance goes hand in hand with a high incidence of maternal mortality. In the Congo, with practically no contraceptive practice, the rate is 1,000 maternal deaths per 100,000 live births, while in the UK the rate is 1.8 per 100,000. This Catholic doctrine causes more misery, in total, than [did] apartheid; there are only 21 million black South Africans but nearly 1 billion Catholics.[3]

Migrations of the uprooted millions

In recent years, world-wide, at least 40 million people have been forced to abandon and leave such homes as they had, because of either environmental problems, or hostilities, or both.

Whatever the cause, their predicament is invariably exacerbated by the local population explosion. Environmental disasters such as crop failures or water shortages may be compounded by harsh topographical or climatic conditions. For example, many of Nepal's people, numbering around 35m by 2000 in a small, mountainous country with their forests gone and most land exhausted, will inevitably be driven to emigrate, but to where?

Neighbouring India and Bangladesh are already overcrowded and have a plethora of problems of their own, some of them, ironically, resulting from being downstream from Nepal.

The concept of environmental refugees, who leave because of various disasters or because the land can no longer support them, is growing, particularly throughout Africa. As demands for energy, water and land expand with population, so the numbers of such refugees will swell, up to 100m according to one UN estimate.

In various parts of the world, life has been made impossible for significant populations who have been forced by hostilities to become refugees. A particularly tragic example is that of Mozambique, which 'had its heart torn out by Renamo, a legion of killers conceived by Rhodesia to destabilise the Frelimo revolution; when Rhodesia lost its own war, Renamo was inherited, tutored and strengthened by the South African regime.

The result is a country in total ruin, with maimed and starving people walking through the game reserves only to be eaten by lions.'[4]

This report, from *World Media* describes well the tragic scenario of today's migrations of the uprooted millions:

> *The waves of refugees now criss-crossing Africa, often journeying from a place where there is little food to a place where there is none, best show the modern human drama of displacement, impoverishment and marginalisation.* No political resolutions, changes of government or boundaries, no stroke of the pen can alter these massive movements of the dispossessed. They pose a global challenge to the affluent world. Africa's refugees number 6m, or 15m including those displaced internally. Yet no one knows how accurate these figures are, since great swathes of Africa are cut off by war and social breakdown. Hundreds of thousands of these desperate people are permanently malnourished. Most have little hope of returning home and live in utter degradation on the outskirts of cities.
>
> Most are peasants who, uprooted from their land, have lost their way of life , their past, and their children's future.[4]

Before long, population explosions are going to face the world with the unprecedented dilemma of how to cope with perhaps a billion or more completely rootless people. The question of the ultimate destinations of all these millions on the move is never seriously addressed. Like so many other Third World issues, it is simply ignored by First World elites as if it were in no way their responsibility. Now that First World countries have, in the main, absorbed all the cheap labour they need, barriers against any further immigration are well and truly in place.

And, in keeping with today's trend towards, and acceptance of violence, it is certain that those manning the barriers will be well armed, in the event of attempted major incursions by desperate people. Already, 150 men, women and children attempt to enter the US from Mexico every night, risking severe reactions from the 'watch on the Rio Grande'. An estimated surplus before long of 100m people in North Africa alone, together, very possibly, with many from parts of Eastern Europe, would face storming 'Fortress West Europe' if, as is likely, they were desperate enough to attempt entry. World-wide, all the wealthy countries, large or small are jealously guarding their frontiers.[5]

When considering possible future destinations for the world's refugees, one of the most important factors is the existing disposition of populations, to enable those regions having the most vacant space to be distinguished. Very broadly, Asia is already 'full', and Africa is rapidly filling up. China's 20% of global population exists on only 5% of the world's agricultural land. The last 30 year's increase alone in the population density of Southern Asia is nearly double the population density of Europe. On the other hand, Latin America as a whole is far less densely populated than Asia: Brazil alone has an area 2.5 times greater than India's. However, North America has by far the greatest amount of 'spare room'; every Canadian and US citizen enjoys around 100 times more space than the average Third World citizen today.

1 Guardian 11/4/92
2 Ditto 10/9/91
3 Observer 3/3/91
4 Guardian 14/6/91
5 Ditto 10/6/91

Chapter 6

FOOD AND FAMINE

The anarchic state of world food production is described cogently in the following extract from a speech by Stanford University Professor Ehrlich to the American Association for the Advancement of Science in Chicago:

> World food shortages are likely to increase in frequency and severity. Food gluts in the wealthy nations are illusory. Instead of cutting agricultural production, Japan is subsidising farmers and pushing up the price of its rice to four times that of the world market value.

> Japan may be wise to preserve every bit of its productive capacity. Ten tons of rice might some day be more valuable than ten tons of Toyotas. The green revolution of increased fertiliser use and better plant breeds is coming to an end.

> From 1950 to 1984 world grain production kept ahead of population growth; since then it has not, and food supplies from the seas are faltering. Huge tracts of farmland are being lost to the growing cities and some 24bn tons of top soil are being eroded annually; water supplies for agriculture are starting to fail as much in the US as in India. Chemical pest control is 'promoting' previously innocuous species by wiping out natural predators; in California in the late 1970s, 24 of the top 25 agricultural pests were creations of the pesticide industry.

> Air pollution, depletion of the ozone layer and global warming are threatening food production. With one quarter of all the world's species likely to be extinct by 2025, the 'genetic library', from which man's food

plants were originally withdrawn, is also at risk. In the last 25 years some 200m have died of starvation or hunger-related diseases, and over 1bn are hungry today. The population is maintained by consuming, dispensing and destroying topsoil, ice-age groundwater and the micro-organisms, plants and animals that are parts of Earth's life support systems.[1]

Food facts

Optimum daily calory inputs for humans range from 800 for infants up to 3,500 for adult active males, averaging 2,500, but with an absolute minimum for healthy, effective lives of 2,000 calories. Around 1bn world citizens in fact exist on a grossly inadequate input of under 1,600 calories per day.

Average Third World daily food consumptions amount to approximately 0.5kg by weight, of which 5% may be protein; diets often consist of 85% rice. First World equivalents are four times greater, at 2kg of food daily, containing 20% protein, ie meat, fish and dairy products. Many First World citizens in fact consume double the amount which the body can absorb, and ill-health results.[2]

Total calory and protein content of all food produced in the world today is, in fact, over double the minimum requirement of the world's whole population. Sussex University lecturer Simon Maxwell states that: *'There is more than enough food in the world to feed the present population; the amount required to eliminate hunger is small, less than 5% of current total consumption. It is not a failure to produce food that causes hunger.'*[3] In 1970 the UN Food and Agriculture Organisation estimated that the world could feed 30 billion, or six times its then population.

Since 1984, grain production has been falling by 1% pa, with the worst reductions occurring in the Third World. All the current forecasts regarding food production within the Third World are desperate: totally inadequate calories, output growths lagging behind increases in population, and resulting essential food imports absorbing earnings from exports and costing enormous sums.

Around 20% of the earth's surface is cultivatable; of this relatively limited proportion, only about one-third is actually farmed. Approximately one-tenth of a hectare per person is required for basic cereal production. In many countries, particularly in Asia, every conceivable useable patch of land has already been pressed into use; China, for example, feeds 20% of the world's population from only 10% of the world's land.

The necessity to increase vastly the proportion of land farmed properly is clearly critical. Without such an increase, unless present deteriorating trends are reversed, erosion, desertification, toxification, and non-farming conversion are expected to actually reduce existing areas of farmland by around 40% by 2025, in parallel with vastly increasing numbers of mouths to feed. Further, this appalling projection of a 40% reduction does not include the less easily predictable loss of land due to sea level rises following global warming.

Besides augmenting areas of farmland, essential increases in food production will call for the application of about 50% more energy early in the 21st century for fertilisers, pesticides, irrigation and mechanisation.

Famine facts

The hideous plight of hundreds of millions of fellow humans has already been referred to under 'Third World suffering' in Chapter 1, but cannot be repeated too often. The knowledge of just how readily preventable all that massive suffering is, renders it a matter of searing, guilty responsibility for all thinking, caring members of the First World in particular. The terrible facts need to be set out again and again: 10% of humanity, half a billion people, equivalent to all Europeans, are permanently incapacitated by hunger. 20% of humanity, a billion people, the equivalent of all 'Western world' citizens, are permanently hungry. 50% of humanity suffer some degree of malnutrition. And, in worst hit areas, every other child dies of hunger-related diseases before reaching age five.

Those of the many millions suffering from malnutrition who die quickly must, regrettably, be counted the lucky ones. The majority fall victims to lingering sickness and, usually, eventual death from the many terrible hunger-related illnesses, virtually unknown in the First World, which are endemic in the Third World. These include kwashiorkor, marasmus, goitre (sometimes resulting in cretinism), pellagra (even leading to madness), anaemia, beri-beri, blindness (from vitamin A defficiency), bilharzia, malaria, yellow fever, and others.

Chronic malnutrition also leads to stunted growth with adult men reaching only 130 cms (4'3") in height; such 'dwarfism' also diminishes the faculties, and capacity for work, and is suffered, for example, by one third of the population of Brazil.[4] Further, a tragic irony of Third World agricultural practices is that either deadly, or improperly used pesticides poison 2 million and kill 40,000 people annually. Susan George points out:

Perhaps the most morally revolting aspect of malnutrition is that it is now proven that the baby who lacks sufficient calories and proteins both before and after birth, will be permanently damaged mentally, even in the unlikely event of it being fed properly subsequently, and that this underdevelopment will be passed on inexorably to its children.

This has been confirmed by studies in Mexico, Guatemala and India, one of which showed that for 500 middle-class children only 1% had an IQ below 80, while out of 500 poor children who had suffered malnutrition, 62% had IQs below 80.[5]

Malnutrition and famine are experienced throughout the Third World, but the African continent is usually hit worst of all. The food situation deteriorated generally in the 1980s, but in 1992 took a dramatic turn for the worse. Across Southern Africa, 100 million people faced drastically falling stocks, with the harvest forecast at only 40% of the normal, and the Limpopo river level so low that irrigation was cut by two-thirds. Losses of the vital maize crops amounted to 70% in Lesotho, 80% in Namibia and 90% in parts of Mozambique. In their desperation, hundreds of thousands were driven to eating appallingly bad substitutes for proper food. These included boiled wild okra, crushed tree seeds mixed with millet, baobab bark ground with river silt, and millet ground and fermented into a porridge called 'mahewa'; none of these contain any protein whatever.[7] The final blow to these tortured people is that the same cruel conditions which afflict them bring death on a huge scale to their treasured poultry, cattle and other livestock.

First World influences

No sphere of human activity is 'out of bounds' for the insatiable greed of the money system. Even food, humanity's most basic need after water, is seen not as a right, but as fair game for profit-making. The plunder of the Third World today, under the cloaks of 'trade', or 'business', is even more widespread and damaging than that of bygone colonial days. A UN report has referred to the concept of agriculture being run primarily for profit rather than for feeding local populations, as setting in motion many fundamental changes, including vast increases in land prices and evictions of hundreds of thousands of people. In their ruthless drive for the most productive locations and the cheapest labour, both the multinational corporations and local elites drive the poor off the land. In so doing, they relegate still further the unwelcome (to them) prospect of land reform—the very change well proven to be fundamental to increased output of food appropriate to local needs, produced by well-tried and environmentally friendly methods.

In her mine of information, *How the Other Half Dies*, Susan George tells us that, in a 1967 speech, Louis Lundborg, chairman of the Bank of America, insisted on profit being the only basis for increased food production, saying 'all our efforts will be channelled to those nations which are willing to take the tangible, and often politically unpopular steps to assure the proper climate for investment.' As a result, 'no business like agribusiness' projects in some countries have returned as much as 30% pa on investment, by producing, not for local, pressing needs, but for export to high-paying First World markets. There is ample evidence that MNCs' agribusiness activities destroy everything they touch: local employment patterns, local foodcrop production, consumer tastes, even village and traditional family structures.[5]

One of the most dramatic influences of the First World on the Third was the introduction of the 'Green Revolution' into agriculture—first in Mexico in 1943, and subsequently world-wide. This bore all the familiar 'quick-fix' hallmarks of so many other 20th century scientific developments, such as nuclear energy. What had begun with ingenious biological developments of 'miracle seeds' was soon overwhelmed by manufacturers' pressures to sell the profitable accompanying adjuncts: vast quantities of fertilisers, insecticides, herbicides (to kill the weeds largely encouraged by the fertilisers), heavy machinery, irrigation equipment and so on.

If the 'revolution' had been introduced more carefully, particularly in the context of smaller-scale, owner-occupied farms, it would very probably have been of lasting benefit. As it is, nature has rebelled against such 'sledgehammer' treatment, and initially impressive food output increases have been reversed.

The scenario of cash-crop production developed for two main reasons: land-grabs by the multinationals to produce for profits in First World markets, and pressures on Third World countries to meet debt demands. The profits from agribusiness may not be as high as from extractive activities such as mining or lumber felling, but, provided the land is not exhausted in the process, at least the resources involved are not totally depleted. Sri Lanka provides a classic example in microcosm of what has happened since, on a world-wide scale: before the British East India Company enforced tea-growing as the virtually exclusive crop in the 17th century, the country had been self-sufficient; similarly Bengal was previously rich in cotton, sugar, rice, butter, poultry, vegetables, pigs and sheep. Dr J E Dutra, president of the

International Union of Nutritional Sciences, has explained that Brazil could feed almost half the world, yet it does not even feed its own people; instead, in 1991, it exported food worth £4.2bn to contribute towards its debt repayment.[8]

The insidious intrusions of First World commercial influences, witnessed by tourists the world over, have not spared the food and drink markets; Coca Cola 'welcome arches' can be seen at the entrances to Third World towns. In so far as Third World citizens have access to TV or other mass media, they are assaulted by advertisements plugging the superiority of 'Western model' junk food and drinks which are low on nutrition but high on profit. That is the only significant criterion for multi-nationals like Nestle, whose advertising budget alone far exceeds the total budget of the World Health Organisation.[5] Attitudes of, for example, the US elite to the increasingly serious world food situation can be summarised by the following: in 1973, Hubert Humphrey said: 'Food is a new form of power, food is wealth, food is an extra dimension in our diplomacy'.

A 1974 CIA Report forecast increasing world grain shortages, which would *give Washington virtual life and death powers over the multitudes of the needy'. In 1981 the US Agriculture Secretary John Block, said 'food is now the greatest weapon we have, and will continue to be as other countries become more dependent on American farm exports and will be reluctant to upset us.'*

Food price rigging

The odious First World practice of maintaining price levels by storing 'surplus' foodstuffs at vast expense has been referred to in Chapter 2 under 'Food mountains'. Susan George tells us that for a limited number of agents in a position to 'call the shots', food is nothing more than a series of commodities on which money can be made, rather like rubber or gold. A former Food & Agriculture Organisation President complained that 'as soon as production approached quantities equivalent to effective demand, markets became clogged with alleged surpluses, which annoyed governments far more than insufficient food production did'. In the EU, governments practise 'intervention buying' on a broad scale when 'gluts' threaten to drive prices down, and even destroy huge quantities of food to keep it off the market if 'necessary'. At times, millions of hectares of land are deliberately not planted in order to keep prices up. In 1992, for instance, some 5,300 British farmers were receiving £96 per acre to take their land out of production;

some are paid as much as £70,000 pa to do nothing.[9] The 1992 Common Agricultural Policy 'reforms' involve compensating farmers who set aside a minimum of 15% of their land, which will result in 1.5m acres standing idle.[10]

Malpractices and waste

In common with so many other essential activities, food production and distribution is plagued by all the familiar problems: maldistribution of land resulting in a lack of personal interest in much of its cultivation, lack of education and training for many agricultural workers and technicians, and the myriad distorting effects of the money market system generally—all leading to long-term inefficient production and improper use of man's most precious asset. For example, over half of all the water diverted or drawn for irrigation in Asia is lost through inefficient storage or distribution; further, the UN estimates that, before long, salinisation or water-logging will afflict half the world's irrigated areas. Because of manufacturers' concerns to avoid over-production which might weaken profit levels, world output of artificial fertilisers is totally inadequate; US citizens in fact apply more fertilisers to their lawns than India uses for all its agriculture. The return of natural nutrients to the soil, if any, is poorly organised world-wide, except in China where the traditional use of nearly all animal and human waste contributes greatly to their productivity. In the US on the other hand, 1m tons pa of natural manure is not only wasted but actually aggravates pollution.

In the Third World, pesticides are conspicuous by their absence, usually due to their high cost; as a result, around one-third of all crops are lost 'on the stalk'. Following harvesting, appalling food losses result from inadequate handling, storage and processing. In 1984, for example, 180m tons of grain, 10% of the world's harvest, was lost in these ways; between 15% and 60% of fruit, vegetables and fish are lost regularly, particularly in hot, humid Third World countries.[11] Because of totally inadequate facilities and absence of veterinary care, a seriously high proportion of livestock dies prematurely in the Third World.

The practice of using grain to fatten various animals, prior to slaughter for human consumption, represents one of the most glaring examples of the thoughtless selfishness of the First World. Not only does it deprive the rest of humanity of food, but as a practice it is, in fact, grossly inefficient, because poultry, pigs, cattle and other animals waste

70% of the food value of the grain they are fattened on. *In fact, just the grain fed to fatten livestock in the First World would suffice to meet the energy needs of the peoples of India and China put together.* Specifically, UK livestock consumes over 10m tons of grain annually, sufficient to provide a basic diet for 50m people; grain fed to US cattle alone would alleviate several disastrous famines. Finally, the ubiquitous money-market system results in the diversion of vast quantities of rich proteins away from human to domestic animal consumption, through the highly profitable trade in pet foods. In the US, the value of annual food sales for 35m dogs and 30m cats amount to around $3bn; in the UK, pet food protein consumption would suffice for 750,000 people.

1 Guardian 8/2/92
2 World Facts and Trends, McHale
3 Guardian 3/1/92
4 Observer 26/1/92
5 How the other half dies, George
6 Guardian 14/3/92
7 Observer 19/4/92
8 Ditto 26/1/92
9 Ditto 9/2/92
10 Ditto 24/5/92
11 Dictionary of Environment & Development, Crump.

Chapter 7

CRIMINAL WASTE ON WEAPONS

In sharp contrast to mankind's much-vaunted 'development', the 20th century has seen an unprecedented succession of disastrous major and minor wars, which have caused immeasurable suffering and benefitted nobody except the arms manufacturers.

The most significant factor underpinning this global mayhem is the ruthless momentum of the money market system, which has vastly expanded the manufacturing of weapons into huge industries demanding customers world-wide. Elites everywhere, anxious either to increase or just maintain their influence, have been only too happy to buy or just to receive arms as 'aid'. Also, tradition has it that wars are almost normal, inevitable, even glorious occurrences; that armed forces are as natural a part of society as football teams; and that making armaments is a wage-earning job like any other.

Further, a cunning psychological transformation was dreamed up around 1945, when what had been honest-to-god 'War Offices' overnight became innocent sounding Ministries, or Departments, of 'Defence'. Needless to say, belying their nice new image, these bodies have been on the offensive on many occasions since.

The term 'Defence' has, in fact, now been adopted throughout the world, as a euphemism for the complete selection of war-like activities. Another particularly tragic example of the extraordinary distortions of language which the 'top brass' can resort to, in their confusion when trying to defend the indefensible, occurred during the 1991 Gulf War. The largest single group of UK soldiers to be killed, nine young men, died from what was officially described as 'friendly fire', when they were bombed by a US plane. In that same war, over half the US casualties were believed also to have been caused by their own weaponry.

Warfare is not biologically inherent in humans. It is, in fact, only the highly profitable by-product of particular cultures.

That aggression is not endemic in man is best illustrated by the following extract from *The Gaia Peace Atlas* (Editor: Dr Frank Barnaby):

> Homo sapiens has been around for at least 250,000 years. Yet war and military might have been known only in the last 5,000 —2% at most of our history. War is neither a part of human nature nor, necessarily, of civilized life. The Anatolian city of Catal Huyuk, for instance, has been excavated back to 7,000 BC. In the 800 years of its existence so far examined, there is no evidence of any sack or massacre, nor a single skeleton showing signs of a violent death.

Small arms are increasingly a scourge, but big weapons represent a potential threat to many millions. Tens of thousands of nuclear weapons are still scattered around the world, many of them up to 40 years old and almost certain to bring about appalling contamination resulting from their deteriorating condition, and from the near impossibility of dismantling them safely. This terrible legacy of the Cold War could persist for decades. Such is the lethal nature of these weapons that it is estimated that even the cancerous fall-out from testing the new ones still being made will cause over 400,000 deaths in the 1990s, and over 2m deaths in years to come.[1]

The real, immeasurable costs of militarisation have to include allowances for 'opportunities foregone, human needs not met, retarded and distorted economic growth, and lost opportunities for international cooperation. Behind the facade of "Defence", armaments contribute to social unrest, limit political freedom and foster alienation and upheaval.'[2] Besides the well-recorded carnage of the great wars in history, the International Committee of the Red Cross has estimated that around 20 million people have perished in over 100 'local' wars since 1945; a further 60 million have been wounded or uprooted, and that approximately 90% of these casualties were civilians.[3] Subsequent to the Vietnam war, more US veterans of that fighting have committed suicide than were killed in the war itself.[4]

Arms purchases are never productive. 'They produce no wealth, and when not manufactured locally do not create jobs. They are nothing but pure consumption...armies themselves are unproductive, and their salaries play havoc with Third World budgets. As defence establishments become more powerful, they demand more and more arms, and often, the generals then take over completely and do as they please.'[5]

The *Guardian* (25/4/92) reported that the Bush administration had cancelled export bans on a wide range of American high-technology products with military applications, as a result of pressure from the defence industry; the equipment includes products for ballistic missiles. Restrictions on the sales of arms to third parties were also eased; the moves could bring up to $3bn in new business to US arms manufacturers. One of the biggest ever recipients of the lethal products of the arms industry was Afghanistan. Arthur Kent, writing in the *Observer* (19/4/92), reported that the superpowers invested their Afghan client with the power of sudden death, not the gifts of reason and mercy. 'The Mujahideen parties based in Pakistan owe most of their might to the Reagan and Bush administrations, and the largest covert support operation in the history of the CIA, valued at over $4bn. The outcome has been a tragic power struggle, a whirlwind of hate, greed and treachery.'

An Afghan writer commented: 'our society was once rich and diverse, but now we have been bred only for the arena of war'.

Lifetimes devoted to weapons

Apart from the all too obvious and terrible end-results of weapons production, their design, manufacture and use involve appalling waste of working lifetimes which the world can ill afford. No less than 80 million persons are involved world-wide, including 25m in armed services, 10m in para-military organisations, 45m civilians in manufacturing or other support roles, and half a million scientists evolving new weapons. All these men and women are, naturally, some of the most highly-educated and trained members of their various societies. They represent a vast reserve of skills and abilities which should and could be put to incomparably better use on constructive and rewarding, peaceful purposes.

The scientists and other professionals involved must, of necessity, be top-class designers. The UK's former Chief Scientific Adviser, Sir Solly Zuckerman, has said 'the nuclear world is the creation of the scientists, not a result of any external demand; they are bringing about the threat of the annihilation of mankind by turning a miracle of nature - the human brain—into a means of self-destruction'. Retired USAF pilot and nuclear expert, Howard Morland, has written:

It is not only money that drives them, but career incentives. Nuclear weapons-builders are highly educated, in-bred bureaucrats; they live in intellectual and physical isolation, in a super-society like a monastic order, except that its members live very well and are paid very well. They see themselves as superior, and have two mottoes: 'Papa knows best,' and 'The public be damned.' They are imbued with the fascination of perfecting techniques superior to any in the world. Hydrogen bombs are considered works of high craftsmanship, comparable to the products of master goldsmiths, cabinet makers, or watchmakers of the past.[6]

One of the most insidious achievements of the military-industrial complex is the dependence of millions, world-wide, on the production of weapons for their livelihoods; this significantly underpins the arms culture. Not only the manufacturers, but whole communities perceive their destinies to be inextricably linked to churning out arms indefinitely, and their trades unions have also been caught up in this paradox. It is well established, however, that equivalent funding devoted to non-military production would in fact provide considerably more employment.

World-wide waste on armaments

The money wasted on the Second World War could have provided every family in the world with a five-room house, every child in the world with secondary education, and every 5,000 people in the world with a fully equipped hospital. Since 1945, world expenditure on armaments has accelerated to such an extent, that the global total in 1990 of $1 trillion represented in real terms a 14-fold increase over that of 1939. Apart from the wanton diversion of funds from desperately needed social expenditure, the actual creation of weapons of all kinds exhausts vast quantities of non-renewable resources, ranging from precious metals to energy in various forms. Addressing the North American Society of Newspaper Editors on 16th April 1953, President Eisenhower said: 'Every gun that is made, every warship launched, every rocket fired, signifies in the final sense a theft from those who hunger and are not fed, those who are cold and are not clothed. This world in arms is not spending money alone, it is spending the sweat of its labourers, the genius of its scientists, the hopes of its children.'

Current global armaments expenditure is equivalent to the entire income of half the world's population; the average world citizen has to part with 4 years' worth of income for military spending.

The world is now spending more on arms than on health and education combined, which means spending, on average, $100 pa to teach a child to read, and then spending $10,000 to teach him how to use a weapon. In the US, three times as much is spent on military research and development as on peaceful r & d; the 'net' expenditure on armaments amounts to one-third of total US government spending. But, if with that is included NASA military spending, interest on the National Debt, due to previous defence spending, and pensions for ex-military personnel, then the 'gross' total of spending, related to defence, amounts to over half of the entire US budget. Just when the US Congress was poised to make significant cuts in this horrendous expenditure, the Gulf War conveniently provided the Bush administration with a pretext to restore 'national security' spending to $300bn pa.

In April 1991, Dr Paul Rogers of Bradford University wrote:

> The current $14bn shopping list includes 25 fighter and other aircraft, 235 tanks, 52 patrol boats, over 100 attack helicopters, 50 howitzers, 750 armoured vehicles and 4,000 rough terrain trucks. They are also purchasing 7,600 cluster bomb units and 70 multiple rocket systems. The MRLS is seen as the most devastating conventional system, involving the firing of 12 missiles in under a minute, delivering 8,000 bomblets, releasing millions of shrapnel fragments; these will destroy targets and people over an area of 60 acres up to 20 miles away. During the Gulf War, the US army fired 10,000 and the British 2,500, of these missiles. As well as the major industrialised countries and Israel, many others are now producing these weapons, including Chile, Argentina, Brazil, South Africa and India.[7]

Military spending in the Third World as a whole has increased three times faster than even that of the First World, approaching $200bn pa in 1990 and thus amounting to around 20% of total world military spending. Third World expenditure on armaments has consistently totalled more than the spending on education and health combined.

World-wide, but especially in the US and UK, and in spite of the ending of the Cold War, arms manufacturers are engaged in a headlong rush to produce ever more exotic weapons systems often extolled as 'clean', 'quick', 'surgical', 'smart', even 'benign'. They represent a fantastic, nightmare collection, on a huge scale, of devices of such sophistication that their laser, 'fly-by-wire', or other control systems can become entangled with each other, creating an invisible jungle known as electro-magnetic-interference. This can render powerless operators or pilots, and cause whole varieties of missiles to either fire themselves or otherwise malfunction, causing even wider casualties or damage than intended.

The world's armed forces are the single biggest polluters on the planet. *The Nation* (8/6/92) quotes from a report by the Toronto University Science for Peace institute, which states that 10 to 30 per cent of all global environmental degradation can be attributed to military activities. The Pentagon, for instance, is the largest consumer of oil in the US. The 200bn barrels it bought in 1989 could run all US public transit systems for 22 years. An F-16 jet fighter consumes as much fuel in 30 minutes as the average US motorist does in a year.

Approximately 25% of the world's jet fuel is consumed by armed forces. World-wide military consumption of aluminium, copper, nickel and platinum, exceeds that of the entire Third World. 6 to 10 per cent of global air pollution is linked to the military, and armed forces are responsible for over two-thirds of the ozone-depleting CFC-113 released into the atmosphere.

The report concluded that under 10% of current resources wasted on arms would suffice to provide safe water and sewage systems world-wide, and reverse both desertification and deforestation.

Profits: the mainspring of arms production

In *World without War* Professor J D Bernal wrote:

> Military expenditure has been invoked to solve one of the recurrent problems of the capitalist economy; how to keep up profits without at the same time flooding the market with useful goods. The answer, as it appears in practice, is to produce useless goods. And from this point of view, weapons are not only useless, but have the additional asset of becoming rapidly obsolescent, so that however many are produced, even larger numbers are soon required.[8]

On his retirement, President Eisenhower warned of the potential menace of the vast and constantly growing 'military-industrial complex' in the US. The top 100 US arms firms employ, in fact, over 2,000 ex-military officers with the rank of colonel or above. Their Boards of Directors—industrialists, generals, bankers, admirals, and others are supported by high-ranking teams of Washington lobbyists, to inject proposals for weapons and garner the contracts. The 75,000 odd armaments firms are the driving force behind US weapons production. They push out a constant stream of every conceivable and inconceivable type, many of which are so complex as to be almost unuseable, or prone to failure. For example, during the first 100 or so flights, the Cruise missile failed 28 times; Pershing trials resulted in 30% failure rates. But one of the major attractions of making weapons, unlike consumer goods, is that accounts are settled regardless of whether the product performs as planned.

In 1930, a Senate committee investigating arms corporations found that profit levels of 100% were common. Now, with the arrival of electronic and nuclear weapons , prospects are even brighter, with the profit rate being 50% higher than in consumer-goods industries. The chairman of Lockheeds, makers of Cruise, Trident etc, has said that, compared to 'traditional weaponry', the 'production of missiles and other weapons of mass destruction is many times more profitable'. In the mid-1970s, Lockheed admitted paying out $106m in commission to various princes, prime ministers and political parties, to assist in obtaining arms contracts in the newly-rich Third World.[9] In the mid-1980s, Reagan's 'Star Wars' project promised defence contractors potentially their biggest ever bonanza, the *Wall St Journal* commenting that 'the scramble for the pot of gold is on'.

The core of the problem of runaway profits is that only 6% of Pentagon contracts are put out to competitive tender.[10] In June 1985, the *New York Times* reported on the latest 'charge-sheet' from the Defence Department's Inspector-General:

Nine out of ten of the largest Pentagon contractors, and 45 of the largest 100, are under criminal investigation; McDonnel Douglas and Rockwell are being investigated for alleged mis-statements of costs; General Dynamics, for sub-contractor 'kickbacks', product substitution, security lapses, defective pricing, cost duplication and false claims; Lockheed for wrong labour charges; Boeing for mis-stating labour and material costs; General Electric for false claims, defective pricing and product substitution; United Technologies for sub-contractor kickbacks, bribery and defective pricing; Raytheon for labour mischarging and product substitution; Litton for bribery and kickbacks, false claims and bid-rigging; Ford for defective pricing and falsifying records; Texas Instruments for product substitution; and Northrop for false progress payments.

Not suprisingly, the lust for massive profits has not been confined to the US. In the UK, for example, a National Audit Office investigation into £6.6bn worth of non-competitive contracts awarded to large armaments firms between 1982 and 1984 revealed excess profits of £400m.[11] Further, at least £100m was 'spirited away' by the international ring of fraudsters involved in the Ferranti 'phantom contract' scandal.[12] The *Guardian* (3/8/91) reported that 'a new UK "conventional" submarine, completed in 1991 at a cost of £405m was found to contain faults leaving it no longer watertight, and unable to fire torpedoes; requiring a further expenditure of £16m.'

Ronald Higgins has written:

That the main impetus for the production of weapons stems from so many manufacturers, all pressing for profits, is well illustrated by a 1975 report which recorded that NATO members were wasting $10bn pa competing between themselves in the development and procurement of weapons. The situation is as insane militarily as it is financially. NATO armies had 31 different sorts of anti-tank weapons, 22 different anti-aircraft weapons, and 7 different tanks. The air forces had 23 different kinds of aircraft. The navies had 100 different sorts of ships of destroyer size or larger, equipped with over 40 different guns and 36 kinds of radar.[13]

The scourge of 'small arms'

Small arms are in a sense the source of all evil in the world of ballistics. *Should a scientist refuse to make a hydrogen bomb, it only takes a man with a pistol to make him change his mind.* The overwhelming majority of assaults on human life and liberty are effected, and indeed only made possible, by the use— or threat of use— of hand guns or similar weapons. These are the death-dealing implements used by bloody-minded, domineering bullies the world over, against almost invariably unarmed, innocent civilians, resulting in millions of illegal executions or incarcerations. Handguns enable dictators to take and maintain power. A former Iraqi staff officer, now in exile, has stated that 'advisers don't dare give Saddam Hussein bad news. If they do, they minimise it as much as possible, because he easily loses his temper and has shot a lot of people for giving him bad news.'[14]

The scourge of small arms is, of course, felt world-wide. Murder rates are horrific in most cities; Naples suffers 500 per year. In the UK, a 1991 survey found that 75% of women felt unsafe at night, and 64% said they would arm themselves were it not illegal.[15] In the US, however, small arms can still be purchased 'over the counter' in some states, and their use is widespread and lethal. If present moves to restrict them are not successful, it is likely that, as with so many aspects of US culture, these perversions of human behaviour could well spread and worsen the situation world-wide. Murders throughout the US now total around 25,000 pa; there were 2,245 in New York alone in 1990. These figures can be compared with the 47,000 killed in action over nearly ten years in Vietnam. The increasing numbers of deaths are in part due to the switch from handguns to semi-automatic weapons, which can spray bullets through thick doors.

More and more young US citizens are becoming involved; 12% of murder arrests in 1989 were of teenagers under 18.[16] Guns are now killing more teenage males than all natural causes combined.[17] Deliberate killings are tragic enough, but accidental killings of bystanders begin to resemble what has come to be expected for civilians in war situations. Deaths from stray bullets in 1990 caused 40 deaths in New York alone. The US National Centre for Health Statistics records that in 1984 there were 1,668 unintentional firearms deaths in the US, of which 287 were children under 15.[18] *The Nation* (17/6/91) reports on a poverty-stricken area of New York:

> It takes much planning and energy to avoid walking into a drug deal, witnessing a shooting, or being shot. A caretaker reports a strange silence, broken by bursts of gunfire during weapon sales…signs of violence are everywhere—in the shells on the ground; in windows so full of holes as to suggest urban warfare; in the home-made targets to test guns, and in memorials to the young who have died. A housing project is nick-named 'Dead Man's Plaza'; nearby someone has written hurriedly, in huge letters; 'Still Alive.'

According to the US Academy of Paediatrics, an average US child watches 18,000 murders on TV before leaving high school. Bullet-proof blazers, jackets and raincoats in all sizes, from toddler to young adults, are selling fast in New York, at from $250 to $600. 'Urban Survival' as a subject has been added to the curricula in various schools. At the end of a period of almost daily shootings, a *Time* magazine poll revealed that, given the opportunity, 59% of New Yorkers would prefer to live elsewhere.[19]

All this mayhem stems from the weapons manufacturers' longstanding success in bolstering the belief throughout a high proportion of US society, that owning a gun is perfectly normal, and indeed a cherished right. The existence of approximately 200m privately-owned guns, including 50m handguns, in the US gives some indication of the rich pickings to be made. The US gun manufacturers are represented by the powerful, and hitherto all but unstoppable, National Rifle Association. It has an income of $70bn pa, including $10bn from gun makers for advertisements to oppose all forms of gun control, including even a proposed ban on new plastic guns which would, for example, allow a hijacker to move successfully past a metal detector.[20]

In 1989, one of the major US gun makers, Smith and Wesson, marketed the 'Ladysmith' .38 calibre revolver at $415, designed 'specifically for the physiological requirements of women'.

However, a report at the time pointed out that, in spite of 12m US women owning guns, 4 are killed every day, and went on to say that the fantasies of women 'fighting back' are, in fact, eclipsed by the following far more likely scenarios, typical of people owning guns, including men: they shoot a lover or spouse in the heat of a quarrel, or are shot themselves; they are overwhelmed by a stronger assailant who turns the gun against them; their child finds the gun and thinks it is a toy; they hear noises, panic, forget all safety instructions, and shoot someone who is not an intruder; they over-react and shoot someone who could have been restrained or pacified; they shoot when they could have chosen to escape; they shoot and harm an innocent bystander; their gun discharges accidently, or misfires; they get depressed and shoot themselves.[21]

1 Guardian 4/8/91
2 World Military/Social Expenditures 1986,Sivard,Washington
3 Guardian 22/1/91
4 Observer 16/12/90
5 A Fate worse than Debt
6 The secret that exploded, Morland, Random House, NY 1981
7 Guardian 28/4/91
8 World without War, J D Bernal, Routledge/Paul, 1958
9 Guardian 27/9/89
10 Observer 26/5/85
11 Guardian 18/5/88
12 Ditto 18/11/89
13 The Seventh Enemy, R Higgins, Hodder/Stoughton 1978
14 Guardian 19/1/91
15 Ditto 13/5/91
16 Ditto 19/7/90
17 Ditto 15/3/91
18 Ditto 19/10/89
19 Ditto 9/10/90
20 Ditto 19/1/89
21 The Nation 15/5/89

Chapter 8

THE CRITICAL FACTORS

We have seen, throughout Part One, that the world is desperately sick in virtually every important respect. Unless fundamental changes are made very soon, life on earth will inevitably be extinguished by the end of the 21st century, or even considerably sooner. Speaking prior to the June 1992 Rio de Janeiro Environment Conference, Secretary-General Maurice Strong said : 'People have only survived on earth for a very minute portion of its history. The phenomenon of life is a rare one and the conditions which support it are very, very exceptional. We are acting in a way which changes those parameters.'[1] At the conference itself he added : 'To continue along this path could lead to the end of our civilisation. We have to face up to the dire implications of the warnings scientists are sounding. They point to the prospect that this planet may soon become uninhabitable for people.'[2]

The most evident, and the most poignant indicator of mankind's sickness, is the dramatic and growing disparity between the haves and the have-nots world-wide; in particular, the denial of practically every vestige of civilised life to three-quarters of humanity in the Third World. The long-running, specious argument, that wealth created at the top will 'trickle down', has been nailed once and for all by the 1992 UNDP report, showing that the income of the richest one-fifth of humanity is 150 times greater than that of the poorest fifth. Inevitably, in these still worsening circumstances, man's instinct for survival will result in violent upheavals by desperate millions having nothing to lose, which will lead only to yet further mayhem and environmental destruction. The same UNDP report forecasts that, failing a fundamental change of hearts and minds, ferocious and prolonged class war will follow, and that the poorest will not be contained behind national frontiers.

Capitalism

The capitalist money system is the root cause of the world's terrible plight. This pernicious system, nurtured in its earlier years by the slave trade, continues to bleed the Third World through domination by the multinational corporations and the thraldom of debt. *The world's desperate need is for co-operative forms of production and distribution for the benefit of all. The capitalist system produces the precise opposite: it increasingly side-lines the vast majority of the world's peoples, while further enriching the few who run it.*

In banking, insurance, stockbroking and the other leading financial institutions, at least 30m well-educated people world-wide spend their entire working lives doing nothing more productive than shuffling figures and paperwork, for the ultimate benefit, primarily, of the elites who employ them. No matter how well-trained they may be, however, they cannot guide or control capitalism because of its mercurial characteristic, which results in unwanted and unpredictable booms and slumps.

During booms, elites put on so much financial fat that they can ride out the slumps with ease. Conversely, these 'recessions' cause havoc amongst the great majority, laying low whole industries and communities and throwing millions of workers on the scrap-heap. A hallmark of the money system is that funds are readily made available for useless activities such as making armaments or building unnecessary commercial buildings, yet are invariably in short supply when required for socially necessary projects such as housing, schools or hospitals. The built-in capitalist compulsion to maximise profits at all costs, compromises all worthwhile human endeavours, and even life itself. The money system pervades every aspect of our lives, and taints everything it touches. The stupidity and divisiveness of capitalism constitute an affront to the dignity of mankind; the whole money system must be abandoned if the world is to survive.

Domination by elites

A tiny proportion of the world's peoples, with insatiable appetites for both power and money and with disregard for all else, are dragging down humanity and its habitat to the brink of societal and environmental collapse. Referring to isolationist First World enclaves, Maurice Strong warned: 'No place on the planet could remain an island of affluence in a sea of misery. We are either going to save the whole world or no one will be saved. One part of the world cannot live in an orgy of unrestrained consumption while the rest destroys its environment just to survive. No one is immune from the effects of the other.'[2] We have seen in Chapter 3 that domination by elites has led to the perpetuation of overblown nation-states, the stifling of innumerable separatist movements, and the paralysing of parliaments by tiny executives. To further consolidate their interests, the seamy world-wide bonds of wealth have developed naturally into unholy alliances of reactionary elites across both the Third and First Worlds.

A prime example of elitist megalomania is that of the US leadership in early 1990s. Ignoring totally global requests to moderate their inordinate pollution of the planet, President Bush stated bluntly: 'The US lifestyle is not negotiable.'

Having dismembered the old USSR to its satisfaction, the White House decided to turn to creating, unilaterally, a 'new world order', which made little pretence of furthering any nation's welfare other than its own. Paul Rogers commented:

> The US foresees a very unstable world over the next 30 years, with bitter divisions of wealth and poverty, coupled with continued proliferation of advanced weapons, producing a dangerous world disorder. This, it is claimed, must require a military response, and the US will need to field the full range of forces, including the new nuclear weapons, primarily for use against China or other Third World targets, in order to maintain its wealth and security.[3]

Tragically, the baneful influence of the US elites is all too evident also within the United Nations organisation. As John Pilger explains:

> The UN is dying. Some will argue that it was never much alive, but this is to underestimate the largely unseen work of the UN in fields that touch the lives of the majority of humanity. For example, the Centre for Science and Technology for Development has shown Third World governments that they need not be intimidated by foreign big business, and that there is a way to 'develop' other than by the cult of 'growth' and by plundering the earth. Such agencies have enjoyed support in the General Assembly, but members' voting patterns are now watched closely by the US, and governments seeking World Bank and IMF blessing dare not go against US wishes. Internal UN policy now is to kill off general research, policy studies or anything suggesting inter-governmental cooperation; the market lobbyists figure that with research eliminated, no one will notice problems like toxic wastes or dangerous pharmaceuticals.[4]

Weaponry

Clearing the decks for the introduction of an alternative world order must necessarily include the question of weapons, because their total elimination is fundamental to success: their existence is both a threat and an affront to humanity. *It is a grotesque contradiction that, on the one hand, man has developed innumerable possibilities for every human being to enjoy full, healthy and rewarding lives, and on the other hand, retains all the lethal paraphernalia for extinguishing those same lives.*

It is indisputable that the sole purpose of weapons—big or small— is to kill people; and yet it is equally beyond dispute, that the over-whelming majority of human beings reject totally the very idea of killing anybody. *So why then have any weapons at all?* Further, it is becoming less usual to hear even the most reactionary leaders actually recommending going to war, and the ridiculous denunciation of opponents of such madness as 'pacifists' or 'conscientious objectors' is similarly dropping out of fashion. Most nations claim to support the principles of the United Nations, whose charter states unequivocally: 'All members shall settle their disputes by peaceful means, including negotiation, mediation, conciliation and resort to regional settlement'. *So why then have any armed forces at all ?*

The environment, populations,food

The many problems in these areas, referred to in Chapters 4, 5, and 6, would be alleviated dramatically by the elimination of the capitalist money system, and all the exploitation and unnatural pressures which stem from it. Judith Hampson reports: 'The world's indigenous peoples, original inhabitants of their ancestral lands, believe not that we inherited the earth from our forefathers, but that we have merely borrowed it from our descendants. Since we hold it in trust for them, it is our moral duty to preserve it.[5] Andrew Lees, of Friends of the Earth, commented: 'The fate of the forests has become a symbol of the battle between North and South, a propaganda battle with each side blaming the other while the destruction continues...the US is playing political poker with the fate of the planet, and Britain is acting as its poodle.'[6]

To the many different existing threats to the environment which are already critical, must be added the likelihood of friction and destructive hostilities between ravenous First World consumers competing for control of diminishing natural resources, unless their exploitation world-wide can be planned and controlled co-operatively and rationally. The critical nature of the explosive growth of populations was summed up by the secretary-general at the opening of the 1992 Rio Earth conference: *'Populations must be stabilised, and rapidly...if we do not do it, nature will, and much more brutally. We have been the most successful species ever. We are now a species out of control.'*[2] One of the tragic examples of our being a 'species out of control' is the global predicament of agriculture. The growing and fair distribution of food has become a critical factor only because profit-hungry 'agribusiness' has been allowed to grab control in so much of the world.

Precedents for fundamental change

The elites and their media would have us believe that capitalism is a permanent part of the natural order of life on earth. To consolidate this myth, they have ensured that the tentacles of their money system reach out and penetrate virtually every daily activity of every individual in the First, and in increasing numbers in the Third World; we have seen the fateful results of these penetrations in Chapter 2. In promoting fundamental societal changes, it is apposite to recall some of the more important precedents which have proved that human existence can not only be maintained, but greatly enhanced in the absence of capitalism. After ridding themselves of their old orders, in, for example, China, the USSR and Cuba, it was demonstrated that, with all their deficiencies and the facing of enormous difficulties and opposition, highly impressive societal improvements could be made after abandoning capitalism.

In so far as the subject of fundamental change is ever discussed, the elites, fearful for their privileges, maintain that abandoning capitalism would have catastrophic results. The 'upheaval' involved would no doubt result in them losing their superfluous and unwarranted pleasures, but, for the teeming billions, the gains would in many cases include life itself; and in all cases, immeasurable improvements in the quality of their existence. In the 20th century alone, there have been very real and catastrophic upheavals in the shape of horrendous wars, exterminations of populations, and other disasters. By comparison, to suggest that to transfer to a sane, peaceful form of society from the chaos of capitalism could be termed an 'upheaval' would be an insult to the memory of the many millions who suffered and died in those terrible events.

The condition of the world at the close of the 20th century is so critical that every facet of human society must be examined and improved at local, regional, and world levels; various proposals are advanced in Part Two below. However, it has become clear that if humanity is to survive, and if an alternative world is to function peacefully, constructively and for the benefit of all, certain fundamental changes are absolutely critical for success. First, a fully democratic, alternative world can only be founded on the genuine equality of all men, women and young people of all races, exercising maximum self-governance at all levels. The existing, almost universal practice of domination at every level by very small groups, usually men, who owe their privileged positions too often to accidents of birth or wealth, must be relegated to history; the very concept of elitism is humiliating, and degrading to human nature. *Of paramount importance for a successful Alternative World is the total and permanent rejection of capitalism.*

1 Guardian 27/9/91
2 Ditto 4/6/92
3 Ditto 2/7/92
4 New Statesman 10/7/92
5 Observer 7/6/92
6 Guardian 8/6/92

Part TWO

ALTERNATIVE WORLD

Utopian?—No!—Achieveable and Essential

Chapter 9

BASIC PRINCIPLES

Building an Alternative World confronts every concerned member of world society with a tremendous, stimulating challenge, which must be accepted if mankind is to both survive and prosper. If any, or all, of the proposals put forward below appear at first to be impossibly difficult of achievement, it must be remembered that perceptions at present are, not unnaturally, blurred by the all-pervasive false values of today's money culture. It is unthinkable that such a shallow, demeaning culture can survive indefinitely, when such an enormous untapped reservoir of socially-conscious citizens exists world-wide, who need, and deserve, a vastly better way of life. Essential, fundamental changes in world society can and must be brought about by publicising their potential worth, and thus enthusing men and women of goodwill everywhere. Their innumerable, diverse abilities could then be harnessed to achieve the needed changes, by powerful collective action. This would be non-violent, because the abandonment of all weapons is one of the cornerstones of Alternative World. At the same time, it could be brought home to many of the elites of today that they too could look forward to vastly more settled lives in an alternative world, through involvement in genuinely constructive activities, rather than their often spurious and uncertain ones as at present.

Need for global change

Fundamental social change is undeniably a formidable task on the scale of a continent, or even one country, but to succeed, Alternative World would need to comprise what its name implies: global change. The

20th century has taught us that individual attempts to effect serious political changes, on both large and small scales, have been all but strangled by the remaining capitalist world, and no doubt would be again. Apart from that negative reason, the positive case for global change is that Alternative World could only function properly, for the maximum benefit of mankind, if every important activity were planned and co-ordinated in a global context. The proposals made below are intended to be applicable to any part of the world. Man's essential physical needs in life are broadly similar everywhere; once these are taken care of, then true local cultural diversity in many forms can flourish—for the benefit of all.

Human equality

The first basic principle of Alternative World is that, world-wide, all men and women are born equal and, lifelong, remain equal in potential for using their abilities to the full, regardless of race, language, culture, religion, ancestry or any other allegedly special factor. One of the greatest advantages of abandoning money is that its possession, or lack of it, constantly undermines human equality and exacerbates differences. Freedom from the money system would enable all individuals to maximise their abilities, and thus lead full and rewarding lives. In particular, freedom from the hampering monetarist excuses of 'lack of funds' would enable societies to provide innumerable worthwhile jobs, meeting a vast range of badly needed requirements.

World scale planning

Whenever the will of the concerned majority prevailed, global agreement to introduce Alternative World arrangements would be signalled, in particular, by setting a date when all money would be abandoned, all weapons destroyed, and new societal organisations adopted (as in Chapter 10). At that stage, representatives from all regions should convene to draft the first global master plan, for the optimum locations of the world's agricultural and industrial production activities in the light of access to resources, distribution networks and other relevant factors. This preliminary, strategic plan would take account especially of the anomalous disparities between the original 'First and Third Worlds'—terms which henceforth would be consigned to history.

Levelling-up

In the light of the strategic plan, significant transfers of resources, including, for example, complete production plants, should be made from 'North' to 'South', so that, at the appointed date, Alternative World could commence on a more even footing than exists today. Clearly it could not be fully even: achieving a truly balanced spread of production facilities world-wide would inevitably take time. A particularly significant, automatic outcome of the abandonment of money is that the terrible scourge of Third World debts would be eliminated forever.

Sharing world resources

The world's most precious resource resides in the mental and physical potential of all its human inhabitants. With the advent of Alternative World, this resource would soon be augmented to the extent of at least 1 billion people, hitherto incapacitated by malnutrition. Further, it would also be added to forthwith, by the hand and brain power of at least 100 million able-bodied men and women, who would be released from both armed services with their support industries, and from all the various financial institutions. The latter, too, would see the freeing of vast numbers of valuable ex-armament production facilities, together with barracks, banks and a host of other commercial buildings for conversion, so far as possible, to dwellings or other useful purposes. The world's existing natural resources are amply sufficient to provide for full lives for all humanity, provided only that they are properly cared for and fairly distributed.

The second basic principle of Alternative World, therefore, is that the entire surface of the globe, land or sea, with everything under or upon it, natural or man-made, belongs jointly to every world citizen. This joint ownership would unite whole populations, both locally and more widely, with the common purpose of conserving and improving their entire environments in the most ecologically sustainable ways. The concept of sharing would be basic to the successful emergence of immeasurably healthier societies, whose citizens could forget enmities, jealousies and the like, and instead progress together towards the natural goal of continuing enhancement of their lives and communities.

Individual rights from society

The third basic principle of Alternative World is that every man, woman and child, fit or disabled, throughout their lifetimes, should receive as of right, from society as a whole, the basic essentials necessary for healthy and fruitful lives.

These should include as a minimum: appropriate accommodation in sound and sanitary buildings, balanced diets with adequate calories, basic clothing and footwear, full health care, all appropriate education and training, and the various other ingredients of really fulfilled existences, as set out in more detail in Chapter 11.

Individual obligations to society

The fourth basic principle of Alternative World, a corollary of the third, is that, after receiving adequate education and training, everyone up to an agreed age should contribute to society a certain agreed amount of work. Without the constraints of the money system, the whole work/leisure culture could be far more flexible, granted steady production and distribution of all the requirements of life in each region.

Again, an important factor would be the fair sharing of both the more arduous and the more interesting occupations, as discussed further in Chapter 12. A further obligation would be that every individual, from time to time, should contribute in appropriate ways to the organisation and smooth running of society, as outlined in the following Chapter.

Chapter 10

WORLD SOCIETY REORGANISED

Besides the abandonment of money and weapons, a third cornerstone of Alternative World has to be maximum devolution of societal controls. The term politics derived from the Greek 'politikos', which means 'of a citizen'. Pericles, leader of Athens city state in the 5th century BC, said: 'We are called a democracy because the administration is in the hands of the many and not of the few...we regard a man who takes no interest in public affairs not as harmless, but as a useless character.'

Discussing man's instinctive affiliations, Raymond Williams has written about 'rooted settlements, lived and worked with placeable social identities, and actual lives in knowable communities, as against the abstractions of modern national cultural identities. The term society began with a very strong stress on direct relations with other people, specifically physical relationships of contiguity, contact, relating. It was a word consciously opposed to the word 'state'—with all its implications of the power structure.'[1]

The case for alternatives to nation states was put powerfully by Amos Oz during his speech accepting the German publishers' prestigious Peace Prize in October 1992:

> I regard nation states as a bad and insufficient system. I think that upon this crowded, poverty-stricken and decomposing planet of ours there should exist hundreds of civilisations, thousands of traditions, millions of regional and local communities—but no nation states. Especially

now, when national self-determination has deteriorated into bloody disintegration of some parts of the world, threatening to turn each of us into an island, there ought to be an alternative vision. There ought to be ways of fulfilling various yearnings for identity and self-definition within a comprehensive commonwealth of all humankind. We ought to be building a polyphonic world, rather than a cacophony of separate, selfish nation states. Our human condition, our solitude on the face of a vulnerable planet, facing the cold cosmic silence, the unavoidable ironies of life and the merciless presence of death, all of these should at long last evoke a sense of human solidarity, overruling the sound and fury of our differences. *Flag-patriotism must give way to humanity-patriotism, earth-patriotism, patriotism of the forests, the water, the air and the light: creative relations with creation itself.*[2]

Regionalism: world turned downside up

To replace nation states, which were shown in Chapter 3 to be anachronisms, totally new administrative arrangements would be called for in Alternative World. The optimum forms of these arrangements could well evolve over a period of time when, happily, the circumstances would be fundamentally different to today's, in that there would be, for instance, no bitterly competitive trading blocs, nor potentially warring armed factions. On the contrary, the primary concern at all levels would be simply the co-operative promotion of human well-being, by planning production and ensuring egalitarian distribution, supporting scientific developments, improved technologies, better working conditions and innumerable other worthwhile, constructive endeavours.

The term 'regionalism' is adopted here in order to focus on the most important ingredient of decentralisation—that is the grouping of peoples into administrative areas according to their natural instincts, in relation to the most fruitful ways to coalesce; and topographical/economic regions would be the most likely starting points. For there to be meaningful planning and efficient co-ordination of all activities world-wide, it would be essential for there to be administrative bodies at each step from local, via regional and, say, 'continental' levels to a world forum. At all levels these bodies should be held in equal esteem, with guidance rather than dominance emanating from the 'higher' ones, but whose decisions would clearly have to be final in the event of any unresolved disputes. The aim would be for all ideas, proposals, draft economic plans and the like to have opinions formed upon them at all levels, which would then, if appropriate, be circulated for consideration in the contexts of the other levels, prior to final decisions being taken.

One of Alternative World's great assets is that these arrangements could start, and remain, flexible, in tune with mankind's continually changing, evolutionary circumstances. For example, the sizes of administrative areas, local or regional, could be readily increased or decreased according to organisational experience. Further, with equality of citizens world-wide, and minimal restrictions on movement, natural flows of talent would gradually take place as the needs for particular skills in certain regions attracted appropriate people from others, thus leading to a 'balancing up' of both cultural and technical capabilities. Such movements could also result in the increased integration of races, ethnic groups, and other allegedly divisive characteristics, leading to more harmonious cooperation throughout humanity. Such organisational devolution and flexibility, leading to enhanced human fulfilment, would be made possible by the abandonment of both nationalism and money, which have resulted, hitherto, in boundaries having been drawn in the contexts of chauvinism, racism, tax collecting, electioneering and other specious factors.

Representation: world without politicians

Devolution in Alternative World must mean the maximum, active participation by citizens in the shaping and running of their lives. Every issue arising, great or small, would need to be discussed as widely as possible in the community, in the certain knowledge that both imaginative ideas and worrying concerns would be considered seriously, and without undue delay. Also, citizens would have the satisfaction of seeing communities reaping the benefits of proposals they had made or supported.

In turn, representatives on bodies at all levels would feel confident of being able to benefit from informed, constructive criticism of issues put before them. Private, caucus meetings of representatives at all levels would be outlawed. The whole nature and tone of the only permitted, open discussions of representative bodies at any level would be quite different to those of today. They would be free of malign pressures from 'financial constraints', special interest lobbying, or issues involving potential armed conflicts. Thus the somewhat forbidding 'high-powered' image of representative bodies today would be replaced by a more relaxed, natural atmosphere in which all members of society could feel at ease, and able to contribute to what in the majority of instances would be common sense decisions.

Although the dispositions and sizes of administrative bodies in Alternative World could, and should, develop flexibly, certain principles would appear to be basic to success. In particular, representation should never be in any sense 'professional'. It should occur only once in a lifetime, for a brief period of perhaps three to four months, in order to provide opportunities for nearly every willing member of society to have the opportunity to serve once as a representative. We have seen in Chapter 3 that the existing widespread practice of 'politics' being a permanent, or semi-permanent job or career, is wrong on many counts, and totally at variance with the maximum involvement of all citizens—the lifeblood of democracy. Similarly, political parties would be extraneous and inappropriate, since their very existence implies partisan differences of interests, while in Alternative World only one interest would be paramount, namely the equal well-being of all citizens.

The various systems of elections, related to the occasional choosing of small numbers of long-term 'professional' representatives, would be inappropriate for Alternative World's frequent needs for large numbers of short-term 'lay' representatives. The most effective method of choice would be random selection by computer from the whole local electorate.

This should be programmed to choose equal numbers of males and females, from all age groups from, say, 15 to 75, in proportions broadly related to the actual population numbers in those groups, with at least one teenage boy and girl always included.

Thus the basic 'local' councils, serving populations of around 10,000 to 20,000, would be formed by perhaps 50 representatives, each serving approximately four months. During their period of service, the more imaginative and enthusiastic representatives would become apparent to their colleagues, who could, in turn, vote to send one in ten, say, of their own number, as delegates to the council at the next higher level. This process could be repeated at 'sub-regional', regional, and 'continental' levels, culminating in delegates to the world forum, but in all cases kept within the serving duration maximum of about four months. At both local and higher levels, representatives would serve full time, having been released from their normal occupations.

In this way, it could reasonably be expected that the higher echelon bodies would be replenished regularly with the more able representatives, who would all have had the invaluable experiences of having served at one or more of the more local levels. In all cases, when not attending committees or full meetings, it would be expected that representatives would augment their knowledge by research into appropriate current affairs of concern, and provide 'surgeries' to meet and assist those they represented. At all levels, both full and committee meetings should be open to public attendance, fully recorded for access by all, and televised if possible. This would encourage everyone, particularly young persons, to become involved, and start thinking about the sort of contributions they would wish to make when their turn came to participate.

At all levels, it would be natural and necessary for there to be administrative staffs to implement the various decisions of the bodies of representatives. For reasons of simple efficiency, it would be sensible for them to continue in their particular departments for several years. However, in the interests of both stimulating exchanges of experiences and ideas, and of offsetting any tendencies towards permanent bureaucracies, these administrators should alternate, before too long, with other occupations, as suggested in Chapter 12.

The media and publishing

The whole spectrum of the media and publishing in Alternative World would have an extremely important role, both in providing comprehensive world news and information objectively, and in stimulating all manner of co-operative societal aims generally.

Exclusive control of the production or operation of newspapers, television, radio, films, audio and visual recordings, magazines and books would need to be vested in the councils of representatives, at whichever level proved appropriate. Actual editing and other production activities, together with the choice and employment of writers, would be the responsibility of professional sections of the various administrations, with whom the representatives would be in close and frequent contact.

Thus the people, through their representatives, would have the opportunity to comment on and influence all aspects of the various programmes or publications, and to make suggestions regarding useful, stimulating and entertaining subjects for articles, films or books. *Replacing the present day remote, reactionary domination of a handful of tycoons over the entire media field by genuinely popular, responsive control, would make a dynamic contribution to the success of Alternative World.*

The current daily production of around 1,000 books and some 20 million words of technical reports clearly constitutes 'information overloading', which often proves highly stressful to those attempting to absorb it. Regardless of quality, the sheer bulk of data currently available, for example on the Internet, inevitably compromises its value. In Alternative World, global liaison between scientists and others, working free from the constraints of special interests, would ensure that research and development in every field of value to society were coordinated to maximise cooperation and minimise overlapping, without excluding differing approaches. Thus readers world-wide could benefit from reports and publications of all kinds which would not only be of premier quality, but would transform information into readily digestible knowledge.

Chapter 11

WORLD WITHOUT MONEY

The most convincing demonstration of humanity's determination to save itself would be to abandon money. To the small proportions of humanity currently in possession of sufficient amounts to enable them to draw from the flood of consumables at will, the very idea of not having money at all may well appear inconceivable. But if the decision to abandon money were to be taken, looking back later, it might well appear no more traumatic than an individual giving up smoking to preserve his or her life.

Almost every aspect of life throughout the twentieth and recent centuries, can be seen, throughout Part One, to have been cursed by the existence of money. *It has become clear that the money system has an inbuilt corrosive capacity for encouraging man's inclinations for evil, while rarely being available in sufficient amounts to support his efforts to do good, which are usually less profitable.* The great majority of the evil or unnecessary activities or institutions, listed in Chapter 2's A to Z, would disappear rapidly if there were no money to nourish them. And the incidence of the few, such as accidents or crime, which might not be eliminated, would be greatly reduced.

The key features of Alternative World are interdependent. In particular, the world's natural and man-made resources are only adequate for full, healthy lives for all if fairly shared worldwide, when money would become redundant. At present, the great majority of the world's peoples either have no money at all, or so little as to be almost meaningless, and that situation has shown no indication of improvement over recent decades. In the well-off sectors of privileged societies, money does indeed have an inglorious function in not only enabling their fortunate citizens to choose how to spend their ample funds, but also in enabling those heading the many branches of the system to continually enrich themselves further. At the close of the 20th century the capitalist money system can be seen to be in a state of incessant turmoil—and more clearly than ever to be beyond the capacity of its leaders to control it. It is a system which glorifies greed and, as a way of life, represents a profound insult to the dignity of man. Freedom from the stranglehold of the money system would enable humanity to make a giant leap forward.

Planned production

Relief from the constraints of capitalism would enable mankind, for the first time, to plan objectively the optimum arrangements of every kind of human activity in the interests of all, rather than the few. All-round, comprehensive planning would become a top priority, and would always take account of both short-term and long-term factors. Administrative staffs at local, regional and other levels would include members of all the appropriate professions, to prepare both production and construction plans which would become the responsibility of the various bodies of representatives to amend and approve. Developed within the context of the global master plan, regional and local plans would be concerned with rationalising the numbers, sizes and disposition of points of production in relation to the convenience of those working in them, proximity to necessary resources, distribution facilities and the like. Pooling of all existing productive units in common ownership would facilitate rationalising them in terms of retaining, enlarging, merging or closing; and deciding the scope, size and locations of required new points of production of all types.

Co-ordinated plans would embrace agriculture, raw materials, engineering and other manufacturing units, construction programmes and every other productive activity of real value to society. A key ingredient in all these plans would be the human element, including accessibility from settlements, health and safety, and liaison with education and training departments to ensure adequate numbers of appropriate personnel in years to come. The priority obligation in all output planning would be that of ensuring adequate, and, so far as desirable, varied outputs of the essential products needed to provide every citizen with the basic foodstuffs, goods and services listed below.

The abandonment of money, and pooling the world's resources would open up dramatic new planning horizons. The frustrations of striving for profits at all costs, cornering markets, over-producing, duplicating, under-producing, fighting price wars and so on, could all be forgotten, along with all the other extraneous and wasteful activities of capitalism. Instead, planners could enjoy the tremendous challenge of starting to meet the whole of mankind's vast and genuine needs, with unrestricted though ecologically-mindful access to resources, and with the world-wide support of ample numbers of capable and keen men and women in all fields of endeavour.

Citizen's entitlement from society

A high proportion of the production of goods and services worldwide is involved with meeting basic human needs. Since these are common to all men, women and children, everywhere, it would be logical for communities to divide up and allocate everything planned to be available to them, aiming to optimise both quotas and choices in all instances. *Decisions regarding such quotas and choices would be one of the main responsibilities of local councils of representatives, in the light of carefully planned use of resources.* Over and above benefitting from the provision of these basic necessities, individuals would be able to fulfil their innumerable different wishes, through obtaining their particular requirements in return for their extra work efforts as described below.

The first human entitlement would be appropriate balanced diets with adequate calories for all, which could be provided either for consumption in the home, or in part at canteens or restaurants. It would be helpful here to recall that modest, evenly-distributed diets have at times served communities adequately; for example during the 1939-1945 war, in the UK, rations per head, per week (in ounces) were: Cheese 1, Tea 2, Butter 4, Sugar 12, and Meat 15.

The second basic entitlement would be housing. In common with all other man-made resources, existing or new housing would be in social ownership. Local representative bodies would be responsible for allocating particular units of accommodation to citizens for as long as appropriate for their needs, and for maintaining dwellings regularly. One of Alternative World's highest priorities would be extensive construction programmes of good quality, permanent housing (Chapter 18), but for some decades housing would be likely to remain a scarce resource, to be valued highly and not wasted. Therefore occupation of every type of accommodation would need to be flexible, taking account of changes in family sizes, occupants' work locations, and other factors. Natural ancillary provisions would include water, energy for heating, lighting and cooking, and telephone. All these would naturally have to be subject to rationing— at levels agreed by representative councils in the light of local circumstances.

The third citizens' entitlement would be the best possible health care for all, with every available medical resource apportioned equally to all in need of attention, together with appropriate preventative programmes (see Chapter 15). Particular attention would be given to all forms of disablement, and to the well-being of the elderly. In the context of maintaining good health in local climatic conditions, adequate quotas of appropriate clothing and footwear would be made available to everyone, including exchange arrangements for children. The fourth major people's entitlement would be lifelong education (see Chapter 14), embracing every level from creche, through schooling to higher education, training, and refresher courses.

Further, to stimulate cultural activities of all kinds, Alternative World would promote the necessary environments, and access for all to theatres, libraries, cinemas, art galleries, museums and the like: it would also promote the widest range of physical education facilities, and all forms of recreation.

Every citizen of Alternative World would be entitled to annual holidays of agreed durations, including accommodation and reasonable travelling. Use of local transport would be available to all citizens, who would also be entitled to daily issues of the regional newspaper and use of postal services.

The above entitlements, which represent the basic requirements of virtually all citizens, would automatically be available to all. A second category of goods and services consists of items to meet particular individual interests or requirements; these would also be available to all, but on the basis of short- or long-term loans. As with major items such as dwellings, these too would be in common ownership and borrowers would be expected to maintain them well before returning them to stores or libraries for re-issue to others. Inventories of such items would be extensive, and constantly widened following popular demand; they could include for example: Bicycles, Books, Cameras, Garden Tools, Home computers, Musical instruments, Pictures, Radios, Records and Tapes, Televisions, Tools, Toys, Video Recorders etc. The administration and quota setting for all the various citizens' entitlements listed above would represent the major part of the responsibilities of the representative bodies and their administrative staffs. Thus the supply of every item impinging on people's lives, from food, housing, education and health, to bicycles, books and toys, would be sensitive to popular demands for alterations or improvements.

Recording citizens' inputs and outputs

In the vitally important area of ensuring fairness amongst citizens in all respects, Alternative World would take full advantage of the latest developments in computers and allied technology. At the administrative centre of each local council of representatives would be housed what might be termed the 'citizen computer'. At the inception of Alternative World, and thereafter for each new infant arrival, every citizen living within that computer's area would be allotted a registration number which, having around 12 or more digits, could, by co-ordination, remain unique to each individual, world-wide.

When a citizen moved home from one area to another, the registration number could simply be deleted, and added to the 'memory' of the citizen computer in the new area.

To operate the system, it would be necessary only for each citizen to have a plastic card carrying the appropriate embossed registration number, almost identical to the 'credit cards' which have proved themselves in the rich world to be both convenient and compatible with electronic scanners. With the exception of foodstuffs and clothing, all the entitlements mentioned above would be available freely to all citizens, without the need for billing or tickets of any kind. In respect of foodstuffs, clothing and household necessities, Alternative World would provide evenly-distributed outlets for every neighbourhood, similar in many respects to the 'supermarkets' so familiar in the rich world, which have the advantages of economy of scale for servicing and administration.

The 'currency' of Alternative World would be 'points', used both to value foodstuffs, clothing and other items, and to quantify extra work put in by citizens over and above their agreed obligatory minimum amounts. It would be necessary for councils of representatives to set 'norms' of points-per-week for food and clothing for all citizens, which might well remain standard over wide areas for considerable periods of time. These would be graded for children from infancy up to adulthood, with the great majority of adults of all ages on a standard amount, with an appropriate increase over the standard for those involved from time to time in particularly arduous work, and likewise a reduction below the standard for any citizens fit to work but not choosing to do so.

In respect of the most important area of food, administrators —

monitored by representatives —would allot value points to every item, so that citizens of all ages would obtain adequate nutrition from their allocation of weekly points. The range of items which could be set out in the supermarkets would depend, particularly, on there being a fair distribution of available supplies over wide areas, at least regional in size. The aim would be to provide a reasonable variety, so that people could choose, for example, different forms of protein, and still complete their shopping with around the desired 2,500 calories per adult per day. At each 'check-out', linked to the citizen-computer, each item's 'bar-code' would register the total points used, and, after insertion of the customer's card, these would be debited against the personal points account.

Every supermarket would have a computer screen, so customers could insert their cards to check their balances, and thus ensure they did not exceed their entitlement. Besides foodstuffs, these arrangements could also include agreed quotas of clothing, footwear and household necessities.

After receiving adequate education and training, every citizen of Alternative World, up to an accepted age, would be expected to contribute to society an agreed regular amount of work, in return for the entitlements set out above. This ruling would apply across the whole spectrum of industries, including agriculture, production, health, education and all other occupations; it would also apply equally to men and women. (Child care work by either sex is discussed in Chapter 12) Further, it would apply equally to all professions and occupations because, although professionals may have had to study hard to qualify, that training would have been free, and their responsibilities are compensated for by the nature of their work, which is invariably more interesting and agreeable than that of, for example, manual workers. In fact, differentiation in points grading between jobs of any kind would be invidious and divisive. The term 'professional', which now has somewhat elitist connotations, is used here for convenience to define those primarily non-manual health, designing, scientific or similar 'white collar' tasks usually performed in smaller groupings. In practice, in Alternative World, all occupations, from architect, through bricklayer and surgeon to welder, would be held in equal regard, all being essential components of society.

The measure of the 'agreed amounts' of work by each citizen would, naturally, depend on the nature of the tasks involved in each of the many different industries and professional departments. The first essential would be for each job committee (Chapter 12) to agree on what daily work output norm/s they considered reasonable, either in relation to their whole workplace, or in relation to larger or smaller groups within it.

These proposed norms could then be discussed with the local or regional council of representatives, who would amend or accept them when they were satisfied that, as nearly as possible, parity of effort had been arrived at across all occupations.

Naturally, these output norms could be varied by the councils whenever circumstances, such as introduction of new technologies, made changes appropriate.

Within each workplace, workers of all kinds would be concerned to cooperate, and to assist each other in order to achieve the weekly output norm for their particular group as quickly as possible, perhaps in 2.5 days if the norm had been set at three days. Once the job manager was satisfied that the called-for quantity and quality of output had been achieved, he/she would insert the cards of the workers concerned into the citizen computer terminal so that their weekly stints of obligatory work could be recorded. Any worker so wishing could then leave, and live on the basic entitlements listed above.

Alternatively, he/she could choose to continue working up to an agreed maximum number of hours per week, and the citizen computer would record the resulting extra output in terms of commensurate numbers of points. These points could then be used to obtain some of the numerous goods and services not already included in the list of citizens' entitlements, each of which would carry points value tags, agreed between administrators and representatives, according to availability. In this way citizens would be able to lease cars or other individual vehicles; make use of transport facilities beyond the free local range; or obtain extra items of foods, clothing or household equipment not already covered by their entitlements.

Living without money

The aim of the system outlined above would be to provide all citizens with an essential foundation and operating framework for their lives, which would enable them to make the best possible use of their very real equality of opportunities. *It would also encourage an appreciation of belonging to a world-wide community, with only limited and precious resources.* However, it would also be important for local councils to institute systems of rewards for outstanding contributions to society.

These could be given for a wide range of achievements, including for example: successful teaching of autistic children, building a road in exceptional conditions, creating a work of art enjoyed by the whole community, or producing a record food crop. These rewards should not become routine, but proposed and agreed within representative councils when clearly appropriate. They would take the form of a reasonable number of points, perhaps the equivalent of 100 hours of work, which would be seen as both just, and worth emulating.

Some idea of the tremendous advantages to be gained by living without money can be gauged from the fact that everyone (particularly those at present living in the rich world) would be relieved of these day-to-day financial worries: bank charges, exchange rate variations, fluctuating interest rates, inflation, means tests, mortgage or rent demands, overdue credits, overdrafts, pension worries, recession fears, salary or wage stoppages, security of cash and credit cards etc, unemployment benefit worries, unpaid bills, various taxes and so on. By contrast, Alternative World's simple points system would be easily understood by everyone and be totally under their control, by virtue of the only accountant involved being the inanimate, incorruptible citizen-computer, accessible to them at all times through use of their personal cards.

Chapter 12

CONSTRUCTIVE WORK FOR ALL

Throughout almost the whole of today's world, the work scene is too often characterised by frustrations, tensions and friction.

The lack of job satisfaction is illustrated by absenteeism, high worker turnovers, drug-taking on the job, vandalism and poor quality work. Employers rarely offer their workers any involvement with decisions, or variety of tasks. Many workplaces resemble battlegrounds between demanding boss and reluctant worker. The constant threats of recession and unemployment further undermine the confidence of workers, and compromise their efforts for better wages and conditions.

Further uncertainty is caused by the practice of retaining workers in spurious occupations—such as manufacturing armaments—simply to bolster the employment figures for political purposes.

New concepts of work

With the advent of Alternative World, work of all kinds would become integrated with society, as a natural part of life as a whole. Above all, this would mean a basic re-orientation of attitudes to work. *It would no longer be 'employment', organised in every respect according to the whims of private employers, and without which breadwinners suffer. On the contrary, work would become a normal activity which everyone would expect—and be expected—to perform, as their contribution to society* (as referred to in Chapter 11). Instead of being carried on in independent units, all work, whether in agriculture, production industries, transport, the professions, service industries or elsewhere, would become the responsibility of the local or regional councils of representatives to plan and co-ordinate for optimum results.

Freed from the twin evils of profit-seeking and wasteful competition, work units of all types and sizes could cooperate with others locally, regionally or globally to share out resources and tasks in the most logical ways. Freedom from the pressures of the money system would enable decisions of all kinds to be taken more objectively, for there to be less tension leading to aggravations and accidents, and for installations of new buildings or machinery etc to be made as required, without being compromised by worries over funding.

Control of all workplaces by society would also facilitate movements of every kind of worker from one type of occupation to another. While it is likely that most individuals would prefer to remain in their chosen fields of work, many might well wish to change to, for instance, more intellectually demanding or responsible work as their self-confidence grew with further education and training. In such cases, or alternatively in cases of shorter term secondments, the resulting cross-fertilisation of ideas and experience would be beneficial both to the individuals involved, and to their new working environments. Such transfers or exchanges of personnel could be particularly helpful, for example, in the case of persons from other areas joining and assisting the departments of administrators attached to the representative councils (as suggested in Chapter 10).

The tasks ahead

The briefest consideration of the vast scale of the tasks ahead, awaiting fulfilment by the world's workers, makes a mockery of the very idea of unemployment for many decades to come. In respect of physical developments alone, it has taken the rich world several centuries to create its various existing environments, and a great many of those need basic renewal.

Today's vastly bigger poor world has little that is comparable, which although in some respects not a disadvantage, represents a mammoth backlog for Alternative World to tackle. The release of resources, presently wasted on armaments and other features of the money system, would augment basic supplies sufficiently to permit commencing the creation of environments worthy of all its six billion or so inhabitants.

Railways, roads, health and education buildings, and a host of other infrastructure requirements would be needed. But the greatest task of all would be the construction, world-wide, of at least one billion good quality dwellings. And each of those billion houses or flats would require several hundred different items of fixed or loose equipment, ranging from sanitary and kitchen fittings, through furniture, crockery, radios, to books and innumerable other personal requirements. At the same time, there would need to be a vast increase in numbers of teachers, in particular, so as to guarantee the enhanced numbers also needed in the other professions such as engineering and medicine. Thus it can be seen that even starting to fulfil all the tasks would occupy every citizen of working age worldwide, and would present the planners and organisers of all the endeavours involved with unprecedented challenges.

Introductions to work

J K Galbraith has written: 'There is no greater modern illusion, even fraud, than the use of the single term "work" to cover what for some is dreary, painful and socially demeaning, and what for others is enjoyable, socially reputable and economically rewarding.'[3] A whole range of sometimes dreary, often arduous jobs, such as waste collection and disposal, and 'general labouring' in almost every industry and occupation, will always need to be performed to keep the wheels of society turning. *Alternative World would introduce the practice that without exception all fit young people around age 18, having completed schooling, would undertake these tasks for one or two years, before commencing higher education or other forms of training for their chosen careers.*

This arrangement would have many advantages: it would enhance citizen equality; it would emphasise that such jobs, being essential, were no longer 'socially demeaning'; it would ensure that the inevitably heavy jobs were performed by those best fitted to undertake them, namely the young; with the presence of permanent foremen and forewomen as instructors, it would serve as an important introduction to work in general by teaching amicable discipline, cooperation over tasks, use and handling of basic tools and equipment, the importance of safety at work for onself and comrades, and other useful forms of experience. Interchanging could be readily arranged, so that each young person obtained some understanding of perhaps four or five different industries. A further, fundamental advantage of the practice would be that it would promote the development of broad-minded, understanding young people, better equipped to contribute later to the successful running of society.

Workplace organisation

In Alternative World, real democracy would be as important in the workplace as in the rest of the community. In all workplaces, large or small, across the whole range of industries and occupations, people would be involved as much as possible, and encouraged to participate in decision-making regarding all aspects of production. This approach would be supported by the realisation of all concerned, that the whole production environment was their own, joint property, to be valued and cared for, and used for the speediest production consistent with good quality output.

A parallel principle of representation to that in the community as a whole would be adopted for the establishment of job committees in all workplaces, namely random selection by computer to give everyone the opportunity to serve. These committees, representing either whole workplaces or sub-divisions of very large ones, would be reasonable in size, with a proportion of their number being replaced at intervals for continuity. Job committees would only meet as circumstances required, for example, to amend or endorse other than routine management proposals. These committees would arrange elections, from and by the whole personnel, of a manager and the minimum necessary number of assistant managers. They would serve for limited periods and could stand, if they wished, for re-election, with a maximum of perhaps two years. Managers would liaise regularly with local or regional councils, to maintain output in keeping with the accepted plan. Freed from the innumerable distractions of financial wheelings and dealings, managers would be able to devote their time solely to obtaining required materials, and organising the most efficient general arrangements.

In keeping with workforces as a whole, managers would contribute to the weekly obligatory working time, and then receive the same number of extra output points as those earned by their fellow workers. Managers and job committees would agree actual working days and hours, including for both the obligatory output stints and subsequent 'individual benefit' working hours. Night work, except in special circumstances, would be avoided. These timings would reflect suitable compromises between individual preferences, and factors pertaining to efficiency such as energy conservation.

Job managers in Alternative World would strive *to foster individual aptitudes and skills; make work as interesting and enjoyable as possible by maximising flexibility and avoiding boredom; listen to complaints and take account of preferences; encourage all concerned to suggest and design new tools, technologies or production layouts;* and put forward recommendations to councils for rewards to outstanding workers (as mentioned in Chapter 11). Further, job committees and managers, in agreement with the appropriate council, would need to agree on balances between labour and mechanisation, bearing in mind the desirability of minimising tedious operations. They would also make use of the experience of those who had been trade union organisers or shop stewards in relation to promoting good working conditions and welfare generally. Trade unions as such, like political parties, would no longer be required in a society where the need for protagonists of employees against grasping employers no longer persisted.

One of Alternative World's important objectives would be to give women every opportunity to lead as full and interesting lives of their own choice as their male counterparts, particularly by providing creches at workplaces, nursery schools and health care facilities for sick children. However, during periods when women, or fathers, had to remain at home for pre- or post-natal or other essential occasions, they would be counted not only as working the basic weekly stint, but would also receive individual benefit points in line with those of their colleagues at work. A further objective would be to make all possible efforts to compensate the permanently disabled for their predicaments by facilitating their joining whatever working environment appealed to them, through appropriate training, ease of access, adaptations to equipment and similar measures.

Finally, Alternative World would lay great emphasis on safety at all workplaces by encouraging workers to be alert for dangers, and arranging for regular inspections by safety teams, with the right to order instant closures until corrective steps were taken. If there were cases of workers wilfully or carelessly compromising safety, or causing any other distress to their colleagues, managers would be duty bound to impose penalties by withdrawing points earned by the wrongdoers.

Chapter 13

HUMAN RIGHTS, JUSTICE

The famous United Nations Declaration of Human Rights represented an admirable and comprehensive code of conduct for mankind. If it had been respected globally over recent decades, we would not have witnessed the terrible wide-ranging assaults on humanity described in Part One. These assaults have been mounted worldwide, by elites sustained by their money system— capitalism. Alternative World would supplant that system, and thus clear the field for the establishment and consolidation of the full range of human rights everywhere.

Rights of individuals

The following more important rights listed in the UN Declaration, Articles 3 to 21, would all be confirmed by the introduction of Alternative World: the right to life, liberty and security of the person, the right to equality, freedom of thought, conscience, religion, opinion and expression, peaceful assembly and association; Freedom of movement and residence, freedom from arbitrary arrest, exile, detention, torture and slavery; freedom from arbitrary interference in privacy, family, home or correspondence; the right to participate in government. All these rights would be brought to life and given real meaning: for instance, in the latter case, over and above it being a right, every citizen would be actively encouraged, and expected, to play his/her part in all levels of government (as explained in Chapter 10).

Similarly, the Economic, Social and Cultural Rights listed in Articles 22 to 27 of the UN Declaration would also be fully implemented, including the following: the right to social security; the right to work; the right to rest and leisure; the right to a standard of living adequate for health and well-being, including food, clothing, housing and medical care; the right to education. Again Alternative World would provide an added dimension to these rights. For example, 'work', which could have many meanings, would be firmly defined as a normal, expected, societal activity in a context of total equality.

Justice among citizens

In today's world citizens' attitudes to society can be defined as 'battening down the hatches' in regard to private property, looking the other way and hoping not to get involved in regard to wrong-doing in public, and leaving it to the police to sort out misdeeds of all kinds, usually without success. In fact, both today's police and judiciary have become increasingly fallible and unpopular, and represent little more than alibis for societies' failures to organise themselves equably. Furthermore, both judiciaries and police forces are often staffed and controlled by discredited and usually harsh elites.

In Alternative World, the elimination of money, private property and weapons would bring about fundamental changes for the better in human relationships. *Above all, primitive instincts, such as 'What I have I hold', would be replaced by a cooperative sense of shared responsibility for all aspects of living—engendered by human equality and the common ownership of everything except small personal belongings.* A totally fresh approach would be based on the concept of 'society looking after itself' in the light of centuries-old morality relating to generally good behaviour. This natural morality, instinctive for the great majority of mankind unless distorted by evil influences, is in fact enshrined in the tenets of the world's great religions.

Thus the attitude of the vast majority of citizens would become one of valuing and caring for every part of their jointly-owned environments. Every citizen's instinctive outlook would be to watch out for potential 'slippage' by fellow humans into wrong-doing of any kind. In these ways, damage to or deterioration of environments would be minimised, and many minor or worse crimes prevented before they occurred.

To emphasise its determination that every member of society should be answerable only to themselves and each other, Alternative World would not maintain either police or judiciary.

The only arbiters of human behaviour would be the local representative councils, which, being constantly replenished by random selection, would be held in the same esteem as the well-tried jury systems of today. The importance of 'popular participation' even in today's context was underlined by one of the few open-minded and well-respected UK judges, Lord Scarman, when writing an obituary tribute to another, Lord Devlin:

> It was basic to his thinking that the true criterion of sound law was whether or not it achieved justice. He saw justice not as some legal concept to be defined by lawyers, but as a requirement set by society which the law must meet. At the end of the day, society—that is to say the opinion of ordinary men and women—should decide what is or is not just.[4]

A form of society akin to that of Alternative World was envisaged in the 1887 prophetic novel, by the US writer Edward Bellamy, *Looking Backward 2000-1887*, in which he wrote:

> We have next to no legislation—we have nothing to make laws about. Our society's fundamental principles settle for all time the strifes and misunderstandings which in your day called for legislation. Fully 99 percent of laws then concerned the definition and protection of private property, and the relations of buyers and sellers, neither of which now exist beyond personal belongings. With no private property to speak of, no business disputes, no real estate to divide nor debts to collect, there remains no civil business for lawyers. Defendants in criminal cases pleading guilty are punished, those pleading not guilty are still tried. Law as a special science is obsolete; it was a system of casuistry which the elaborate artificiality of the old order required to interpret it; everything touching the relations of men to one another is now much simpler.[5]

The whole new range of circumstances in Alternative World would eliminate practically all temptations and opportunities for wrongdoing. More positively, it would make universally available both long term education, and numerous opportunities for cultural and physical activities, which would provide the best antidotes to any criminal tendencies. However, whenever any forms of crime were commmitted, it would be the responsibility of those present at, or with knowledge of, the incidents, to make 'citizen arrests', obtain statements from witnesses, and take the culprit before the local council of representatives. Since these councils would consist of some 50 full-time members, they could well appoint a 'sub-committee' of 10 or 12 jurors as quickly as possible, while memories were still fresh, to hear the evidence. Those brought before such juries could depend on being considered innocent until proved guilty. In the event of guilt, the death penalty would never be an option, and every effort would be made to minimise both the number and duration of incarcerations. Preferably, alternative, non-custodial sentences would be imposed. These could include exposure to ridicule by fellow citizens or workmates by inclusion of portrait photographs in 'rogues galleries', or simple fines in the form of subtraction of points from the culprit's personal account within the citizen computer.

Chapter 14

LIFELONG EDUCATION

The non-existence or terrible inadequacy of education in the poor world was described in Chapter 1. The resulting immeasurable loss of human intellectual potential represents the greatest waste of global resources, especially because, following brain damage from malnutrition, it is largely irreversible. However, the widespread absence of education is not the only problem in today's world—its very presence is also, in certain respects, an obstacle to progress. Although many subjects by their nature are non-controversial, the teaching of others such as history or economics is almost invariably biased in favour of the status quo. There have been many instances of governing elites arranging omissions or changes in their own histories in order to present their young with glossier versions of events. But, more importantly, almost world-wide, today's educational regimes collude with the media in presenting the young with the concept of present day capitalist societies as the only possible form of environment for humanity to exist in. Schools and universities tend to be mirrors of society, rather than searchers after the truth; even in more 'liberal' countries it is exceptional for a teacher to be bold enough to suggest that there might be an alternative to capitalism.

Childhood education

The basis of education at each level in Alternative World would be the provision for every young member of world society of equal opportunities to develop their intellects and abilities to the full, in vastly better academic environments than exist today, if they exist at all. *They would be taught about all aspects of society in Alternative World, and how they could begin to participate and make useful contributions to running it. They would be encouraged to cooperate rather than to compete; to be partners rather than adversaries.* Underlying the concept of 'lifelong education' would be that of the whole of society being one big school. This would imply arranging, within reason, for the gaining of some experience by young people—outside the classroom—of various aspects of adult working lives. It would also suggest a 'freeing-up' of society, so that all young people would feel at ease when asking advice or guidance from older citizens, whether previously known to them or not, on any subject at all. By the same token, it would become natural and accepted for older people to absorb some of the latest knowledge acquired by those younger. In these ways the artificial divisiveness of 'generation gaps' could be eroded, to the lasting benefit of society as a whole.

By way of a refreshing change from the gross commercialism of education in the US, the principal of a New York City secondary school, Deborah Meier, made this comment on the educational reform debate:

> The challenge is a thrilling one: to make every child the possessor of a kind of intellectual competence once available to only a small minority. This inspiring, and new, task means granting all young citizens the conviction that they can have wonderful ideas, invent theories, analyze evidence and make their personal mark on this most complex world. Such a transformation of the idea of why children go to school would transform the very nature of democratic life.[6]

A succinct definition, in *Looking Backward* by Bellamy, of factors favouring giving man 'the fullest education he can absorb and enjoy', includes 'the right of his fellow citizens to have him educated as necessary to their enjoyment of his company', and 'the right of the unborn child to educated parentage.'[5]

Alternative World would restore the bygone respect for teachers as persons of the highest importance, since the crucial responsibility for the nurturing of future citizens is to such a large extent in their hands. It would be recognised that the key to success in education at all levels lies in the best possible relations and understanding existing between pupils and teachers. It would also be recognised that conscientious teachers' tasks are very demanding, and they should be given all possible aids to ensure their job satisfaction. Freed from the constrictions of monetarism, there would be greatly increased numbers of teachers, so that none would be overloaded, and pupil/teacher ratios could be optimised. School and university buildings would be built and maintained to the highest standards. Educational equipment aids would be supplied as required—to assist but not to supplant teachers. Lending libraries would be stocked liberally with the widest range of textbooks.

Alternative World would recognise the importance of schools as cradles of democracy, by ensuring that pupils had reasonable opportunities to participate in decision-making relating to the running of their schools generally, and actual teaching methods in particular. To this end, teachers would be expected to invite their pupils, from time to time, to answer questionnaires regarding their methods, and then to discuss with them the desirability of any changes. This practice has been described by the Head of Exeter (UK) University School of Education, as leading to much better performance by both teachers and pupils. In a report [7] Dr Burden states: 'Pupils will be asked if teachers are friendly, helpful, and whether they consider pupils' feelings and suggestions. They will have the opportunity to comment on the way the teacher organises lessons and the methods used. Experience shows that if children are involved in the establishment of rules, they are more likely to keep to them.'

All tiers of education would be administered by the departments directly responsible to the local or regional councils of representatives. Both the overall sizes of schools, and of classes within them would be strictly limited to those agreed by all concerned to be in the best interests of both pupils and staff. It would be an axiom of Alternative World that all children attended the co-educational school appropriate to their age level nearest to their home at the time, without choice. If any parent/s had good reason to argue that a particular school was not operating to such a good standard as the majority of others, then it would be obligatory on the council's administrators to put matters right forthwith without regard for any over-sensitive feelings.

Education up to secondary level would be comprehensive, with a balance between the sciences and the humanities, and without premature specialisation. The main objectives of education would be to detect, to bring out, and then to train the capacities of creative thought. Parents would be encouraged to make use of work-place or local creches, to introduce children to cooperative activities from infancy. Similarly, nursery education from age three would be obligatory, since it has proved to be such a valuable foundation for future schooling. Both creches and nursery schools would be housed, equipped and staffed to the same high standards as all other educational establishments.

Adult education

The introduction to work (see Chapter 12) undertaken by all young people aged 18 to 20 would provide a natural transition from school life to adulthood. Through broadening the mind by involvement with the 'nitty-gritty' of society, it would result in those choosing to undertake higher education being more mature, and thus better equipped to take full advantage of it. The significance of 'Lifelong Education' is that compulsory childhood schooling would be followed by the freedom, the facilities, and the encouragement for all citizens so wishing to participate in both 'higher' and 'further' education from their 20s, right through to their 70s and 80s. *The huge release of resources away from destructive and wasteful activities which would follow the introduction of Alternative World would readily permit—many times over—the provision of buildings, equipment and teaching staff to cater for whatever demand this lifelong freedom created.*

The first, emergency task of Alternative World in the education field would be to eradicate illiteracy globally, at all ages.

The provision of teaching environments for all schoolchildren everywhere would naturally give priority to reading and writing for them. The immense task of assisting the many millions of adult illiterates would need to be tackled in different ways according to circumstances, but it would be a task of paramount importance if all the other benefits of Alternative World were to be fully realised. Adult literacy campaigns in parts of the Third World, albeit so far on limited scales, have proved that students can well succeed in initiating older persons into literacy. A ten-year target period, for example, for the achievement of universal literacy could be publicised to catch the imagination of everyone, world-wide. School leavers would be encouraged to help run the crash courses involved as part of their introduction to work periods.

Once young people had completed their introduction to work periods, they would be free to enter places of higher education, granted only a sincere and evident intention to benefit themselves and thus society by so doing. In the interests of equality, as much intermingling of students as possible from all parts of the world would be encouraged, to maximise cross-fertilisation of ideas and cultures. Course durations would vary up to four or more years; initial groundwork courses of general education would be recommended before specialisation.

One of the most important tasks of the departments of education would be to assess the approximate needs for the many different skills and disciplines in the years ahead. With the vastly greater resources available for all the arts and sciences in Alternative World, serious over-production of particular disciplines would be unlikely; however, it would clearly be desirable to be able to guide young people's choices to some extent so as to ensure the output of as good a balance of abilities as possible. While studying, students would receive the same basic entitlements as other citizens; during spare time or vacations they could earn extra points on appropriate jobs at output rates agreed between them and the local councils of representatives.

In relation to higher education, it is apposite to quote from J D Bernal:

> In a civilisation where the whole basis of knowledge is expected to change several times in a generation, the passing on of established knowledge becomes palpably inadequate and, also, from its ever increasing bulk, impossible.
>
> It is lucky if most of what is taught is true, or supposed to be true, at the time it is taught. It is certain that it will no longer be considered true by the time those who are taught it are half-way through their lives. What is needed, therefore, is a different and lightened content of education. The emphasis will be on discovery rather than knowledge. It will be, not so much the passing on of established truths, as showing the way to criticise and discover new truths; in other words, the active part of the scientific method.[8]

The multi-disciplinary universities in Alternative World would be 'centres of excellence', with all necessary libraries, technical equipment and other resources. They would provide for the following needs: first, basic undergraduate training in chosen subjects; second, refresher courses to enable citizens to catch up with new knowledge within their existing disciplines; third, re-training in different spheres of work for those in contracting occupations, and for those simply desiring to change occupation because their original choice had proved inappropriate; fourth, further education in any desired subjects for citizens of all ages wishing to broaden their horizons.

Chapter 15

UNIVERSAL HEALTH CARE

Today, the appalling lack of health care throughout most of the Third World, and the poorer parts of the First World, continues to cause the decimation of shamefully high proportions of humanity. In particular, it results in the extinguishing of young lives, even before their potentials have had the faintest chance of developing. Average First World expenditures on health amount to 100 times that in the Third World. The US figure approaches 500 times greater. Most Third World citizens never so much as see any medically qualified person throughout their entire lifetimes; by contrast, some First World individuals benefit from the undivided attention of whole teams of surgeons, anaesthetists, and nurses during lengthy transplant operations. 15 million helpless infants suffer agonising deaths yearly, or 40,000 every single day, from almost totally preventable diseases. These, with their approximate annual numbers of resulting fatalities, include diarrhoea - 5m, tuberculosis - 3m, measles - 2m, malaria - 1m, tetanus - 1m, whooping cough - 600,000, polio - 50,000. The World Health Organisation has estimated that mass immunisation campaigns would virtually eliminate all the killer diseases —at the trivial cost of around $2 per child. The failure to quench the greed of the multinationals, selling powdered milk baby foods to the Third World, continues to cause 25 times more infants dying than those that are breast-fed.

Alternative World health

Health has been defined as being not merely an absence of illness, infirmity, anxiety and helplessness, but rather a state of complete physical, mental and societal well-being.

Alternative World would make a reality of that definition, by making every required resource available —just as for education. The saying 'Money no object' would take on a real new meaning, since there would be no money— and therefore no shortage of it—to be an objection. The world would be freed from today's gargantuan wastes of manpower, steel, cement, aluminium and innumerable other valuable resources currently squandered on armaments, and other examples of profligate wastefulness of the money system. Thus, the whole of mankind could build schools, universities, health centres and hospitals, with all their ancillary laboratories, operating theatres, dispensaries and so on, and still leave resources to spare.

Within those laboratories, Alternative World would promote the fullest programmes of research to develop both ameliorative treatments and total cures for all the various diseases which currently plague mankind.

In keeping with the vast deployment of all the necessary physical resources in the health field, Alternative World would take immediate steps to make commensurate global increases in the numbers of medical personnel. The eventual grand total of health workers of all kinds would, as with teachers, simply reflect the uninhibited demand for their services.

Since training human minds absorbs trivial amounts of resources besides other human minds to instruct them, it would be absurd to compromise successful health care because of any shortages of doctors, nurses, surgeons, laboratory technicians or others.

Further, as again with teaching, successful treatments often demand more individual attention than is commonly available today, even in the First World. Also, medical work is often very demanding, and the resulting desirability of reasonably short duty periods would further increase the needs for personnel. Medical training schools would be established urgently, but, even with tremendous efforts, a decade or more would inevitably pass before anything approaching adequate numbers became available globally. During this period, all possible steps would be taken to assist already qualified and willing medical personnel to help in establishing health services in what had been the Third World.

Universal health care in Alternative World would be built on two equally important foundations. First, the physical. This would include good housing, served by pure water supplies and efficient drainage systems; adequate food and clothing; air and soil free of pollution. Second, the psychological. *This would include self-confidence, based on an awareness of the equal value of every individual; a real sense of involvement with*

society; control of one's destiny without frustrations and uncertainties; free-
dom from worries about money and unemployment; enjoyment of pleasant
environments, which would promote relaxation through cultural activities
and leisure generally. Both these vital foundations would be profoundly
important for creating favourable conditions for healthy minds and
bodies; they would immediately result in dramatic reductions in the
present catastrophic global toll of deaths, and of both mental and
physical illnesses.

Organisation of health care would be undertaken at two distinct
levels: local health centres and regional or district hospitals. Health
centres would be sited for ease of accessibility by population groups
ranging from around 2,000 to perhaps 5,000, according to circumstances. They would contain facilities for doctors' consultations, and
clinics of all kinds, an operating theatre, X-ray room, a dispensary,
and living accommodation for at least one doctor and one nurse. The
first function of these health centres would be preventive medicine.
This would be exercised by obligatory physical examinations at regular intervals, involving scans and other checks known to be rewarding in terms of early diagnosis. Preventive advice in various forms
would also be given on many aspects of health maintenance including, for example, first aid, exercise, child care and the like. The second
health centre function would be to provide as many medical, dental
and minor surgical treatment services as possible to save citizens having
to go into hospital.

In keeping with Alternative World's aims of equality and fair sharing of resources, hospitals would be kept to reasonable sizes and dispersed as evenly as possible, both to facilitate access by relatives and
to minimise emergency ambulance journeys.

The aim would be to achieve broadly equal standards of excellence,
rather than some, often remote, hospitals becoming outstanding in particular fields. The role of hospitals would be limited to those tasks
beyond the capacities of the health centres, involving more sophisticated equipment and in-patient care. All hospitals would be built and
equipped to the highest standards, and would always have more than
enough beds and staff for the needs of their catchment areas, so ad-
missions would never be a problem. Doctors and nurses could be in-
terchanged at times between hospitals and health centres, both to
meet changing demands and to broaden experience. Since there would
be no financial constraints, but only prudent resource-use considerations, hospital management could take the common-sense form of
committees elected from those most concerned, namely doctors, surgeons and nurses. These management committees would be responsive

both to current patients' suggestions, and to the local council of representatives in broader contexts.

In the interests of stabilising and eventually lowering world population, particular attention would be paid to family planning clinics at the health centres, where the responsibilities of men, too, for contraceptive measures would be emphasised. All sectors of populations would be catered for at health centres, but if priorities ever had to be allotted, they would go to women for pre- and post-natal care, and to young children. Many problems dealt with by social services departments or citizens' advice bureaux today, would fade away with the abandonment of money. However, a need for counselling on a variety of subjects would always be likely to exist. Since unresolved worries often result in health problems, it would be logical for there to be an 'advice clinic' at each health centre where psychologists or other appropriate professionals would be available.

Alternative World would pay particular attention to the needs of disabled people of all ages; every opportunity would be taken to assist them to lead as normal lives as possible. In cases of disablement, or frailty due simply to old age involving people being confined to their homes, ample numbers of social workers would make frequent visits and would make arrangements for home help and provision of meals for as long as necessary.

Chapter 16

NATURAL RESOURCES, FOOD, THE ENVIRONMENT

We have seen in Chapter 4 and elsewhere how the grossly irresponsible money system continues to savage both global resources and the environment for short-term gain, without any consideration for the future. During just 30 years, from 1950 to 1980, annual world paper consumption increased fivefold to 230m tons, involving over one third of the total timber harvest. Paper production consumes huge amounts of energy—in the US for instance, it uses 10% of all energy used in industry.

The great majority of paper disappears into astonishing quantities of 'newsprint' produced by rival elites, who may be competitors yet who are all devotees of capitalism. Thus the millions of daily acres of newspapers which are not wasted on unnecessary advertisements are covered with almost exclusively negative news often slanted against the best interests of mankind.

Conservation of resources

Those fortunate enough to be involved with the introduction of Alternative World will face a tremendous responsibility in deciding how best to use all the world's manifold resources.

In sharp contrast to today's careless approach, they would need to consider the welfare of many generations to follow them. In the context of greater longevity, looking ahead four to five centuries would only imply five to six lifetimes. The first world forum of representatives would need to institute a detailed global survey, resulting in an 'inventory' of all known, and likely potential resources world-wide. Detailed proposals for the long term use of every type of resource could then be drawn up by the planners. In the interests of democracy, and so that the widest understanding of the issues could be gained, those proposals would then be circulated throughout all the various representative councils world-wide, for amendments and approval.

Global resources fall into two distinct categories: renewable and non-renewable, which call for different types of decisions.

Renewables, relating primarily to the earth's surface, include: topsoil, food crops, forests, flora and fauna, and water. In very approximate, round figures, half the world's surface above sea level is currently unused, being mountainous, frozen, desert, or excessively saline. The other half is, currently, divided roughly equally between forest and potential food-producing areas, the latter, where used, being subdivided approximately as to one part crop land to two parts pasture or grazing land. It can be taken for granted that the planners would recommend retaining the vast majority of forest areas, and reinstating, as soon as possible, those that had been destroyed, particularly in areas of climatic significance. Taking account of greatly reduced, but truly essential needs for timber, they would also designate appropriate areas for harvesting and re-planting.

The optimal purposes of all remaining usable land would then need to be agreed. It is known that the existing global total of land used for food production could be increased by at least 50%. Further, huge areas of both arable and grazing land have become degraded for various reasons resulting from private ownership and market forces. Freed from financial inhibitions, all necessary steps could be taken to restore such areas to good condition. Having expanded farming land to the utmost, the balance between arable and grazing land would then call for agreement. Current heavy consumption of meat, almost entirely by the better-off in the First World, is vastly in excess of protein requirements. The huge amounts of grain presently fattening livestock would be better used for human consumption.

Anal gas emissions from the world's 6bn cattle worsen global warming through nearly 60m tons per annum of methane; together with sheep and goats they have degraded over 70% of global grazing lands.

Since obtaining proteins through animal consumption is an inefficient process, an informed global discussion would need to be instituted in order to decide, first, whether it was sensible for the world to produce any meat at all. If, having taken account of nutritional, ecological and other considerations it was agreed to produce nominal amounts, a modest weekly meat ration for each world citizen could be agreed. An appropriate balance between grazing and arable land could then be struck, which could differ significantly from that obtaining at present, and thus increase dramatically the potential for wheat, rice and other food crops.

Alternative World would take fullest advantage of its common ownership by all humanity, to devote loving care to the restoration of the earth's surface to full health in all respects. In particular, the highest priority would be given globally to preventing further topsoil erosion—the insidious devastation let loose by market forces which now threatens future food supplies. Great emphasis would also be placed on the world-wide preservation of flora and fauna, which would be facilitated by the absence of financial temptations.

Problems with both quantity and quality of water supplies have become all too evident in many parts of the world. These very difficult problems would become considerably more tractable following the abolition of both money and nation states.

Reasoned negotiations could arrive at fair distribution arrangements where regions shared common sources. Alternative World would promote water conservation through flood control and elimination of waste, and by fair distribution, including curbing excessive use by some industries. Research would develop new possibilities for water supply, such as long distance 'grid' distribution, and by furthering deep tube well technology. If, eventually, a viable transfer method evolved, the annual 100m tons of fresh water in Antartic icebergs would suffice to produce 2bn tons of grain.

The world's non-renewable resources, mostly below ground, can be subdivided into fuels (Chapter 17) and minerals with industrial applications. At present consumption rates, known global fuel reserves have been estimated to be sufficient for the following periods: coal 200 years, gas 50 years, oil 30 years. The more important minerals include: bauxite, copper, diamonds, iron ore, lead, nickel, tin and zinc; considerable reserves of many of these are also known to exist upon or beneath sea-beds. The resource-use planners would need to list the current global consumption of each of these, and other less well-known minerals. Next, global totals of all the current consumptions by all forms of weaponry manufacture could be deducted, leaving projected net, 'peaceful' consumption figures. Following that, global lists of all the other current applications of each resource would be prepared. These would highlight forms of resource use which would be saved by eliminating wanton waste on all forms of luxury developments. Next would follow a schedule of applications not necessarily considered luxuries, but which the planners proposed should be either eliminated, or greatly curtailed, in the interests of conservation.

This schedule would include those prodigious current wasters of mineral resources: cars, lorries and motorways. Alternative World would explain to that small proportion of global society now owning cars, that they are an aberration which the world should never have had in such numbers, and must largely abandon (see Chapter 18). Emphasis would be placed instead on excellent public transport, including especially railways for both passengers and goods, and the provision of hire cars for occasional use by those earning the necessary points (see Chapter 11).

Finally, a master plan would be prepared which would set out the reasonable annual outputs of every worthwhile form of production, ranging from basic heavy industrial machinery or ships, to lightweight household equipment. Against this would be shown the consumption of all the different resources involved, together with the resulting likely exhaustion dates for each, which might range from 50 to 500 years ahead. This plan would then be circulated for discussion by councils of representatives world-wide, so that binding, democratic decisions could be taken governing the future use of all global resources. Alternative World would encourage citizen representatives to arrive at such decisions in a spirit of unprecedented self-denial, in the interests of many generations yet unborn. Even the unlikelihood of a resource having an exceptionally long-lasting expectancy would not justify using it up more than strictly necessary. Also, the predicted likelihoods of technological developments leading to substitutes should be looked upon as a bonus for future citizens rather than an excuse for extra consumption.

World food supplies

It is in the fundamentally important field of feeding humanity that Alternative World would be able to achieve dramatic improvements more quickly than in any other. This is because, as we have seen in Chapter 6, total calorie and protein productions already exceed the world's total basic human requirements. Once the inhuman capitalist priority of profits before life had been eliminated, it would be possible to mount an immediate global emergency programme of distributing food to all suffering the criminal tragedies of malnutrition and starvation. This would be a short-term measure only, until it became possible to transform world agriculture and food distribution on to a sound, balanced footing. Farming in most of today's Third World is skewed deliberately by agribusiness towards export-oriented mono-crops, and in the First World it is often inhibited by the stop-go uncertainties of the market system.

Alternative World would introduce as quickly as possible an integrated global plan for all food production, processing and distribution, based on maximum diversification of crops and, so far as possible, self-sufficiency within regions. In common with all plans, the human element would be crucially important, and the fact that all workers in agriculture and ancillary industries would be joint owners of the land would be fundamental to success. The only near equivalents to full societal ownership have been the rare examples of land reform, which resulted in dramatic improvements in output. For example, reforms in China in the 1950s had almost doubled agricultural yields by 1975, to a level 60% higher than India's. By 1987, China was able to feed a population 50% larger than India's, 20% better, and with 30% less cultivated land.[9] Although ideologically hostile to the concept, the World Bank itself has estimated that land reform could increase agricultural output by, for instance, 10% in Pakistan, 20% in Malaysia or Colombia, and 80% in North East Brazil.

In common with other industries, the most efficient machinery and equipment would be made available for circulation within groups of farms, to minimise wastage. Alternative World would create agricultural colleges to train 'agro-technicians' and disperse them globally, so that farm managers and workers could themselves receive up-to-date training and guidance in all aspects of agricultural techniques. Farms would be organised to be within reasonable distances from small towns, which could provide cultural and recreational amenities, besides having some light industry. The latter would facilitate interchanging from time to time between farming and factory work.

Besides expanding total farming areas, improved methods of cultivation would always be the aim. Measures would be taken to recycle sewage and return phosphates to the soil; to adopt improved breeds of plants; to rationalise the economical use of fertilisers; to organise improved forms of handling, storing and distributing foodstuffs to minimise waste; and to eliminate pests. Eliminating the tsetse fly in Africa, for example, would reclaim an area for farming approaching the size of the US.

Further, since only about 10% of existing Third World farm land is irrigated properly, Alternative World would give priority to creating new irrigation systems, sometimes assisted by reviving old ones. For this purpose, mechanical plant would be widely used, unless prevented, for example, by exceptional terrain. In these circumstances, large numbers of manual workers would be mobilised to excavate canals and tunnels, build dams, and upgrade river banks against flooding. Other measures to amplify efficient food production would include increasing wheat production, which requires only half as much water as rice, and integrating fish breeding with irrigation systems. Ecologically balanced steps would also be taken to extend ocean fishing, since the sun's energy produces more living matter in the seas than on land.

Saving the environment

Throughout Part One of this book can be seen the many different seeds of potential for the destruction of mankind; in particular, armed conflicts could degenerate into nuclear holocaust. None of these appalling developments is necessarily inevitable, however, provided today's world leaders can to some extent control themselves. By contrast, mankind's doom resulting from environmental crises can already be said to be all but inevitable, because all the disastrous, often irreversible processes involved are already well under way. Relief from the horrors set out in Chapter 4 can be gained from the realisation that they could be reversed, and gradually rectified, by the elimination of the profit-seeking money system.

First World leaders today continue not just to tolerate, but actually to promote all-round environmental destruction, pleading that to do otherwise would be 'too expensive'. This in spite of an official estimate that it would cost no more than 3% of world GNP to rectify most of the problems. The much-vaunted 1992 global environment conference, attended by the world's most prestigious leaders, achieved little beyond various half-hearted promises, some already broken. Alternative World would ensure that every aspect of the environment was treated with the highest respect, guided by two main principles. First, malpractices of all kinds would be stopped immediately, and forbidden in future. Second, in so far as any manufacturing or other activities with potentially harmful side-effects were to be considered beneficial for society, then whatever resources were necessary to counter those side-effects would be brought to bear on the problem, financial constraint being a thing of the past. Above all, in common with natural resources generally, discussed above, it would be of critical importance for a mandatory world plan dealing with all environmental issues to be adopted.

A global ban on all tree-felling would take immediate effect, until balanced conservation and harvesting plans had been agreed. All necessary resources would be applied urgently to reduce serious flooding, and to conserve water for irrigation and domestic use. Construction work on all unfinished large dams would be halted, in most cases permanently, unless impartial studies showed completion to be in the best interests of society. Stopping felling and taming rivers would also assist reduction of soil erosion, but the eradication of this desperately serious blight would call for a global campaign.

Eradication of atmospheric pollution, involving global warming and damage to the ozone layer, would also receive the highest priority. Since coal is still plentiful and so valuable for electricity generation, its inevitable side-effect of CO_2 emission would have to be accepted, and countered by applying the most effective known flue gas 'scrubbers' world-wide.

Because of chlorine's severe effects, all forms of CFC sprays, which society could well live without, would be banned permanently; a harmless alternative for refrigerators would be prescribed for use globally. In view of their prodigious emissions of carbon and nitrous oxides, space rockets and supersonic planes would be prohibited for ever. For the same reason, the use of ordinary planes, lorries and cars would all be reduced severely. These measures would result both in improved atmospheric conditions and in significant savings of non-renewable fuels.

Alternative World would adopt a highly critical stance in relation to industrial processes involving noxious fumes, effluents or other poisonous side-effects. If the products were of a luxury or otherwise unnecessary nature, they would be prohibited. If appropriate councils of representatives decided that some 'dirty' industries were essential to society, then every suitable resource would be brought to bear, preferably to substitute a pollutant-free technology, or to purify the effluents to the maximum possible extent. There would be a firm ruling that such toxic wastes as could not be avoided would have to be both rendered as harmless as possible, and then disposed of within the region of origin, and never exported elsewhere.

Apart from saving materials and energy, in order to minimise waste every type of packaging, bottling, canning and other forms of containerisation of all kinds of products would be reduced to the bare minimum. Citizens would be expected to take away most goods loose, and to bring their own containers to the supermarkets for refilling from hygienic bulk food dispensers, so that canning could be virtually dispensed with. Similarly, they would bring their own glass or plastic bottles for refilling with milk or other drinks, and would never take away a full bottle without replacing it with a similar empty one. As a result, recycling would become largely redundant. It is in any case an unsatisfactory solution which tends to promote the 'throw-away' approach, and, especially in the case of glass, can absorb almost as much energy as the original product.

Recycling would, however, be promoted for all metals which unavoidably became scrap, and for the significantly smaller quantities of newsprint and other paper which would be produced in Alternative World.

The most lethal of all waste-producers, nuclear generation, would be closed down, world-wide, as rapidly as possible.

However much its protagonists minimise the risks of accidents, when they do occur, the results are so horrendous that mankind can no longer tolerate them. There would then remain no option but to devote whatever resources proved necessary in order to dismantle all nuclear installations, and to render both them and all their terrible waste products totally safe indefinitely. Finally, Alternative World would call a halt to further despoliation of the planet through the indiscriminate spreading of towns and cities.

Chapter 17

ENERGY, AND ITS USES

The First World, with around 30% of global population, consumes 80% of all energy today. Over 2bn world citizens depend on rapidly diminishing supplies of firewood as their primary source of energy. They are denied any possibility of enjoying all the various uses of electricity which the rich world takes totally for granted: lighting, heating, cooking, washing machines, refrigerators, televisions, vacuum cleaners and all the numerous other household aids. If there is no firewood to be found, even after many daily hours searching, and they are able to obtain modest amounts of crude kerosene for cooking, the fumes will cause them both lung and eye damage. At the other end of the energy use scale, profligate consumption of many tons of high grade aviation fuel takes place every minute of every day throughout the rich world as 'Jumbo' jet planes struggle to get airborne with their massive loads.

In common with so many other valuable resources, the world's stocks of non-renewable fossil fuels are being exhausted at an accelerating rate. Their consumption is all too often governed by barely credible preferences being given to short-term profits. In 1992, for example, the UK government considered it perfectly acceptable for the newly privatised electricity generating companies to change over to burning allegedly 'cheaper', but less plentiful gas, even though the resulting fall in demand for their traditional fuel would mean millions of tons of coal being lost for ever in the abandoned mines.

Throughout the First World, political leaders preside over a headlong rush towards the extinction of basic fuels, without a thought for future generations.

At current, accelerating consumption rates, natural gas and oil are expected to last around 50 years and 30 years respectively.

Therefore the final exhaustion of these prized and versatile fuels will occur around 2025. We have seen in Chapter 4 that the various environmental disasters including soil erosion, forest destruction and climatic deterioration will also reach ultimate crisis levels at around the same period. Thus during the remainder of the 20th century, and the first quarter of the 21st, mankind faces a whole series of doomsday scenarios, unless urgent action is taken to reverse them. Further, although coal resources are currently expected to last some 200 years, once oil and gas have gone that expectancy could well be greatly reduced.

Alternative energy policies

There are three distinct priorities for energy conservation and use: first, the necessity to treat the remaining reserves of fossil fuels with the greatest care; second, to maximise efficiency in the use of all forms of energy, world-wide; third, to promote the development and use of all possible alternatives, and so far as possible renewable forms of energy. In Chapter 16 we have already seen the need for a significant reduction in the waste of resources involved in the manufacture of certain road vehicles. Because of the urgency, also, of reducing fuel consumption, Alternative World would immediately cease further manufacture of cars and heavy lorries, and withdraw the maximum number as early as possible from the roads (see Chapter 18). Oil fuel would remain available for medium and large passenger vehicles, local goods delivery, farm tractors and mechanical plant for housing and other essential building and civil engineering works, such as irrigation. However, even those vital activities could not depend on oil fuel supplies indefinitely, and a start would need to be made on developing alternative energy sources or technologies for them.

In common with all the other fields of endeavour, the elimination of the restraints of the money system would open the door for the most rewarding approaches to the problems of energy. Private profit interest would no longer exist to compromise promising developments, such as restricting the development of hydrogen as a fuel by the oil companies. Every needed resource world-wide would be applied to make suitable and adequate energy available to mankind everywhere. The world forum of representatives would prepare a global energy plan for ratification by all the regions, and thereafter adoption would be mandatory. The plan would first ensure that the remaining supplies of all three of the main fossil fuels would be shared out equally, world-wide. Because regular energy transfers over long distances tend to be wasteful, the plan would aim at regional energy self-sufficiency wherever possible, with mutual assistance when necessary.

Energy use efficiency

One estimate of over-all global energy conversion efficiency has suggested a figure as low as 6% to 8%, with an absolute maximum of 20% after taking account of such factors as friction, heat losses, wear, malfunction, poor fuel oxydisation, transmission losses, overloading and inadequate insulation.[10] Whatever the actual figure may be, the scope for improvement is clearly enormous. Studies have shown that, simply by applying already known technologies, efficiency world-wide could well be increased by at least 30%, leading to commensurate energy savings. An authoritative US study in 1989 showed that improving efficiency nationwide could be 7 times more cost effective than introducing nuclear generation. Very large, widely separated generating stations,which result in serious transmission losses even at very high voltage, indicate the desirability of smaller-scale, localised generation, using whatever energy source is appropriate.

Alternative World would promote the widest possible application of 'CHP', or combined heat and power schemes which have already proved their value in many locations. CHP makes use of the otherwise wasted exhaust heat from fuel-fired generating stations by means of 'district heating' systems piped around neighbouring housing or industrial estates. This technology can double efficiency; if used more widely in the UK, for instance, annual savings of around 30m tons of coal could result. The most dramatic energy savings could naturally be obtained by eliminating altogether such inefficient users as cars and heavy lorries. Similarly, significant savings could be made in hot climate areas by eliminating air-conditioners. The gross inefficiency of this technology is underlined by the fact that it absorbs five times more energy to lower air temperature by one degree than it does to raise it by one degree. In the US and Japan, for instance, peak electricity loads are determined by air-conditioning demand. Since prior to the 20th century all societies managed their lives without air-conditioning, and most still do, Alternative World would not permit its use except for hospitals and other genuinely special cases. Dramatic energy savings could also be made by curtailing nightlong lighting of streets and other forms of unnecessary illumination.

Freed from the inhibitions of 'budget restrictions' and the like, it would be possible to devote all necessary resources to exploiting the the tremendous opportunities for greater efficiency in almost every sphere of energy use. Alternative World would ensure that, in cold climates, both new and existing buildings included the best possible standards of thermal insulation. Since compact fluorescent tubes use only 20% of the energy required by conventional bulbs for equivalent lighting, and last around 12 times longer, their use would be introduced everywhere, both in new and existing buildings.

Items of household electrical equipment offer scope for energy efficiency improvements; it has been estimated that if low-quality refrigerators were replaced throughout the US, the output of some twenty generating stations could be saved. Similarly, the efficiency of electric motors, with such a vast variety of applications, could in many cases be improved.

Both through greater efficiency,and through elimination of wasteful usage, mostly in the rich world, as outlined above, the net energy gains to the world would be huge, if incalculable.

To those gains would be added the enormous energy savings which would follow the elimination of both the manufacture of weaponry, and the wasteful use of fuel by armed forces everywhere. The combination of these two totals would represent a formidable proportion of existing world energy use. That grand total of presently wasted energy could be diverted, and used in the best possible way by bringing living conditions in the present Third World up to acceptable standards, without seriously encroaching further on existing world energy stocks

Renewable energy sources

Very shortly, when oil and natural gas are gone, and before long, when coal too is gone, the world will have no choice but to exploit alternative, renewable sources of energy.

Alternative World's master energy plan would give high priority to both developing existing technologies further, and to researching all possible new ones. Once 'levelling-up' had been achieved by the transfer of necessary resources including energy, from North to South, the world could face its energy future on a fairly equal footing. Fortunately, largely because all renewable energy derives in different ways from the sun, opportunities for exploiting that energy are reasonably evenly spread around the globe. For example, very broadly, the greater availability of solar heat in equatorial regions could be said to be balanced by the greater possibilities for hydro- or wind-power in Northern or Southern regions.

Renewable energy sources can be divided into two categories. 'Primaries' can be defined as those which require initial construction of necessary installations such as solar panels, but subsequently continue to function indefinitely by natural processes. 'Secondaries' can be defined as those which, besides initial installations, require various additives to supplement natural processes. 'Primary' sources may be subdivided into those involving water, wind, the sun and other forms of heat.

Hydro-electric schemes already produce around 25% of all power produced globally. Reference was made in Chapter 4 to the highly harmful environmental effects of many of the world's huge new dams. Unless it could be established beyond doubt that no ecological damage would result, Alternative World would put a stop to such developments. Instead, efforts would be concentrated on medium-sized and small 'run of the river' dams which could supply local communities and reduce transmission losses.

Power generated by turbines within estuary barrages, driven by the rising and falling tides, have been proved in a number of examples world-wide to be technically satisfactory. However, as with massive dams, it would always be necessary for possible harmful ecological side-effects to be taken into consideration.

In line with all the other possibilities for producing energy, all necessary resources would be provided to promote wave-power generation, particularly by building full-sized trial installations. One of the many possible types was designed and described, by Professor Salter of Edinburgh: 'Nodding "ducks" would float in long lines absorbing over 80% of wave energy. Free-floating, they would slowly drift towards shore, while using their generated power to electrolyse water and thus produce hydrogen. At a convenient point most of the hydrogen would be taken off for use as fuel in various ways, and the balance used to tow the line of ducks out to sea to start the process again.'[11]

Wind as an energy source is unique in being available world-wide, night and day, and in overcast conditions. However, its main compromising feature, intermittence, has to be taken into account. Since in Alternative World all resources would be owned in common, it would be vastly easier to both integrate wind generation with other forms, and to provide various means of storing wind energy for use during calm conditions. Great emphasis would be placed on research to improve and extend such storage technologies, which currently include pumped water, flywheels, compressed air, batteries and hydrogen. It has been estimated that 100,000 well-dispersed, large wind generators could supply all Europe; California expects shortly to meet 10%

of demand from wind power. Research would also be focused on the aesthetic aspects, to make future, necessarily prominent but essential 'wind farms' as visually acceptable as possible.

Solar energy absorbed by the earth annually, approximates to 20 times the energy value of all the world's existing fossil fuel reserves yet at present we fail to use more than 0.5% of that potential. An important contributing factor to that failure has been the selfish, profit-guarding behaviour of the money system: 'When the solar-cell industry began to flourish during the 1970s, the world's major oil conglomerates lobbied strongly against it. They then proceeded to buy out most of the independent producers and research and development organisations. By 1983, the four largest photovoltaic manufacturers, which commanded half the global market, were wholly owned by major oil companies.'[12] Once Alternative World had 'freed up' man's natural inventiveness, a vast range of possibilities would open up for solar energy. At one end of the scale, large installations could generate electricity for distribution, as a few already do. A Japanese estimate has suggested that around 300 square miles of solar cells, sited in deserts, could produce as much power as is currently consumed world-wide. At a more modest level, photovoltaic cells, such as those used on spacecraft, could produce instant electricity for domestic cooking, refrigeration and stored energy for lighting.

Such a technology would have obvious application in the present Third World, and would represent a simple, yet tremendously welcome, resource which could be readily transferred from North to South once Alternative World had been established. Apart from the humanitarian impact, such a transfer could put an early end to the present appalling destruction of the earth caused by the incessant, desperate search for firewood.

The geothermal energy in the upper 5km of the earth's crust is equivalent to 40m times that in the world's oil and gas reserves. It can be used to produce heat or power. Either subterranean hot water is pumped up or natural steam can drive turbines. Man-made steam is produced by drilling into hot rocks and pumping in water which emerges as steam from other boreholes.[12] Currently only 0.1% of the world's energy needs are met in these ways, so the opportunities for research and development are clear.

Several 'secondary' renewable energy sources could well be developed further, particularly by minimising the amounts of 'top-up' energy needed to supplement the natural processes involved. Hydrogen is a particularly promising, clean fuel, simply produced from the reaction between electricity and water, but requires further research particularly in relation to the bulk of the tanks required. 'Green' fuels have been developed from various crops; so far petrol solvents, diesel oil, and lubricants have been derived from sugar beet, vegetable oils, straw and oilseed rape.[13] Alternative World scientists and representatives would need to weigh carefully the pros and cons of using potentially food-producing land for fuel production.

Every effort would be made in Alternative World to keep waste of all kinds to the absolute minimum. Whatever domestic, industrial or agricultural waste proved to be totally unavoidable, would all be put to the best possible use in some form as fuel. Again, unconstrained research and development would undoubtedly produce solutions beyond those already proven.

Methane is a valuable gas produced from most decomposing processes, and can be used at high efficiency in specially designed engines. In fact, in 1990, the US was producing more power from bio-generation than from nuclear energy.[14]

Chapter 18

BUILT ENVIRONMENTS

Conditions in Alternative World would provide an unprecedented opportunity for planners, architects and designers generally, to create genuinely 'user-friendly' environments. Within one, or at most two centuries the characteristics of physically developed areas the world over could be transformed from their present often inefficient and ugly nature to areas giving pleasure and satisfaction. *Freedom from the dead hand of private ownership of land and property would make possible the essential broad approach to what is undoubtedly mankind's most significant activity: creating physical environments which, through their inevitable permanence, will affect many generations yet unborn.* Because all planning and construction works would be the responsibility of local or regional councils of representatives, they would as closely as possible reflect the best interests of society by taking full account of every aspect of citizens' needs.

References have been made under 'concrete jungles' (Chapter 4) and 'bloated mega-cities' (Chapter 5) to the avalanche of appalling environments world-wide, which have resulted from the largely haphazard developments of the 20th century.

Uncontrolled mushrooming of city populations up to many millions has plagued the Third World worst; for example, Lima grew from 2m in 1960 to 7m in 1990, or 50% of Peru's total. A rare example of the benefits of planning control has been Havana, whose population of 2m remains as in 1960, ie 20% of Cuba's total. Without even the excuse of exploding populations, the First World also continues to desecrate itself; for example, if physical developments of all kinds continue as at present, it is estimated that 20% of the UK will be concreted over by 2050.

Not only have buildings themselves left much to be desired, very often vital services have been omitted altogether; in the world as a whole 40% of urban populations, and 90% of rural populations lack sanitation altogether.

Planned development world-wide

Alternative World's planners would be able to adopt a totally fresh approach to all physical development. They would appreciate that the disorder they would too often inherit is nothing more than the inevitable legacy of the anarchic capitalist system. That system would be seen to have been not only inherently antagonistic to positive community planning, but supportive mainly of individualistic plans for personal profit.

20th century towns and cities might appear to be terribly permanent, but nothing on earth is immutable. Several great cities in early history disappeared completely; hundreds of towns and cities throughout Europe were largely destroyed between 1939 and 1945. Great swathes of housing and industrial buildings in First World cities, left derelict by capitalism's regular attacks of depression, have, in some cases, been demolished and cleared away. The fact that most or all of those demolitions took place for wrong reasons does not exclude the concept of planned clearances being made for the right reasons. For example, because Mexico City grew irrationally from an old village in a location with insuperable seismic and climatic problems, serious consideration has been given to abandoning it completely.

To lead balanced and rewarding lives, town and city dwellers need to be able to visit and enjoy the many different facets of the country-side from time to time. *At present, many cities are so vast that their citizens are virtually trapped in them, as if in a quicksand, many for their whole lifetimes. However well-planned and attractive urban areas can be made, the aim should be to restrict their size firmly to around one million inhabitants, or far less where possible, and to ensure the rural integrity of their surrounding areas.* With the advent of Alternative World, equality of rights and opportunities would be established for all, everywhere. As a result, massive emigrations of city dwellers would surely follow, as people abandoned overcrowded slums to return to the healthier areas they had originally been forced to leave.

The first world forum of representatives would need to establish a planning commission charged with the task, in close liaison with all the regions, of developing an optimal global plan for physical developments. This plan would need to take account of the disposition of resources, including food, energy and water, and a host of other relevant factors, before making recommendations regarding slimming down certain existing conurbations, and locations for new human settlements. In this context, it would become essential to take account of the bizarre imbalances in existing population densities world-wide, that is, numbers of people related to 'usable' areas of land available to them. Non-usable areas include mountainous, desert, swamp, waterless and other forms of inhospitable territory, together with forests which must be preserved. The resulting proportions of total land areas which can be used by mankind for agriculture or physical development amount to under one-third in all the current Third World continents. Thus expressed, population densities in South East Asia are around 100 times higher than those in North America. A further indicator of astonishing space disparities is provided by the fact that the US has, per capita, 20 times more agricultural land than China.

Population densities are commonly expressed as persons per hectare, which happens to be the area of a football field, and is thus easy to visualise. When standing at its centre, everyone on such an area can be readily identified, and a few moments walking brings one to the centre of the next similar area. By 2030, according to present trends, every hectare of usable land in 12 present Third World countries, by then having over 3bn inhabitants, will have to 'carry' from 6 to 30 persons. The comparable 'loading' in the UK, for instance, would appear likely to be about 2 persons, and in North America approximately 0.1 persons.

In the light of such data, it is likely the planners would be predisposed to recommending new settlements in particularly North, but also South, America, and in whatever other comparatively 'empty' parts of the world their research revealed. Citizens in densely populated areas would have every right to move to less crowded regions if they wished, but the scale of such movements would be very difficult to predict.

Past migrations have usually resulted from persecution or economic pressures; in the absence of these, millions might well prefer to remain in the environments they grew up in.

Therefore, although populations in the existing crowded areas would be sure to fall in due course, following birth control and some emigration, it is clear the planners would need to recommend particularly strenuous development efforts in those regions, accepting that much housing and other accommodation would have to be shared for the first few decades.

Alternative World's physical development policy would be the creation of both new towns and sub-divisions of existing cities, large enough to be self-sufficient in respect of education, culture, health, leisure and working occupations. New Towns would always be sited on land least suited to farming; the aim would be for 90% to 95% of usable land to be agricultural.

Existing cities would be 'humanised' by retaining such good features as existed, demolishing the ugly and worthless and sub-dividing them into a number of self-contained 'towns', separated by parks leading in turn to the surrounding countryside.

One of the planners' most important aims would be to arrange the locations of industry world-wide so as to achieve an overall balance of work opportunities. Apart from certain 'heavies' such as ship-building, whose locations are pre-determined, the majority of industries could be dispersed evenly around regions so as to maximise choices of occupations. At present, many millions of workers world-wide have come to accept the depressing scenario of daily 'commuting', often long distances from home to workplace and back. It is a practice not only wasteful of their time and often health, but above all highly wasteful of energy for transport. In Alternative World, since industrial processes would be obliged to minimise all forms of pollution, only very few operations would need to be sited 'down wind'. The majority could be dispersed evenly around communities, just as schools for in-stance, so as to be within easy reach from the homes of their workers. Further, since housing would be plentiful and occupancy flexible, cit-izens changing jobs could move easily into homes adjacent to their new occupations. Thus commuting could be relegated to history. Common ownership of all forms of physical development would enable local and regional plans to be truly comprehensive. The disposition of schools, community buildings of all types, leisure facilities, housing and industry would all be conceived in terms of facilitating citizens' move-ments within and between them, whether on foot, bicycle or by public transport.

Housing

Alternative World would single out the design of housing for very special attention, because it is the environment in which everyone, inevitably, spends such high proportions of their lifetimes, and in such close proximity to each other. The critical importance of maintaining consistently high standards of housing would be recognised as fundamental to the creation of contented, co-operative and productive societies. The steady increase world-wide in the numbers of older, less mobile members of society adds further to the importance of dwellings. In this context, housing layouts would contribute so far as possible to regenerating the concept of the 'extended family', promoting opportunities for mutual assistance without compromising privacy. Housing design and management would reject tendencies to group the elderly together, and aim instead at a mix of generations which would be beneficial to each other.

All housing would be built to high structural standards, which are in any case obligatory in many parts of the world for earthquake or cyclone resistance. Permanency makes for optimal use of resources, and spares future generations the burdens of unnecessary maintenance. Each dwelling would have as much basic sanitary equipment as resources allowed, but, as a minimum, a toilet and a sink. Sound insulation, both within and between dwellings, would have a high priority, particularly because of high occupancy rates. These would favour designs making it possible to sub-divide rooms during the early years, until housing output had met demand. The immense numbers of dwellings required would call for maximum standardisation to facilitate mass prefabrication. It would be recognised that, far from being a disadvantage, good designs bear repeating; witness the well-liked 18th and 19th century UK terrace housing, in which sufficient individuality is often expressed simply by different coloured front doors.

In Alternative World, the whole of the world's surface would be the joint property and responsibility of mankind, and recognised as being a highly precious and easily wasted asset. Because of the necessity to preserve all possible areas of land for agriculture, and because housing is inevitably a heavy land user, it follows that all new housing, worldwide, should be built at high densities. Shoddily built, overcrowded slums have created the false impression that high densities are synonymous with low standards; in fact, much luxury housing in the First World is high density. More importantly, the use-efficiency of resources for sewerage, water, electricity, street lighting, paved access and other facilities all relate to the number of dwellings served and therefore benefit from high densities. In this context, the building of large dwellings on individual plots would be outlawed, whether in 'leafy suburbs' or in open country.

The importance of building housing at high densities is underlined by the following: other than agriculture, the two main users of land are a) housing and b) community facilities. The latter include: playing fields, parks, education, health and administration buildings, supermarkets, industry and transport. Whether in cities or towns, group b uses are all essential, and experience indicates that for healthy, productive communities they require a relatively stable average of around 10 hectares per 1,000 population. By contrast, depending on the density chosen, housing for 1,000 persons will consume widely fluctuating areas of land, varying from 1 hectare at a density of 1,000 persons per hectare, up to 20 hectares at a density of 50 persons per hectare. Besides wasting precious land, low density housing inevitably involves longer distances for people to traverse to reach the various group b facilities.

Alternative World would recommend that the great majority of new housing take the form of two- or three-storey, narrow-fronted terrace dwellings. One suitable application includes a private patio with planting space at the rear, with further, separate accommodation above a toilet and utility room beyond. Such a layout could result in fully acceptable densities of up to 180 dwellings per hectare, accommodating over 1,000 persons per hectare. With low water use sanitation (using kitchen and washing water for flushing) the highly economical arrangement could be provided of one private toilet, washroom and sink for under two metres run of sewer. If small numbers of flats were called for, these could be provided in three- or four-storey blocks, adding visual variety but inevitably consuming more resources to build, particularly in seismic areas.

Transport

In Alternative World, the common societal ownership of both all points of production, and consumer outlets would mean that all forms and sites of activities could be rationalised, and thus the needs for transportation of both goods and persons reduced to the essential minima. Joint ownership of every type of transport facility would promote both flexibility and energy savings. All forms of transport would be planned and coordinated by departments responsible to the local councils of representatives, and thus all systems would be responsive to community needs. Main emphasis would be placed on surface public transport worldwide, for both goods and passengers, over long and short distances, in rural and urban areas.

The aims would be to maximise carrying capacities, and minimise numbers of individual drivers while retaining all staff desirable for safety, yet providing such comprehensive services that cars and long-distance lorries would become largely redundant. Environments would be planned and laid out to encourage individual movements either on foot or bicycle, by provision of safe, sometimes covered path- and cycle-ways. Elimination of commuting would greatly reduce local passenger transport demand.

Priority would be given to railways of all kinds, from long distance to local light systems or tramways in urban areas, all carrying both goods and passengers. Widest use of electric traction using power from renewable energy-sourced generation would minimise pollution. Container systems would be developed for maximising efficiency in transferring loads from mainline to local delivery transport.

For inland regional goods movements, canal systems would be both revived and extended. Two-unit push barges can carry as much weight as two freight trains or 100 heavy lorries, with far less fuel consumption. Passenger coaches and medium-sized trucks would be used for local transport to supplement rail services; monster articulated lorries would be outlawed. Since hydrogen can be produced renewably from electrolysis of sea water, and exhausts water vapour only, its use would be promoted for barges, trucks and coaches which could accommodate the somewhat bulky tanks required.

There are now around 500m cars in the world, and their numbers are increasing by nearly 20m annually. Each year, cars are responsible for 250,000 deaths and vastly more injuries; their exhaust fumes will soon be the biggest contributors to global warming. In Europe alone, 12m discarded cars weighing 9m tons are scrapped annually. 30% of car journeys are under one mile, 50% under two miles and 75% under five miles. Alternative World could not continue to tolerate such appalling pollution and waste of human lives and resources. However, there will always be some legitimate uses for cars, and the right to use spare 'points' to lease them has been mentioned in Chapter 11.

Therefore, research would support the further development of electric cars, which, in the interests of both safety and economy, would be unable to exceed, say 30 miles per hour. Their batteries could be recharged from renewable energy sources.

Since air transport can only be energised by rapidly disappearing oil fuel, which pollutes directly into the most sensitive levels of the atmosphere, Alternative World would phase out all aeroplanes as quickly as possible. Elimination of the money system would automatically eliminate the vast existing numbers of 'business' flights. In so far as 'face to face' meetings were absolutely essential, they could follow surface travelling. However, because medium- and long-distance communication between representatives and planners at all levels from local to the world forum would be absolutely essential, well-tried electronic sound/sight systems for 'air-wave' meetings would be promoted. To complement world-wide expanded rail networks, passenger ships would be reintroduced as required. Resources would be made available to assist the conversion of shipping generally to non-polluting energy such as hydrogen, supplemented by computer controlled sail systems.

Chapters 9 to 18: References

1 New Statesman and Society 19/6/92
2 Guardian 5/10/92
3 New Statesman 8/5/92
4 Guardian 11/8/92
5 Looking Backward, E. Bellamy, Penguin 1982
6 The Nation 21/9/92
7 Observer 7/7/91
8 World without War, J D Bernal, Routledge 1958
9 New Internationalist, November 1987
10 World Facts and Trends, J McHale, Macmillan 1972
11 Nature, June 1974, Vol 249
12 Dictionary of Environment, A Crump, Earthscan 1991
13 Observer 9/2/92
14 Ditto 28/10/90

CONCLUSION: A WAY FORWARD

It is all too evident that the overall state of the world worsens year by year. Warfare, repression, genocide, starvation, mass migrations and environmental destruction continue. Societal inequalities, poverty, unemployment and moral decline persist. Shameful bullying of poorer Third World countries becomes entrenched, their acute problems increasingly ignored even by the more serious Western media in favour of endless degrading coverage of titillating trivia. These, and the many other disastrous failures of today's 'world order' described in Part One are tragic but not inexplicable: they are the almost inevitable products of capitalism.

During recent decades, by using every form of overwhelmingly powerful military and economic pressure short of actual war, the capitalist elites have succeeded in extending their pernicious influence virtually world-wide. Having done so, standing on the shifting sands of monetarism, they now feel the need to bolster their self-confidence by proclaiming that 'The demise of socialism proves the superiority of the market system.' In doing so, they ignore the fact that true, democratic socialism has never really had a chance to exist; and we have seen in Chapter 2 the all-pervasive ill-effects on humanity of their much vaunted 'market'.

Alternative World rejects emphatically the negative view that humans are innately self-seeking and therefore 'market-orientated'. On the contrary, given the opportunities, very many men, women and young people will always express and act on the natural instinct to work together cooperatively for the good of society. It is important, too, to remember that capitalism has had the opportunity over several centuries to improve the lot of all humanity, but instead has done nothing but entrench widespread suffering for the majority and enrich the few. It is a system which has without doubt forfeited any right to continue dominating the world, and should be replaced by cooperative societies such as Alternative World at the earliest opportunity.

The Western elites encouraged and even demanded that the Eastern Bloc and the Soviet Union open up to the 'free market' as the Soviet leadership sought to revive growth in their stagnating economy. The result has been the familiar attributes of capitalism across the world: corruption, homelessness, hunger, unemployment, violent crime, child prostitution and so forth.

Those developments in Eastern Europe formed part of a world-wide pattern of ruthless aggression by multinational corporations seeking locations having both cheap labour and natural resources. This process has gone hand in hand with unprecedented injections of capital by the World Bank and others into areas such as China, offering potential high returns, but studiously avoiding those in greatest need such as Africa.

These global reactionary offensives, consistently supported by media barrages trumpeting the demise of Socialism, have to some extent succeeded in throwing progressive forces world-wide on to the defensive.

This is not to say that anti-establishment activities have died out completely. For example the inspiring 'World Court Project', aimed at persuading the International Court to outlaw nuclear weapons, received over 3.3m signed declarations of support world-wide, and in July 1996 the Court announced that both the threat and use of nuclear weapons would generally be illegal under international law. In spite of the ending of the Cold War, opposition by the NATO nuclear powers has culminated in the US State Department earmarking $800,000 to thwart such a judgement.[1] At the same time, many dedicated and brave people world-wide, often risking their lives, continue to confront a whole range of assaults on the global environment.

However, it has to be recognised that these, and other such valuable activities, are essentially defensive. They do not amount to actual attacks on the root causes of the world's problems, nor do they postulate alternatives.

We have seen in Part One that the world's plight is desperate; there is absolutely no time to lose in taking corrective action. However. realistic account has to be taken both of the insidious anti-socialist hold over many millions by the various forms of reactionary media, and the current undeniable weakness of genuinely progressive forces.

Thus it becomes apparent that both exposures of the evils of capitalism. and constructive advocacy of the benefits of cooperative societies, are likely not only to fall on largely deaf ears, but also to lack adequate support.

So what is to be done?

The author's belief is that the answer lies in the one 'chink in the armour of capitalism', namely the aberration of the continued existence of weapons of all kinds.

Many parts of the world are cursed by increasing levels of unprecedented violence. This already appalling picture looks set to steadily worsen, owing to the numerous degenerative factors listed in Part One. In the US, for example, there are now 300,000 licensed gun dealers, and over 30,000 dead from gun shots yearly; these include some 4,000 killed by 10 to 18 year-olds including, for example. a Los Angeles boy of 14 who shot his mother in the forehead in a dispute over a chocolate biscuit.[2] Further, many children, wearing bulletproof vests, bring guns to their schools, some of which have been driven to installing airport type metal detectors.[3]

At the 'macro' level, since the toll of 55 million dead in World War Two, well over 20 million are estimated to have died in subsequent hostilities. These 'conflicts' can, in some cases, be more appropriately termed 'slaughters', as, for example, the Indonesian extermination of one-third of the total population of East Timor in the 1980s. Even after bouts of fighting die down, some 10,000 Third World civilians are killed annually by indiscriminately scattered mines, and countless more are maimed.

An overview of today's conflicts presents a very different picture to that of 1914 or 1939. Now, the great majority are in fact 'civil' wars, in which either autocratic elites suppress their fellow citizens, or rival elites battle it out with each other. In either case, the great majority of the weapons are supplied, highly profitably, by the First World, sometimes as 'Aid'. These supplies are often so plentiful that guns are commonly carried by children as young as six. 'Some had spent the whole of their formative years carrying a gun. When the war ends, they've never been to school. All they know is how to shoot.'[4]

Continuing use of weapons in conflicts is clearly essential for the armaments manufacturers in order to justify their existence. Today however, the actual business of fighting has in effect been 'contracted out' to the Third World. Thus the superlatively-equipped armies, navies and air forces of the First World have (happily for them) become largely parade-ground forces, for whom the very idea of actually fighting anywhere is anathema. To forestall adverse publicity from deaths of their own troops in action, First World politicians are increasingly reluctant to commit forces at all, except sometimes aircraft at a safe height . Even their occasional contributions of personnel to UN peace-keeping missions are very sparse.

It is crystal clear that the many millions of desperately-wronged victims of conflicts in the Third World can feel nothing but revulsion for all the increasingly sophisticated weaponry used to torment them. At the same time, millions of concerned citizens in the First World undoubtedly not only fear the increasing violence in their own societies, but also grieve for those suffering and dying elsewhere in the world.

It is equally clear that all the appalling mayhem in the world is only made possible by the existence of weapons. A logical case has never been made for men to have ready access to death-dealing weapons for solving disagreements between themselves. If all weapons were consigned to oblivion, there would be no alternative to solutions through discussion.

We saw in Chapter 7 that violence is not biologically inherent in humans. Warfare has only been known to have taken place during the last 2% of the duration of mankind's existence. Only misery and desolation has been proven to have resulted from it consistently, with never any beneficial outcomes whatsoever. A significant proportion of respected scientists believe that mankind's very existence might well be in jeopardy during present lifetimes because of gross interference with the world's ecology alone. In such a context it is insupportable that we should not only ignore these warnings, but should actually aggravate an already delicate imbalance. This we shall do if we continue to squander an outrageous proportion of precious resources to perpetuate the ways and means of destroying fellow human beings. Can it credibly be accepted by all sensitive, thinking men and women world-wide that such a macabre distortion of mankind's creative genius should continue to be perpetrated indefinitely ?

We have seen in the Introduction that many traditions form the greatest obstacles to mankind's progress. because they reflect nothing more meaningful than thoughtless repetitions of what has been done habitually in the past, regardless of whether they were beneficial or not. The whole culture of weapons and armed forces rests solely on tradition, and as such has no logical justification whatever; it represents a gross affront to the dignity and intelligence of mankind. Further, its astronomical expense not only bleeds societies seriously, but represents a total waste. The argument that the world must continue staffing armed forces and making weapons for ever in order to provide employment is too crass to merit comment.

If there ever was any honour in 'serving one's country' as a professional combatant, there is certainly none now; for, during the 20th century, the proportion of innocent, defenceless citizens killed in hostilities has risen from 14% to 90%. The comparatively 'disciplined' culture of national armed forces killing each other has given way to the anarchy of all manner of wild-cat, mafia-type eruptions of violence over a wide range of issues. These include narcotics, scarce resources, even jobs, all involving civilians and fuelled by a global flood of second-hand weapons, many abandoned or even sold by the previously disciplined forces.

Abandonment of all weapons would, in fact, have a profound 'freeing up' effect on world societies by removing, at a stroke, the capacity of elites and their state machines to coerce fellow citizens, through threats of the ultimate use of force. By the same token, it would improve dramatically the opportunities for truly democratic societies to develop along the lines of 'Alternative World'. However, in order to initiate movement towards the total rejection of all weapons, it is proposed here to simply build on the belief that the vast majority of men and women everywhere are sickened by the accelerating orgies of killings, and that they all have an inbuilt preference for living rather than dying.

It follows that there should be initiated world-wide DEMANDS for the total destruction, and permanent abolition, of weapons of every size and type on or before 1st January 2001. These DEMANDS would be in similar terms in every country; addressed to the only bodies capable of giving effect to them, namely the governments of each country; by the people most capable of pressuring such governments, namely the citizens of each country.

It would be inappropriate for the campaign to take the form of petitions, which would characterise human beings as supplicants. Rather, it should be based on well-founded, confident DEMANDS by men, women and children world-wide for recognition of their inalienable rights to live at peace with one another, free from the fear of sudden death.

The DEMANDS would provide for a clear understanding by every government and every citizen, that for global weapons abolition to be realisable and lasting, it would have to apply throughout every country without exception. This provision would not only be patently fundamental to success; it would also assist in identifying those countries 'dragging their feet', in announcing their agreement to abandon weapons on 'D-Day', as pariahs to be pressured by the rest of the world community.

The choice of 1/1/2001 as 'D-Day' would have the important psychological advantage of representing a New Year/New Century resolution of totally unprecedented significance. A period longer than the four years suggested (from the time of writing) might well make it difficult to maintain the high level of enthusiasm world-wide for the campaign which would be essential for success. At the same time, around four years would be sufficient for plans to be drawn up for diversification of labour, from both weapons production and armed services, to peaceful activities.

It is reasonable to believe that the novel concept of millions of world citizens acting together contemporaneously in a deeply common cause could well excite and catch imaginations widely, and stimulate positive emotions of global 'togetherness', and loyalty to humanity as a whole, rather than just one's individual country. Such an initiative could also well rekindle the enthusiasm of many thousands of peace organisations and activists globally who have to some extent been thrown on to the defensive in recent years. Such local enthusiasms could also well culminate in supportive activities such as marches and demonstrations of unprecedented sizes, and pledges of non-violent direct action such as blocking weapons-factory gates, to provide powerful support for the DEMAND.

Such irrefutable efforts to promote the triumph of good over evil should reasonably be expected to gain widespread support, including that of believers of every faith world-wide. While appreciating the prodigious problems confronting a successful outcome of such a campaign, it is necessary to keep them in proportion. The vast majority of mankind, including in the First World, neither likes weapons nor profits from them.

Further, a highly significant pointer to what can be achieved by concerted popular demand evolved in the UK in 1996, following widespread revulsion to the massacre of children in a school classroom. Though not yet enacted, the total elimination of all privately held handguns throughout Britain looks set to become an historic, inspiring example for other countries, especially the US, to follow.

The essential foundation for such a campaign would be an inspiring Manifesto, which would generate confidence in the potential for success. This could become one of the world's most historic documents;

one on which the future of much of humanity might well depend. It would need to be succinct; appropriate for translation and use in every community of the world, rich or poor. It would need to include clear guidance on how the collection of signatures (or crosses), pledges of non-violent direct action and other forms of support for the local DEMAND could best be made.

The Manifesto should make it clear that the DEMANDS would be for the total, permanent elimination of ALL weapons, including nuclear, chemical, biological, planes, ships, tanks, guns of every type and size, land mines and others . It should affirm that use of weapons represents a denial of humanity, and has never solved problems, but rather worsened them.

Further, the manifesto would explain clearly that closure of weapons factories and dismissal of armed services personnel would NOT need to result in unemployment. On the contrary, it has become estab-lished statistically that equivalent funding spent, for example, on building housing, schools and the like would provide work for MORE men and women. Employment would become meaningful, precious material resources would not be squandered, and lasting community facilities would be provided .

A small, ad-hoc committee would need to initiate the campaign, for which, because of its broad appeal, sufficient start-up funding should be readily forthcoming. That committee would first need to agree an initial draft of the Manifesto. This could then be circulated to a small number of appropriate prominent persons world-wide, who would be asked both for comments, and whether they would be prepared to join a launch committee, or at least lend their names as sponsors.

Decisions could then be taken on printing the finally agreed Man-ifesto in appropriate languages, on involving the media, and numerous other organisational issues which would evolve naturally. These would require the immediate establishment of a small full-time secretariat .

The first task would then be to identify an existing or ad-hoc body in each country which would be prepared to promote the campaign locally. It is recognised, and all too evident, that in many countries such activity would result in persecution, unless given resolute support from more liberal sectors of the world. Such support would need to take every possible form. The General Assembly of the United Nations should be called upon to recognise the basic morality and logic of the DEMAND, and its correspondence with the UN' s own constitution, and call for the protection of all promoting it.

The initial support of persons well-known globally would be invalu-able. However, to maximise support within countries, it would be im-portant for local organising bodies to obtain sponsorship of the Manifesto from individuals in their particular countries who are well-known, popular and respected, such as sportsmen or media personalities .

Liaison between country organisers and the secretariat would be important for exchange of information, advice and progress reports. To this end many forms of communication could be used, including the Internet. At the same time advantage could be taken of the dramatic increase of tourism, including in countries with repressive regimes; in this way invaluable personal contacts could be made in support of the campaign.

The time is long overdue for the vast, peace-loving majority of mankind to stand shoulder to shoulder and INSIST that the whole culture of problem-solving by violence is archaic and an insult to their intelligence.

A WORLD WITHOUT WEAPONS OF ALL KINDS WOULD PROCLAIM A NEW LEASE OF LIFE FOR HUMANITY!

Anyone who, having read this book, would like to write to the author about any of the issues raised is welcome to do so through the publisher, Housmans Bookshop Ltd, 5 Caledonian Road, London N1.

1. Ex-Services CND News letter, May 1994
2. Guardian 22/8/96
3. Observer 19/9/93; Guardian 6 & 8/11/93
4. Oxfam News, Winter 1993

Edward VII 109
Egypt, water supply 135
Ehrlich, Professor, food shortages 151
Eisenhower, Dwight D, ex-President, arms waste 162, 164
Elderly, living conditions, First World 46
Electoral expenses, US 125
Elizabeth II, Queen, fortune 73
Ellerman, D 18
El Salvador 48
Environmental degradation by military globally 164
Escobar, P, Colombian narcotics operation 70, 74
Ethiopia 19, 32, 116
  water supply 135
Euphrates 135
European Community, fraudulent transactions 76

Factory farming 71
Falwell, Reverend Jerry, electronic church 102
Famines 25
Ferranti, 'phantom contract' scandal 165
Fertilisers, world output 157
Fielding, Henry 50
Financial institutions, employees growth 88
Financial services superstructures 54
Food and Agriculture Organisation 19
Food mountains 72
Forbes, Malcolm, exceptional birthday party 74
Fortunes 73
Fraud 74
Free trade zones 76
Frelimo, Mozambique revolution 149
Friedman, Milton, 88, 106
Friends of the Earth 172
Frontiers, problems arising 118

Gaia Peace Atlas 160

Galbraith, J K, 'work' 196
Gambling 76
Ganges 135
GATT 18
GCHQ, Amnesty International and Christian aid 48
Genentech, malaria vaccine 92
Genetic engineering 77
George V, tax concession lobbying 109
George, Susan 28, 39
  bankers 59
  malnutrition 155
  food as commodity 156
Germany, toxic waste 141
Ghazi, Polly
  rainforests 129
  greenhouse effect 133
Gilmour, Sir Ian, conflicting UK Treasury forecasts 52
Global Success Corporation, newsletter 84-85
Goitre 153
Golden handshakes 78
Goldsmith, Sir James 107
Gorman, Teresa 66
Grand Metropolitan, advertising expenditure 58
'Green Revolution', introduction 155
Green, Sir Owen, 'bottom line' 88
Greenpeace, 'greenhouse effect' 127
Guatemala 29, 36
  malnutrition 154
Guinea-Bissau 113
Gulf War 19

Haemophiliacs, insurance 82
Halpern, Sir Ralph, golden handshake 78
Hampson, Judith, world's indigenous peoples 172
Hanson, Lord, exceptional salary rise 79
Hardin, Professor 17
Harris, Bruce 37
Havana, population stability 227